Preventing and Managing Teacher Strikes

William A. Streshly

scarecrow education ϵ

The Scarecrow Press, Inc.
A Scarecrow Education Book
Lanham, Maryland, and London
2001

SCARECROW PRESS, INC.
A Scarecrow Education Book

Published in the United States of America
by Scarecrow Press, Inc.
4720 Boston Way, Lanham, Maryland 20706
www.scarecrowpress.com

4 Pleydell Gardens, Folkestone
Kent CT20 2DN, England

British Library Cataloguing-in-Publication Information Available

Library of Congress Cataloging-in-Publication Data

Streshly, William A.
    Preventing and managing teacher strikes / William A. Streshly.
        p. cm.—(Scarecrow education)
    includes bibliographical references (p.).
    ISBN 0-8108-4178-9 (pbk .: alk. paper)
    1. Strikes and lockouts—Teachers—United States. 2. Collective
bargaining—Education—United States. I. Title. II. Scarecrow education
book.

LB2844.47.U6 S77 2001
331.892'813711'00973—dc21

                                                                2001042677

Printed in the United States of America

∞™ The paper used in this publication meets the minimum requirements of
American National Standard for Information Sciences—Permanence of
Paper for Printed Library Materials, ANSI/NISO Z.39.48–1992.
Manufactured in the United States of America.

Contents

Foreword

As president of the union, I once traveled—along with our district superintendent, director of personnel, and the president of our board—to a small central California town at the behest of a school district that was about to enter its tenth year of eye-gouging, ear-biting, rabbit-punching labor negotiations. Now, don't misunderstand me, that can be fun for a while; but these folks looked and sounded as if they'd run headfirst into a brick wall once too often and were exhausted by the anticipation of doing so once again.

We all paired up with our counterparts in the district and spent an interesting day discussing the merits of cooperative bargaining. At the end of the day we met in the district conference room, and each of us was permitted to deliver a valedictory observation. Many of them had that "Yeah, Yeah! That's easy for you to say" look in their eyes. Speaking last, I drew their attention to a chart projected overhead, which listed on one side the district's revenue limit increase for the past ten years. On the other side were the raises, which had been won through traditional bruising negotiations for the same period of time. Typically, the raises amounted to figures like 2.4 percent, 1.8 percent, 6.2 percent, and so on. With the panache of an aluminum siding salesman closing the deal I showed them the totals for both columns. After ten years of Hatfield and McCoy wars, which had frustrated management, embittered teachers, and stupefied the community, the total difference between the revenue increases and the raises was one-half of one percent. I allowed a minute for this to sink in and said, "It looks to me as if you folks simply like to fight."

The following week we got a very nice note stating that they had settled their negotiations and were in the process of establishing a cooperative labor model. That was more than fourteen years ago, and they're still cooperating.

A story is told about Robert Fulton and his steamship that clearly illustrates the resistance all sides must be willing to transcend when deciding to launch cooperative labor relations. Fulton's boat was tied to the dock, and on the dock were hundreds of people. There were hot dogs, beer, balloons, and a brass band. About five hundred yards up the river there was a small knot of men shouting, "It'll never work, it'll never work!" At the appointed hour the cannon exploded, the people shouted, and the steamship churned out into midstream and began to chug upriver. While the crowd on the side cheered mightily, the little knot of men up river immediately begin to chant, "It'll never stop, it'll never stop!"

All organizations have their naysayers and cynics. When we inaugurated cooperative relations a veteran teacher vilified me with every name you can't print in a family journal. Several years later when we were about to choose a new superintendent, this same teacher approached me in the local Costco and beseeched me not to hire anyone who could not work in the cooperative labor model.

The late Erving Goldabber was a great negotiator. In his early years he was hired by Walter O'Malley to work with the Dodgers in order to smooth the transition of Jackie Robinson into major league baseball. At various times he worked in the Middle East, Ireland, and the Balkans. He also led a team of negotiators that successfully resolved seemingly intractable imbroglios in more than fifty school districts throughout America. Goldabber pointed out that teachers and school districts are collaborations. They are like family in that neither side is going away, their destinies are intertwined, and each should be a resource, not an enemy, of the other. If this is so, and I believe that it is, then we should get on with the business of finding alternatives to the derogatory and hurtful incivility of traditional labor relations.

James Madison observed that "If men were Angels, no government would be necessary." Since men are not angels, we have constitutions, rules, statues, regulations, codes, norms, stop signs, etiquette, and, yes, union contracts. This book is not a blueprint. It is more like a guidebook for those about to travel into, or return to, a land of internecine tempest. To be sure there are recommendations, caveats, and a few absolutes, but in the end it primarily encourages the adoption of a very different way of looking at labor negotiations in America's school districts. We do not need to annually exacerbate the already strained relations between the public and its educational system.

For those who are considering cooperative labor relations, there are several important requisites to consider. Among them, three are critical:

- The capacity to walk a mile in the other guy's shoes
- A commitment to dealing with the issues, not with personalities
- Both the ability and the intent to trust

Of these, trust is the most important—and the most vulnerable. Once it is violated, it may never be regained, so both sides must guard it zealously.

You can successfully negotiate with anybody, unless he is committed to killing you or crazy. Therefore, you must decide whether there are those from either camp who bring private agendas to the table. They will poison the process. Traditional bargaining not only requires but also rewards leaders with a considerable quantity of ego. Why else would they be willing to step into the fray? Cooperative labor relations complement a very different style of leadership. Like the gunslingers in the Old West who were obliged to check their guns at the sheriff's office, you must check your egos when you sit down to share in the governance of the district.

Finally, as you will discover in this book, cooperative labor relations require a good deal more time than traditional bargaining. More than good luck, I wish you measurable forbearance and good skills.

Jerry Franklin
Former president,
San Marcos Education Association (CTA-NEA)

Introduction

Three years ago I interviewed a group of school superintendents in the aftermath of the disastrous San Diego teachers' strike. All were in agreement that the district had mismanaged the strike. One by one, the veteran school chiefs pointed out strategic errors that hastened the walk-out and ultimately resulted in a resounding union victory.

"Wait a moment," one young superintendent interjected, "I thought there were no winners in a school district strike."

"Wrong," responded one of the superintendents in a matter-of-fact manner. "Strikes are a natural part of the industrial model of collective bargaining we are stuck with, and winning should be the goal of the district's leaders, just as it is with the union's leaders. In San Diego, the union won big because the district did not mount a winning campaign."

"But don't both sides lose in a teachers' strike? Don't all of the players lose a degree of respect or credibility in the eyes of the taxpayers?"

"Sure. There are casualties," explained the older man quietly, "but to say there are no winners in a strike is nonsense. Winning or losing has to do with the broader aims of the school district's strike strategy. The district wins when the strike fails to accomplish the bread-and-butter demands of the union leaders. It's as simple as that. The result is a rank-and-file faculty less anxious in the future for the adventure of the picket line. Unions that win are more likely to go out again—with less provocation—and vice versa. I wouldn't be surprised to see San Diego teachers go out again—or at least use the threat of strike liberally when-ever their demands are not met."

1

The overarching goal of a district's long-range strike strategy must be exactly the same as its labor relations goal in the off-season when hard-core contract negotiations are not in session. That is, the district's goal must be to establish *stable, long-term, peaceful relations* that promote all of the operational and political goals of the school system. I emphasize *long-term peaceful relations* because strategies of appeasement in coping with teacher strikes usually result in years of labor turmoil punctuated by moments of peace.

In stark contrast to the San Diego district, a Northern California district won its teachers' strike by methodically adopting and implanting proven strategies for dealing with confrontational unions. As a result, the strike eventually collapsed, and teachers returned to work with no concessions by the district. Instead, the leadership proclaimed that the union would "continue the struggle at the polls"—a big win for democracy as well as the children and parents of the district. More than a decade has passed, and the union, which had walked out regularly in the previous decade, has not threatened to strike since. Although labor relations in the district have not matured to the collaborative stage described in chapters 4 and 5 of this book, the union has adopted a much greater willingness to arrive at compromise. One short-range consequence was that the electorate voted several of the board members out of office at the next election. As I discuss in chapter 6, this is not an unusual community reaction, and board members must understand that this is the risk they take. Most of the board members I have worked with were not influenced by the possibility of losing their public offices. In the words of one trustee, "The pay is terrible. The only reward is the satisfaction that I've done something to help our schools."

The young superintendent in the discussion above wondered aloud why strategies for dealing with teacher strikes were not as well documented as the more popular collaborative strategies. Contentious unions are a fact of life in some districts. Why don't the experienced administrators in these districts share their insights? The answer lies in the stigma the profession places on administrators (and board members, for that matter) who have not been successful in forging cooperative relations. "It's the battered-wife syndrome," one superintendent explained to me. "The superintendents think it's their fault, and they don't want to talk about it."

Tragically, this frame of mind gets in the way of good management decisions. Administrators who think of a strike as the manifestation of failed leadership cannot possibly win at this phase of the collective bargaining game.

WINNING THE PEACE

This book is about developing winning labor relations strategies that will allow you to work successfully with public school teacher unions. It dis-

cusses thoroughly the popular and desirable "win-win" collaborative models. Most importantly, however, it points out the critical compromises that must be firmly in place before proceeding with these models. So-called cooperative labor relations have been embraced by many unwary boards and superintendents, who found out only later that they had been trapped by their zealousness and skewered by their naïveté.

I should begin by admitting that this book is not traditional, research-based, professional literature. Instead, it is composed primarily of the insights gained by practicing school administrators in the trenches as well as experienced teacher-union leaders in those same trenches. It reflects their biases as well as their idealism and pragmatism. Much of what ensues, therefore, is not necessarily politically correct, and it is more journalism than research. Nevertheless, the wise and experienced professionals I interviewed support the accuracy of these observations and their derivative tactics and strategies. In reality, this is a book about why political correctness doesn't work in an arena as complex and volatile as modern-day school district labor relations.

Not long ago I went to a symposium on school district negotiations attended by negotiators from both the unions and the school boards. Because I had served as a professor at San Diego State University for the past eleven years, I masqueraded as a neutral observer. Only a few at the symposium were aware of my previous twenty-four years as a school administrator, including fourteen years as a superintendent for districts varying in size from 2,500 to 25,000 students. My experiences with teacher unions were varied and stimulating—ranging from the development of a sophisticated, interest-based bargaining model to administration of a dirty, industrial-type combat model complete with a full-blown teachers' strike. All of these experiences, including those of the small rural school district where I began my first superintendency and where I learned the fundamentals of school district labor relations, were intense lessons in the art of playing the school district collective bargaining game.

Only some of the old timers at the symposium knew this background, and they agreed to stay silent. So I was able to probe boldly, and I received honest, candid answers. I was astonished by the apparent consensus that has developed about how bargaining *ought* to take place.

Negotiators now widely agree with the aims and philosophy of interest-based bargaining (or collaborative bargaining, or win-win, or whatever you want to call it). I was even more dumbfounded to learn that these various factions that seem to agree are still doing battle using confrontational adversarial bargaining techniques and strategies. The old model hangs on tenaciously. I was reminded of the poignant story—probably apocryphal—about a kindly grandfather helping his grandson learn to ride a bike. After numerous frustrating attempts to follow his grandfather's overly detailed instructions, the boy wailed piteously, "I know *how* to ride a bicycle, Grandpa. I just *can't!*"

THE COSTS OF CONFRONTATIONAL BARGAINING

Failure to understand the dynamics of traditional confrontational bargaining in the public school arena is the crux of the problem. Labor unions are obliged to pursue the membership's interest in bread-and-butter issues—salary and benefits. Since these are major money items, a natural conflict of interest develops. Boards want more programs; teachers want more salary. What follows is the union's attempt to put pressure on board members to enhance chances of a settlement favorable to the union. Up to

I THINK IT SAYS, "WE'RE NOT GOING TO LEARN HOW TO READ THIS YEAR."

this point the process sounds like a traditional, private-sector, industrial model. But the difference is significant. Businesses in the private sector are under economic pressure to settle. Employee performance during difficult negotiations can trim profits. Work slowdowns and strikes can have major financial consequences including bankruptcy. Not so in public school systems. School board members feel no economic pressure to settle with the unions on any issue. The most prolonged and disruptive labor conflicts in school systems have almost no financial consequences. Districts will receive their tax revenues as usual, and when the strike is

over, students will return to schools as usual. In fact, superintendents often claim they "make money" on their strikes.

The only pressure a teachers' union can inflict upon the school board is
political pressure. Consequently, all concerted actions relating to negotiations are purely and simply public relations campaigns, including pickets
and strikes. The "costs" of difficult, traditional, industrial-style collective bargaining with teacher unions must be measured in terms of public
relations—relations with parents, taxpayers, teachers, administrators, and
the rest of the community. While the economic costs of a teachers' strike,
for example, are minimal, the human costs can be catastrophic.

These costs begin with the damage inflicted on a district's relationships
with its parents and community. The credibility of the school district's administrators is tarnished, and respect for the teachers is lowered. Waging
the "PR war" requires union leaders to "fire up" the teachers and parents
by proclaiming the district to be "mismanaged." This usually is accompanied by vague accusations that administrators and board members are
wasting taxpayers' dollars on unimportant priorities. Unfortunately, this
strikes a responsive chord in the minds of many members of the community, because numerous aspects of the public school program are considered "frills" by those who don't understand their value. The school programs that are considered by some to be frills include athletics, music, art,
vocational courses, food services, transportation, special education, counseling, psychological services, staff supervision (administration), curriculum development (administration), and on and on.

These accusations are usually unfounded, but they "rally the troops"
and dishearten the district's stakeholders. In this PR war for the minds of
the voters, the district is required to counter by pointing out that teachers
are already well paid, and, based on the number of days they work, are
actually far better off than most of the constituent taxpayers. This tends to
incense many hardworking members of the community, especially those
numbering in the majority with no children in the schools. This tactic is
also largely untrue, but it is necessary to add balance to the propaganda
war. Otherwise, the school district leadership is in for a monumental defeat. I've highlighted the focus of the PR war on money and finances because, although teacher unions often try to convince the public that other
less selfish demands have precipitated the job action, nearly all strikes
boil down to salary and benefits.

Ironically, the public usually believes *both* the union's attack rhetoric
and the district's defense propaganda. Once the smoke has cleared and
the contract is settled, the district's stakeholders, as well as state and
national newspaper and television audiences, are more convinced than
ever that public schools are governed by wasteful board members and
bungling administrators. And to make matters worse, the classrooms are

staffed with overpaid and underworked teachers. School principals, the consummate defenders of teachers, once known for excellent "bedside manners in dealing with parents," are finding it more difficult than ever to convince these parents that their children are in the hands of competent professionals.

In addition to the damage wreaked on the school district's community relationships, the school system itself sustains considerable injury. Formal confrontational negotiations restrict and confuse communications. To play the negotiations game properly, unions must regularly discredit the vision and direction of school board members and administrators. Why? If teachers and parents have confidence in their school district's leaders, it becomes very difficult later on during salary negotiations to convince them that these same people are wasteful bunglers. Efforts to generate negative PR only when negotiations are taking place would be transparent and ineffective. The union would lose a major weapon in its arsenal of PR tactics for putting political pressure on the school board to settle a contract.

The rules of industrial-style negotiations also help set a tone of distrust and undermine confidence in the organization's leadership. The old National Labor Relations Board (NLRB) protocol for forbidding management from bringing a single "take it or leave it" offer to the table requires both sides to be less than honest in their initial proposals. The school board must offer less than it is willing to pay, and the union must demand more than what it actually desires. Since these two figures are often miles apart, the result is confusion, suspicion, and distrust. Hardworking, unsophisticated teachers are hurt and confused when they hear that the school board's initial offer contains very little salary increase in spite of the fact that the district's revenues are increasing. In the other camp, equally hardworking and unsophisticated school district leaders are shocked that the union is demanding a salary increase that would bankrupt the district. The truth of the matter, of course, is that both sides are lying. It is required by the bargaining process.

This self-destructive ritual continues in the United States despite the fact that teachers have not seen appreciable increases in salary and have experienced little improvement in their working conditions. As I point out in chapter 2, the widespread unionization of teachers in the late 1960s had no apparent impact on gradually rising wages. In 1998 dollars, wages for teachers actually declined during the decade of the 1970s, when teacher unions were reaching the peak of their influence. In fact, only in the last few years have teachers even approached the break-even point— and this doesn't take into consideration the money lost to significantly higher union dues or strikes. Historically, school boards in America have had a mixed record in dealing fairly and squarely with teachers. However, by World War II, nearly every state in the union had passed laws guaranteeing teachers everything from tenure to sick leave. The state legislatures working closely with the National Education Association (NEA) and their affiliates addressed the problems encountered by teachers in the past and passed laws ranging from protection from abusive parents and students to duty-free lunch hours and guaranteed minimum salaries.

In those days, the teaching profession was on a roll. Remember, the NEA at that time was a comprehensive educational organization, including administrators as well as teachers. Its focus was advancing the profession as a whole, not the advancement of teachers at the expense of administrators. The organization was seen as the "voice of education," a solid, united front—a powerful and respected presence in all state legislatures. Those legislatures became much more prescriptive about improving the working conditions of teachers and school employees. Much less was being left to the whims of local school boards and politics. Americans were beginning to realize that the continued position of the United States as a world leader demanded reforms of this sort. By the time militant unionization of public employees came marching in, following John F. Kennedy's executive order allowing collective bargaining for federal civil servants, most of the protections that industrial unions in the private sector had fought for were already enacted in state education codes, preempting the need for extensive industrial-style labor contracts.

At the same time that state legislators were overhauling working conditions for their teachers, the U.S. Supreme Court jumped in to protect teachers' rights to free speech and association. The court also defined the property and liberty interests of teachers that trigger the due process protections of tenure. These protections were guaranteed regardless of the existence of a negotiated contract. Since the advent of the new adversarial teacher unions, not much improvement has taken place. The bitter irony at the turn of the twenty-first century is that state legislatures are now increasingly attacking tenure rights and other valuable protections won in the days before teacher unionism.

Probably most dispiriting of all, the extended conflict within school districts caused by the traditional industrial-type collective bargaining model effectively denies teachers the full satisfaction of teaching school. In the private sector, the union's focus is on working conditions, meaning the number of hours worked, number of minutes allotted for breaks, criteria for leaves, penalties for tardiness, and so forth. In public schools, unions claim they are protecting teachers from unscrupulous administrators; administrators claim to be preserving power for the elected school board. It doesn't take a specialist in organizational development to recognize that none of this promotes collaboration or joint efforts to accomplish mutually held goals. Quite to the contrary, it is not uncommon for old school union leaders to counsel their local minions not to become involved in the governance of a school district. They reason that collaboration with administrators in governing the district will compromise or "co-opt" the union in its role as advocate or protector of the teachers.

The old collective bargaining model persists in school districts, not because the players are unaware, but because they think they are successful playing the confrontational game. They lack appreciation of the dynamics of a cooperative approach to bargaining. Some of the dynamics are grounded in common sense and experience; others are well researched by scholars such as Fisher and Ury, Kerchner, Lieberman, and others. In practice, however, the approach a school district takes begins with two key players, the local union president and the district superintendent, and their organizations. Chapter 1 explores these relationships.

1

The Union
and Administration:
Collaborators or Gladiators?

A favorite expression among labor relations professionals is "It takes two to tango," or if you prefer, "It takes two to tangle." A "tango" is a metaphor for a collaborative labor relationship between the union and the school district. To "tangle" refers to the more traditional confrontational collective bargaining model. Most leaders, of school districts as well as unions, endorse in principle the collaborative models but recognize their inherent implementational difficulties. Plainly, it is easier to tangle than to tango, and both models can be satisfying, even fun, for the participants on both sides.

THE SUPERINTENDENT AND THE UNION PRESIDENT

A cooperative labor agreement in a school district is a mosaic of diverse interests and people. First of all, the superintendent and the union president must agree in concept to work together in the interest of all the district's stakeholders. These two key figures must be committed to forging a nonadversarial process for coping with the interests of the teachers, the primary producers in a school system, and the community, represented by the board. But the process becomes more complicated. The superintendent must have the strong support of the school board. It would be nice if the board gave its support unanimously, but most superintendents will settle for a solid, stable majority. However, even with a majority, a school board split on the issue of collaborating with a labor union can undermine the development of the process in its fragile first decade. Every labor glitch will be the target of criticism from dissenting board members. It is not unusual to hear a frustrated school superintendent describe a board member who single-handedly torpedoed a nascent effort to establish cooperative labor relations in a district.

Like the superintendent, the union president also requires the support of a representative executive board. Opposition in this body can be as difficult for the union president to endure as dissent in a school board is for the superintendent.

SCHOOL BOARDS AND UNION OFFICERS

Assuming the superintendent and the president are supported by their respective boards, the boards must reach out and gain the support of their constituent power structures within the community and within the faculties. *If any part of this political collaboration is missing, cooperative, collaborative labor relations or interest-based bargaining simply won't work in the long run.* Before significant energies are expended to further develop a collaborative process, this coalition must be hammered out.

There are incentives. Here history plays a part. Widespread satisfaction with the labor relations in the district, or widespread dissatisfaction resulting from adversarial negotiations, can provide impetus for a management–union collaboration. The influence of neighboring districts whose faculties achieve a greater sense of pride and satisfaction from their professional duties as a result of feelings of greater control and respect can also play a part in convincing teachers, administrators, and board members to search for a better way of doing business.

PRECONDITIONS FOR SUCCESS
IN COLLABORATIVE LABOR RELATIONS

The relationship between the union leaders and the district leaders must be more than a meeting of the minds. Several preconditions must also be present. A mutual respect for the power, influence, and authority of the other must exist. Said another way, each group of leaders must recognize the power of the other to enable or thwart their efforts. The aim should be to develop a détente, a true balance of power. One superintendent and union president declared, "We have a loaded gun at each other's head!"

Creating a document that carefully describes how each side maintains its power and rights helps make the proposition more palatable to skeptical union members at the outset—"We can always go back to the old way of doing things." As the collaboration matures, discarding the agreement will become more painful to both parties, especially if dissolving the collaboration means a loss of teacher control in the district and a return to the bargaining process with an increasingly unsavory reputation both in the profession and in the community. Entering the agreement fully armed gives the two sides an honest chance to take time out, leave the ring, and give collaboration a chance. Chapter 5 details the launching of a collaborative model and includes examples of documents that memorialize and institutionalize the agreements.

A REAL BALANCE OF POWER

An important key to détente is a willingness on the part of school district leaders to meet union force with equal or greater force. As I pointed out in the introduction, most school board members and administrators equate a teachers' strike with failure on their part to carry out the labor relations mission properly. As a result, they approach strike preparation and strike management tasks with little enthusiasm. They believe they have lost before the game has begun. They think that no matter what the outcome of the strike, they have failed. This may be the mortal flaw in American school districts' typical response to teacher strikes.

With a few exceptions, whenever the teachers' union has challenged a school district with a strike, they have won—using the criteria of traditional industrial labor disputes. Teacher strikes are professionally and skillfully managed union aggression against woefully unprepared amateurs. One district superintendent lamented, "It's like the Green Bay Packers playing one of our Pop Warner teams." A growing number of superintendents and observers of public education are coming to the conclusion that this imbalance of strategic power need not exist. School board members and administrators must prepare themselves well for labor relations. In other words, they must be prepared "to win the peace."

This means that administrators who fail to develop a working collaboration with the teachers' union must be prepared to conduct traditional industrial-style labor negotiations in a way that protects the district from financial insolvency and narrowly limits the scope of union involvement. The idea is to reserve as many resources as possible for quality programs. And if district interests require taking strong positions that result in concerted action by the teachers' union, then the board and management have a responsibility to carry out strike management activities with the same sort of professional commitment they have for the school's primary mission. In plain English, the objective is to *win* the strike—with no apologies!

FIGHT FIRE WITH FIRE

Aggressively countering pressure tactics is more than tit for tat when a district is facing a hostile teachers' union. It is a necessary precondition for long-term peace among the two organizational factions comprising the school district. Usually teachers are told by their union leaders that there will be no losses to them personally as a result of the strike other than the up-front loss of some salary, which will be returned to them in the long run. This type of statement counts on the district to be an impotent adversary when the union commences its hostile strike activities in earnest. A true balance of power or détente cannot exist when one of the adversaries has such little regard for the capabilities of the other.

CAPITALIZING ON COLLABORATION

Another important precondition for successful collaborative labor relations is the development of a joint union–administration council that considers school district matters, makes decisions, and formulates administrative policy at the cabinet level. This sort of mechanism is probably the hardest for school administrators worried about protecting their authority to swallow. However, if there is board support—and a true balance of power—it is the most powerful means of assuring that the new collaborative system works and that it makes a dynamic, positive impact on the quality of the school district. In time, administrators recognize that the variety of interests represented in this jointly led, cabinet-level decision-making body creates a milieu that results in better decisions and administrative regulations than would have been developed by administrators behind closed doors. Much of the success of the Los Valecitos Unified School District described in chapter 11 is attributed to a formal deliberative body of this sort.

District leaders and union leaders must educate nervous middle managers worried about loss of status or power when union leaders meet with the superintendent's cabinet to discuss district problems. Similarly, union leaders must educate nervous classroom teachers worried about protection from malevolent administrators as their union representatives increasingly support jointly derived district decisions instead of the customary griping and crabbing. Later these communications efforts will expand to include major work by the union to deal with the legitimate gripes and concerns of faculty at each building. Teachers feel more comfortable bringing their concerns to local union reps who, as the system becomes more sophisticated, are able to counsel employees with regard to district processes and procedures. This means addressing aggravating staff problems quickly and nipping them in the bud.

SETTING CRITERIA FOR SALARIES

Of all the basic preconditions for successful collaborative labor relations in school districts, solving the teacher salary issue is the most consequential. Experienced negotiators agree that union leaders give lip service to lower class sizes and whine about the need for agency fees to protect them from freeloaders, but they'll never be able to get their teachers very excited or upset about these language issues—at least not enough to carry out a strike. But dickering over money upsets us all since most of us perceive wages as a measure of how much the district board members and administrators value us. In collective bargaining, as in life itself, "Money is the root of all evil." School districts with stable, long-term, collaborative labor relations have established some sort of interest-based, criterion-referenced, nonpositional method for determining pay increases. In other words, these districts are able to describe what their salaries should look like compared to others in the market. What is the "going rate," and how do we compare? The goal becomes "a fair increase," instead of "as much as we can get." My discussions with school district and labor leaders across the country have convinced me that without the "basics" in place, attempts at interest-based bargaining will wind up on the rocks within a few years. This subject will be discussed in fuller detail in chapter 5, "Launching Collaborative Labor Relations with the Teachers' Union."

But first, how did we get where we are now?

2

+

Unfulfilled Promises

Unionization of public servants has always been viewed skeptically by students of government and economics. Even great labor champions such as Franklin Delano Roosevelt and legendary AFL-CIO president George Meany drew the line at unionization of the public sector. These leaders felt that allowing public servants to withhold essential services in order to gain leverage at the bargaining table was unacceptable. This prevalent attitude among state and federal leaders began to change in 1959 when the State of Wisconsin passed the first collective bargaining law for its public employees, including teachers. The rapid growth of teacher unions, however, did not begin until three years later when

President John F. Kennedy issued Executive Order 10988 giving federal employees the right to organize and bargain collectively. Barely three months later, twenty thousand teachers walked out of the New York public school system in violation of the state's Taylor Law forbidding strikes.

DECLINE OF RESPECT FOR TEACHERS

JFK's executive order and the New York teachers' strike preceded a decline in the prestige of American public education in general and teachers in particular that has continued to this day. The decline has run parallel to a concomitant rise in teacher unions' power at both the state and federal levels. These were not unforeseen consequences. In 1962 the National Education Association (NEA) denounced the New York strike as "unprofessional." Association leaders of that day anticipated the hostility naturally engendered when a community is held hostage by its teachers and a process as fundamental to society as education of the young is hindered. However, in a few short years, the NEA and the American Federation of Teachers (AFT) became locked in mortal combat for membership.

RISE OF THE NEA

The industrial labor union tactics of the AFT rapidly became more popular with urban teachers. Between 1962 and 1967 the NEA won twenty-six elections, and the AFT won fourteen. But the NEA gained only 21,000 members among its suburban and rural districts, whereas the AFT gained 74,000 members, primarily in the larger cities. Internal battles began within the larger NEA organization. The long-cherished concept of professionalism was being ridiculed. Teacher leaders, who had never heard of school vouchers and in those days found it unfathomable that legislators would suggest furnishing public funds for private schools, claimed teachers only wanted higher salaries and better benefits—not a higher standard of respect.

Forced to change its tactics and philosophy, the NEA began to look and act more and more like the AFT. Moreover, adopting traditional industrial labor union tactics resulted in traditional union demands for closed shops or agency fees. This, to the new union's glee, resulted in hundreds of millions of additional dollar revenues for the union's political operations and allowed its administrative staff to become the highest paid administrators in U.S. public education. By 1980, the NEA was viewed by many school boards as an even meaner, more pugnacious union than its traditional union counterpart, the AFT. As George Orwell noted in the final scenes of

Animal Farm, it soon became very difficult to tell the men from the pigs. In fact, in a strange twist, the AFT began to support peer review, formerly considered to be the domain of professional associations rather than labor unions.

AN AWAKENING

Until 1997, the NEA resisted the practice of peer review. In July of 1997, just before the proposed merger of the two unions, the NEA representative assembly embraced peer review—a sign that the NEA leadership was finally recognizing the low esteem its tactics had won for the teaching profession. A growing number of union members realized that a bellicose position by the union invites attack from all corners and supports opponents bent on dismantling public education. The unheeded warnings of association leaders back in 1962 were at last being recognized. Increasingly, teachers of all political bents are now wondering whether the gargantuan, all-powerful teacher unions will only accomplish the execution of the golden goose.

The conventional legislative rhetoric about collective bargaining for teachers in the 1960s and 1970s focused on control. Pro-unionists were able to convince more conservative legislators that collective bargaining laws would actually help prevent strikes over union recognition and at the same time limit the scope of bargaining. Legislators were faced with a paradox: support a law they opposed in principle, or defeat the law and face possible chaos fomented by teacher unions in their school districts.

By 1990, all but eighteen of the fifty states had enacted collective bargaining laws for teachers. Largely due to negotiated closed shop or agency fee agreements, membership in the largest union tripled to 2.2 million members in 2001. The much smaller and originally much more militant AFT, on the other hand, increased more than fifteen-fold to nearly a million members. Combined, the NEA and AFT have become a giant political force in America. Together they collect more than 1.3 billion dollars annually from their members.

THE EXPANSION OF SCHOOL BUREAUCRACY

So, who has reaped the benefits as these unions have metastasized from small benign organizations respectfully supporting the educational establishment to giant bureaucracies striking out in all directions at anything that remotely pertains to education? Certainly not administrators. They have largely been the victims of school bureaucracies forced to expand in response to the new union challenges. The result is a dramatic increase in the gap between school district leadership and the teaching faculty.

Administrators are not the only victims to feel the pain of increased bureaucracy. Two former executive directors for NEA state affiliates in Nebraska and Kansas gave their reasons for quitting the union by explaining that embracing the traditional labor union mission was unleashing a destructive force in public education. They felt that the effect of collective bargaining on public education "has been to make it more bureaucratic. Under collective bargaining, teacher unions, school boards, and administrators have adopted very formal and exceedingly structured ways of dealing with one another at the bargaining table" (Boyton and Lloyd, 1985). These men admitted that public education has problems, but pointed out that the problems cannot be addressed in an atmosphere of competition and isolation. "It's nearly impossible for adversaries to solve problems together." Like others who have witnessed the havoc wreaked by collective bargaining on schools and children, these two ex-NEA executives insightfully endorse collaborative labor relations.

Many districts experience what seems to be year-round negotiations, tying up the efforts of district leaders and requiring the employment of more bureaucrats. Contract management difficulties have rendered team building nearly impossible at school sites in many districts. This is not to imply that administrators don't cope successfully. They do. But most confess that the bureaucratic hindrances forced upon them have taken their toll.

UNFULFILLED PROMISES TO TEACHERS

As a whole, teachers have not benefited from the rise of unionism either. According to NEA (1998) estimates, average teacher salaries in dollars adjusted for inflation across the country actually declined during the most explosive union growth. Only now do teacher salaries compare favorably with the salaries of the mid-1960s. And when one takes into consideration the expensive union dues paid over three decades, most teachers have seen no gain in salary. When one takes into further consideration the progressively hostile legislatures and rapidly decreasing community support, one could argue that teachers have gotten nothing for their money.

THE IMPACT OF LABOR TURMOIL ON EDUCATIONAL QUALITY

Evidence is mounting that harmonious labor relations comprise a major precondition for successful educational programs (Lieberman, 1997;

Chalker, 1990; Maitland and Kerchner, 1986). Studies suggest that the traditional collective bargaining process in school districts

- increases school bureaucracies,
- effects the decision-making processes in ways that adversely affect the educational programs,
- suppresses teacher participation in program development, and
- lessens teacher support of teacher programs.

When school administrators and teachers must bargain formally over instructional issues, too much strain is placed on the positive human relations needed to produce good schools. In one district that moved away from the adversarial approach and adopted a collaborative approach, teachers commented, "Now the buck stops with me." Another commented, "We can't point to the superintendent. We're all in this. Look at where we are in education in the U.S. now. It's deplorable. It is our responsibility to follow through. We're responsible now and we're going to make damn sure these kids learn." The shift in authority accompanying the adoption of the collaborative labor relations mode resulted in the elimination of the traditional "we–they" teacher–administrator dichotomy. Administrators and teachers realized that the philosophies of Maslow and Herzburg, once thought to be the stuff of musty textbooks, actually work. People want to be productive, and if they are given proper incentives and a climate of labor–management trust, they will eagerly and productively tackle their jobs.

WHITHER THE BIG UNION

The big question is, Where are the NEA and the AFT going? Can these organizations move away from traditional unionism? Probably not, simply because it is not in their financial interest to do so. By 1996 approximately three thousand NEA and AFT administrators and officers earned well over $100,000 annually in salary and benefits (Lieberman, 1997). This came at a time when average teacher salaries were less than $40,000. Both unions have officers with a variety of personal agenda not always in the best interests of a nation seeking to improve its educational system. For example, the NEA uses the resolutions it adopts to support its budgetary expenditures. Resolutions for the 1997–98 school year included support for such diverse issues as statehood for the District of Columbia, the International Court of Human Justice, the nuclear freeze, family planning, and atmospheric pollution.

Buried among a long list of other more or less worthy resolutions was one supporting the implementation of peer assistance and review programs in districts. The jury is still out as to whether this will make a significant difference. But it does open the door for more advanced organizational relationships to develop. My personal skepticism is based on my observation of the implementation of other praiseworthy resolutions. For example, in 1997–98 the NEA adopted the "right to know" as one of its guiding principles "to unite educational employees for effective citizenship." The resolution stated clearly that the NEA "believes that open meeting and public disclosure laws are essential to permit the monitoring of governmental actions." At a bargaining training session that took place several months after the 1997–98 representative assembly convention that adopted the resolution, I asked the union consultant and a public employee relations board executive whether the NEA would allow the negotiation of public policy and public money that takes place in collective bargaining sessions to be held in open public meetings. In other words, Would the union agree to let the public monitor these governmental actions? The answer, of course, was a quick and definite "no." They explained that allowing the public to know what the two sides were discussing would destroy the process—"Too sensitive for the public." They thought I was silly for asking. Neither man was aware of the "Right to Know Resolution," but both were sure that governmental discussions of public policy matters were exempt from public disclosure laws when dealing with labor unions.

I admit I was being facetious, because I knew what the union's answer would be. However, I still believe it is a serious question in a country that prides itself on allowing its public to know what's going on in local government. At the very least, allowing union negotiations with school districts to be observed by the public would have a calming effect on the process. Allowing the press to participate would thwart the traditional "troop rallying" strategies unions use to agitate their memberships, and school districts would be relieved of the usual massive efforts to put a "spin" on the news.

Big unions are probably here to stay. However, they will contribute positively to the operation of school organizations only if the positional model of bargaining is abandoned and replaced with a collaborative model.

I'm often asked, What if the union or the board or the superintendent or the executive committee want part of collaborative labor relations but not all? What if they want to participate collaboratively in a broad range of important district policies and procedures much the way a collaborative labor relations model would work, yet they want to "bargain" wages and benefits? I explain that this is a trap. The district ends up in the worst of all positions, bargaining against itself. To make matters worse, when it runs out of money, the teachers are eventually insulted when demands for salary increases are rejected. In the long run this becomes a move *away* from collaboration and closer to labor turmoil. The next chapter will discuss why this happens.

3

✦

Fence Straddling:
A Recipe for Disaster

During one scene in *Oklahoma!*, Ado Annie exclaims to her boyfriend, "With me it's all or nuttin'!" She then righteously demands, "Is it all or nuttin' with you?" School leaders who have been experimenting with collaborative labor relations over the past twenty years have come to the conclusion that mixing collaborative labor relations with traditional bargaining doesn't work, and it's best not to try. Now, I'm not suggesting that you give up the idea of promoting collaboration at the first sign of recalcitrance from your union leaders. Quite the contrary: I believe school leaders must constantly push for quality, and as I discussed in the last chapter, school organizations cannot achieve their highest quality potential when fractured by confrontational industrial-style bargaining.

One superintendent, for example, described how his administrators and union leaders worked out a benefits package that turned out to be a boon to many of his faculty, as well as a savings over the long run to the district. But to do this, union and district officials needed to work together closely, often coming to decisions about one or more elements of the plan, then reversing their positions when additional data was uncovered. Very little of this superintendent's process is even possible in the positional "offer–counteroffer" atmosphere of the bargaining table. The result there would have been a small increase in benefits in trade for less salary increase or some other quid pro quo agreement. Let's face it: The traditional model requires a careful separation of the nobles and the serfs, the masters from the servants, those who serve from those who are served—and is totally at odds with what we know about the mutual support and service among all employees that fosters quality and productivity in organizations.

The ideal public stance for a board and administration is to endorse collaborative employee relations and publicly invite the unions to join with the administrators to forge an official document outlining cooperative and collaborative approaches to all matters dealing with the employment of teachers. At the same time, the board and administration must make it clear that the two games, confrontational positional bargaining and collaborative interest-based bargaining, are no more compatible than football and hopscotch. There simply is no way to combine a little of each. It's all or nothing.

TRYING TO MIX COLLABORATIVE AND
POSITIONAL BARGAINING

Over the past few years, a number of sincere but naive school districts have agreed to collaboratively work out contract language dealing with working conditions and other nonmonetary language—leaving only salary and benefits to be hammered out at the table. The district consequently has one foot in collaborative relations and one foot in confrontational relations. One district superintendent in Southern California announced buoyantly at a county superintendent's meeting that she had sewn up her teachers' contract for three years "with openers only on salary and benefits" using collaborative problem-solving strategies. Less than two years later, her openers were at an impasse, the district was in turmoil, and the teachers were threatening to strike. She learned the hard way that giving up the board's leverage with language in the spirit of cooperation leads to disaster.

The scenario I described is the worst of all worlds and must be avoided at all costs. What went wrong? In the final analysis, *the district only has money to put on the table.* All the rest is in the union's poke—union rights, working conditions, evaluation procedures, termination, leaves, grievances, and so on. Think about that for a moment. If the union collaboratively bargains over its chips (work), all of these issues and union interests will be addressed in a spirit of cooperation and mutual support, resulting in a big "win" for the union side and a "loss" for management. Then, when the money issue is addressed using the old confrontational industrial strategies, the district is caught with nothing to bargain over except money. Since the union doesn't have any money to put on the table, the district is forced to bargain against itself. Quid pro quo, the essence of balanced positional bargaining, is lost. The district is trapped.

THE COLLAPSE OF COLLABORATION IN SAN DIEGO

A classic example of this occurred during the rhetoric preceding a strike in San Diego. The union carped at the district for not raising its salary offer in response to their counteroffers. "We have lowered our salary demands twice in an effort to reach agreement," union leaders wailed. "The district has not responded." The union was not offering any quid pro quo concession in return for additional salary because the other language issues had already been settled—only money remained as openers. The only "concessions" the union offered were a series of discounts on the original salary raise proposal. The district was clearly trapped. With none of their chips on the table, union negotiators had backed the district into a corner with no options.

Predictably, the ensuing strike lasted only a few days until the lost salary was about equal to the raise that was on the table. Also predictably, the final settlement was very close to what the district would have been obliged by good faith bargaining to pay if the teachers had settled before the strike. Teachers, administration, parents, children, all of the district's stakeholders suffered a monstrous loss, although the union claimed a "glorious victory." Some San Diego teachers, of course, disagreed. Calling themselves "Your Concerned Peers," they circulated a rough-hewn flyer pointing out the net financial results of the strike (see exhibit 3.1).

It's only fair to add here that union officials don't agree that they settled for peanuts. They explain that they got some contingency language that would pull in all "backfill" money from the past two years in California. "Backfill" is used to describe revenue equalization aid and deficit reduction monies granted to districts according to their eligibility. The California Teachers Association (CTA) hopes it will add another 3 percent to the settlement. In the long run, they argue, the teachers will come out ahead.

Exhibit 3.1.   Anti-union Flyer

HERE'S SOMETHING SDTA WON'T POST

Dear Fellow Teacher:

Are you going to let the association do your thinking for you? Compare the figures below and determine for yourself if the strike was worth it:

Based on a teacher with 15 years' experience
on salary class E
Total Salary Per Year

Time Period	Settlement 5%, 2%, 2%, 5%	District Offer 5%, 3%, 3%	Difference	Total Gain for 3 Years
Sept 95–June 96	$50,848[a]	$50,448 (5%)	$400	
Sept 96–June 97	$51,872[b]	$51,962 (3%)	$–90	
Sept 97–June 98	$53,800[c]	$53,521 (3%)	$279	
Total	$156,520	$155,931	$589*	
Strike Salary Loss			$1371	$782

[a] = 5% raise beginning July 95; additional 2% beginning March 96.
[b] = Additional 2% beginning March 97.
[c] = Additional 5% beginning February 98.
*There are 552 contract days in this three-year contract. $589 dollars divided by 552 days means we struck for a little over a dollar a day. You can see for yourself what happens when we deduct the loss of pay for being on strike. There is no gain.

Think about this: Why hasn't the association distributed this breakdown?

Respectfully,

Your Concerned Peers

A MISSED OPPORTUNITY

The San Diego City Schools strike illustrates what happens when a district enters collaborative labor relations but doesn't succeed in getting the money off the table. In order to get the money off the table the union leadership and the district leadership must come to an agreement about the *criteria* for those salaries *before* salaries are negotiated. Otherwise the district is negotiating in a vacuum. Critical questions must be answered: Should raises be based on the increase in district revenues? Or the prevailing wages of surrounding districts? Or both? How does the faculty's desire for smaller classes and better working conditions fit in? Successful approaches for accomplishing this task have been developed and are discussed in detail in chapter 5. For now, we will focus on what went wrong in San Diego. For several years, the district enjoyed collaborative labor relations under district superintendent Tom Payzant and teachers' union president Hal Boyle. After Payzant left to take a job as assistant secretary of education and Boyle stepped down from his union presidency, the collaborative deal started to unravel. Previously Boyle and Payzant had worked informally to keep the pact together. However, in those early days, the concept of collaboration was more informal than formal. Observers agree that the collaborative pact was held together primarily by two powerful personalities. Few of the steps to institutionalize district–labor collaboration, as described later in chapter 5, were initiated. When Payzant and Boyle left their posts, the State of California was suffering hard times. Consequently, the reopeners in the contract inherited by the new superintendent produced nothing. The year before the strike, negotiations ended up in fact-finding. And, of course, the major issue was wages, although a second issue having to do with just cause for dismissal and discipline was also now on the table. The district balked at a modest salary increase, and the scene was set for what would eventually become a full-blown strike more than a year later.

A SHORT HISTORY OF COLLABORATION

Because of its short history with collaborative bargaining, the subsequent impasse and strike were even more antagonistic and hostile. Employees felt betrayed. One union leader explained, "The district was talking collaboration, and we saw our employees go three years without a raise! What's more, almost every other district in the county gave some raises during that period of time even though everybody had hard times. Everybody made an effort to say, 'Hey, times are tough. We'll do what we can.'"

Whether we like it or not, money is interpreted by our faculties as a symbol of how we value them. That's why the questions surrounding the criteria for establishing salaries must be asked, studied, and answered to the satisfaction of both the district and the union. And those criteria must be communicated to every staff member at every school jointly by the school's administrator and the school's building rep or other union official. Union officials and administrators close to the San Diego strike both speculated that the strike would not have occurred if Payzant and Boyle were in charge.

INSTITUTIONALIZING COLLABORATION
IN A SCHOOL DISTRICT

This presents a critical question: Is this a personality thing? Are collaborative labor relations dependent upon two adroit politicians making deals and schmoozing their constituencies? Or can realistic rules be forged? Can you set up something that will last?

If a superintendent is not committed to collaboration, will it always fail? I posed that question to one of the CTA's field specialists. He shrugged, and said, "I think personalities are always going to play a part in it." He went on to say that the CTA's interest-based bargaining and interest-based decision-making training is based on the premise that the district and union leaders want to do it. In other words, all parties concerned want to improve their collective bargaining situation.

I interrupted and asked, "What happened in San Diego?"

He replied, "If you don't make that decision-making process a part of the culture of the district, then it will just reside with the personalities. The Tom Payzants and Hugh Boyles made that thing work."

"Wait a minute," I said. "I know for a fact the San Diego Administration and Teacher Leaders were trained in collaborative strategies."

"But the training didn't emphasize making it a part of the culture in the district. It focused on the Harvard project and on interest-based bargaining techniques."

I said, "I don't understand. Isn't that what we're talking about?"

His eyes narrowed, and he pointed a finger at me. "Okay. But you can't let it stop there. It has to be part of the decision-making process at the *sites*—you know, throughout the district."

The veteran labor leader continued to describe examples of districts that did it right. He mentioned another district further north as one where all of the stakeholders are committed to the process. "They trained the bargaining teams, the certificated management, and the classified management. Then they went beyond that and trained the classified reps and the classified supervisors, the CTA reps and the building principals and vice principals."

His point was this: Districts that succeed in implementing and *maintaining* collaborative labor relations have institutionalized interest-based decision making throughout the district. "The district up north conducts training sessions for board candidates before they become board members." To sum it up, he added, "So when the superintendent leaves, the process doesn't leave with her."

One major key to durable collaborative labor relations is institutionalization and training. A number of districts have accomplished this. Others have tried and failed. From the perspective of a union observer, the original success in San Diego was because of personalities, not institutionalized processes. The San Diego administrators whom I interviewed agreed more or less with this assessment but added one other critical element. "When Payzant left," according to one district official, "the board took over. Ron Ottinger's [board member] pet project to lower class size cost a ton of money."

He went on to explain that the unions were not at all supportive of the board's class size reduction initiative, but it didn't look good politically for them to oppose it. However, this, combined with the fact that the district's administrative salary schedule was one of the best around, added further fuel to the fire set by the enforcement of rigid COLA (the state's cost of living adjustment) language in the reopeners. In chapter 5, we will examine COLA along with other criteria for adjusting salaries in more detail. It is sufficient to say at this point that any agreement that results in a perceived inequity is fuel for discontent—especially if management decides to punish the union by forcing it to live with an obsolescent agreement in a contract.

THE LESSON OF FENCE STRADDLING

As a result of the district's history of fence straddling, prospects for collaborative labor relations for San Diego are not good. According to one San Diego administrator involved with negotiations, the union has already said, "Oh, just because we had a strike this last time, don't think we're not gonna have another." Another administrator commented, "The faculty feels that they kicked our asses last time, and they feel pretty good about it."

When I asked whether he thought teachers would go out again during these negotiations, he smacked his lips and stated deliberately, "I think, basically, the rank-and-file teacher does not want to go out on another strike. But they feel empowered now on this [way of negotiating]."

Obviously, the time was right for beginning cooperative labor relations when Payzant and Boyle were in power. Payzant had the confidence of the board and Boyle the confidence of the union, and the two of them were committed to "working things out."

A NEW SUPERINTENDENT'S ADVANTAGES

When Tom Payzant arrived as the new superintendent from Oklahoma City, he had several advantages that led to his success in establishing collaborative labor relations.

First, the San Diego teachers were still suffering from the disruption of the 1976 strike. The faculties felt far less victorious in the years following what proved to be a very unsettling labor dispute. The unions were much less confident that they would be able to rally the teachers for another job action, a factor that severely limited their leverage.

Second, Tom Payzant had presided over a strike while in the Oklahoma City superintendency. Many people saw the somber intellectual as a man coming in to break the union—or at least one capable of doing battle with the militants. In other words, union leaders didn't feel they could frighten him with threats of disruption and walkouts. From the beginning, Payzant dealt with the unions from a position of strength. This latter point should be emphasized. When either the district or union leaders approach the other to propose collaboration, they must be ready to abandon the industrial-style bargaining model. It's all or nothing. But there is little incentive for one side to abandon the adversarial model when the opponent is not a worthy adversary! For example, the San Diego teachers' union in 2001 has little reason to embrace collaboration when its experience with it in recent years has been poor and its victory in the previous strike was so satisfying and gratifying. The specter of a new superintendent with strong traditional negotiating experience capable of beating the unions at their own game might change this, but at the present time the district leaders do not pose a serious threat.

Third, Payzant's intellectuality was matched by a mature union president who enjoyed the confidence of the faculties. Politically speaking, deals struck between the two would fly—and they did.

Finally, and this is not to be understated, Payzant's tenure was accompanied by a period of relative stability in California school finance. During this period, the San Diego district enjoyed generous cost of living adjustments to its revenue calculations. Consequently, it was not difficult to pass on comfortable wage hikes for several years in a row, further enhancing the Payzant–Boyle image in the eyes of faculty and administrators, as well as the board of education.

4

School Reform and the Evolution of Labor Relations

Veteran school administrators grimace every time another school re-form bandwagon rounds the corner. Whether we call it "reform," "school improvement," "restructuring," "teacher empowerment," or "quality management," the message is the same: We must do something to increase the creativity and productivity of our teachers. School leaders try to hide behind the folklore of tenure ("We can't get rid of bad teach-ers"). Others adopt a self-loathing stance, complaining of low salaries that result in too many inferior personnel. Of all the apologies proffered, com-plaints about industrial-style teacher unions are probably most valid. Co-incidentally, they are also the problem we probably can remedy most ef-fectively and quickly. Unleashing creativity and productivity among teachers requires a system that deals with them as professionals, and it begins with professional employee–employer relationships. Since employee unions constitute a major part of the educational system, school reform efforts without teachers' union reform will amount to trivial institutional therapy. Clearly, no reform effort can be successful if it ignores reform in labor relations. Truly successful, quality organizations are those that promote the full potential of each constituent human being. The ideal is achieved by organizations that encourage their employees to dedicate themselves to *continual enhancement* of their organization's missions.

Much has been made of successful Japanese industrial organizations assisted by American statistician W. Edward Deming (1986). Few students of business management will dispute the impact the Japanese success has had upon industrial organizations around the world, including those in the United States. Most, however, will point out that the Japanese industrial reformers were not forced to contend with self-centered, hostile American-style unions and concomitant worker apathy toward quality. Although labor relations in American industry are changing, much of it has to do simply with the decline of unionism. I, for one, am frightened by this prospect. The total demise of unions would reopen the door to hostile, self-centered management and massive employee exploitation. No one wants that. What Americans want are better unions.

Sadly, the collective bargaining model adopted by teachers when they entered the bargaining arena four decades ago was the one that seemed at the time to be working for most of the private-sector unions. The good news is that modern school labor leaders, like their industrial sector counterparts, are recognizing the need to build better labor–management relations. The optimists among the observers of the school labor relations scene see gradual movement away from confrontational positional bargaining toward cooperative, collaborative bargaining models. School district and teachers' union leaders alike recognize that educational reform in U. S. schools cannot be separated from labor reform. Excellence in school districts goes hand in hand with cooperative, collaborative staff relations that reach from the top to the bottom of an organization (Murphy and Hallinger, 1990).

FROM PATERNALISM TO COLLABORATION—A CONTINUUM

Ken Parker, a leading NEA teachers' union bargaining specialist who has been through many years of serious teachers' union labor strife in New York and California, describes the readiness of a school district for collaborative relations as five points along a continuum. (See exhibit 4.1.)

The continuum, according to Parker, begins with *paternalism*. The superintendent provides for employee needs and regulates employee con-

Exhibit 4.1. Continuum of Employer–Employee Relationships

Relationship	Significant Characteristics
Paternalism	On the surface there is a good relationship between parties; the superintendent provides for all employee needs and regulates employee conduct; the relationship is based on the authority of the superintendent and is totally conditioned upon his or her goodwill; all the power rests with one person.
Enemy	There is hostility toward the other party, a refusal to recognize its existence; the relationship is characterized by continuous challenges and threats to the other party.
Adversary	There is a strong resistance to the other party, an arm's-length relationship with minimum acceptance and very strong defense, support, and maintenance of positions, proposals, and so on; either party could accept destruction of the other but would not seek it; some element of challenge to the other party still exists.
Advocacy	There is an acceptance of the other party; both parties are respectful of the rights of the other but employ strong defense, support, and maintenance of their own positions, proposals. Both parties are nonthreatening to the other party.
Collaboration	There is strong *mutual* acceptance of the other party, and the dominant approach is that of problem solving; the relationship is nonthreatening or nonchallenging; there is a willingness to submerge an advocacy relationship to gain broad objectives beneficial to both parties rather than to just one.

duct. Paternalism could be described as a "father–son relationship" and is based on the authority of the superintendent. The second point on the continuum surfaced in the 1960s when many states instituted collective bargaining plans for teachers. Relationships between teachers and administrators in numerous districts nationwide changed radically to that of *enemies.* This phase of the continuum, which still exists in many "adolescent" districts in the nation, is characterized by a reluctance on the part of school district leaders to recognize the legitimate existence of unions, and by incessant threats and challenges made by union officials. In time, the enemy phase becomes a less hostile *adversary* situation, maintaining a strong resistance and an arm's-length relationship. However, in the adversary phase, district leaders accept the legitimate existence of the union, and union leaders concede that district leaders need room to administer programs effectively. A détente begins to take shape.

In the absence of major conflict triggering a setback, the adversary phase of the continuum will eventually mellow to the fourth phase of district maturation, *advocacy.* This is the last point on the continuum to which a labor–management relationship can mature without revamping the philosophical approach to bargaining. At this point, major mutual concessions by the leadership of both factions should be possible, given a desire to accomplish this goal. At this point the district accepts the union and respects its rights and roles. Union leaders in the advocacy stage support and maintain their positions and proposals but do not challenge or threaten the district's leadership. In many respects, this phase of the continuum represents a mature, workable arrangement that allows a traditional line and staff organization to function effectively with minimal abuse of employees by administrators and minimal disruption of the organization by employees.

Parker maintains that once a mature relationship has developed during the advocacy phase, district and union leaders are ready to move to the final point on the continuum, *collaboration.* To achieve this ideal, the district must be willing to give up part of its authority to the employees who are accomplishing the mission of the school district—certainly an ideal endorsed by leaders of today's quality movement. Likewise, the union must be willing to submerge the advocacy relationship to gain broad objectives beneficial to both the employees and the district. When this relationship is achieved, district operations are characterized by organizational mechanisms designed to solve problems. Problem solving becomes the standard operating procedure for matters of concern both to the district and its unions.

If your district is at stage 4 or 5 of the continuum, then skip chapters 6, 7, and 8, which deal with strike preparation and management. Focus on chapter 5, "Launching Collaborative Relations with the Teachers' Union."

If your district is at stage 2 or 3, you will undoubtedly be involved in traditional bargaining. The key here is to do it well.

Critics of industrial-style collective bargaining for public school employees are often confused with opponents of collective bargaining. I was once invited to a Republican women's club to talk about the sorry state of labor relations and public schools. My audience was shocked when I revealed that I supported collective bargaining for teachers. I went on to explain that the current master–servant model of employee unions is not appropriate for public schools. Instead, a new professional union model should be developed. This would give collective bargaining the potential for inspiring a greater number of professional educators in the school organization to become leaders and to contribute more significantly to the betterment of an organization. I admitted that the model most frequently used today in negotiations with teacher unions is just plain stupid. (This helped me regain rapport with a few members of my audience.)

"The collective bargaining model we use," I explained, "was borrowed from the industrial sector simply because we didn't have any better ideas at the time." I explained that in the absence of good ideas, a state's public employee relations board (PERB) would look to the National Labor Relations Board's (NLRB) precedence for guidance. The latter organization was set up by the Wagner Act in the 1930s to deal with old-time industrial unions. At the onset of collective bargaining in any given state, school administrators were immediately trained in draconian industrial-model strategies. Administrators in those early days even talked of initiating teacher time-card procedures. From the very beginning, attention was focused on "minutes of instruction" and "duty-free lunches" and myriad other time-related topics that clearly defined the teaching profession in factory-worker terms. It is unequivocally clear that improvement in the design and implementation of collective bargaining is sorely needed to resolve the issues facing schools today.

I am convinced, as are other critics of today's bargaining model, that collective bargaining will continue to be an integral part of school governance. As I mentioned earlier, it's here to stay.

I am also convinced that reforming the current collective bargaining model, including the laws that support them, is necessary before we can produce the school reform our country is demanding. And this means changing the way we do our bargaining. But if your district is saddled with a recalcitrant union that insists upon a traditional model and refuses to explore alternatives with you, then you have no alternative other than to participate in the process as required by today's laws. The next few paragraphs outline the major concepts, processes, and procedures of the industrial-style negotiations model and offer suggestions pertaining to that approach. I will not discuss the processes exhaustively since many fine books are written on the subject. It is vital, however, that administrators conducting negotiations with teacher unions be well prepared both in the state laws governing collective bargaining and the art of bargaining.

EXCLUSIVE REPRESENTATION

A fundamental element in all collective bargaining processes is the selection of an exclusive bargaining representative. This is accomplished by an election, usually conducted by the committee of state officials in charge of regulating collective bargaining (the state equivalent of the NLRB). The representative is normally an affiliate of one of the large national unions (NEA or AFT). It also can be an independent local teachers' organization, however. Once the exclusive representative has been identified, it assumes the obligation of representing all teachers, whether they are members of the organization or not.

Similar processes are conducted for the noncertified members of the staff. Usually the unions involved are affiliates of the American Federation of Labor-Congress of Industrial Organizations (AFL-CIO), although in recent years, the teacher unions have pushed to organize these folks. Often the noncertified staff is clustered into more than one bargaining unit, frequently represented by more than one union. For example, the secretarial-clerical staff may form a bargaining unit and elect a union that primarily represents office employees or state employees. District maintenance personnel, carpenters, and plumbers, on the other hand, would probably form a separate bargaining unit and affiliate with one of the trade unions. In any event, once the exclusive representative is elected by the bargaining unit, it is responsible for representing the interests of every member of that bargaining unit, including employees who choose not to belong to the union.

SCOPE OF BARGAINING

Scope of bargaining refers to those aspects of public school employment that the school board is required, by law, to put on the table when negotiating with the exclusive bargaining representative. In the private sector, these aspects are determined by the NLRB. They include wages, hours, terms, and conditions of employment. In most states, the scope of bargaining for school employees is spelled out in statute. Usually, the basic list is very similar to the NLRB's list: wages, hours, terms, and conditions of employment. Frequently, it is up to the state-level labor relations board to determine whether the school operations fall into categories that are bargainable. Some teacher associations, for example, argue that the curriculum should be negotiable as well as the number of students in the classroom.

High on the list of traditional concerns of teachers brought to the bargaining table are procedures for transfer, evaluation, promotion, and grievances. High on the list of concerns for union officials are agency fees, release time for union officers, and binding arbitration.

THE NEGOTIATING PROCESS

Collective bargaining laws generally specify a process patterned after the one established by the National Labor Relations Act of 1935—with a few minor modifications to adapt the process for public agencies.

Sunshining

The first step, usually a requirement for all public agencies, involves "sunshining" the initial bargaining proposals so that the public has a chance to inspect the issues before negotiations begin. This process really has little meaning, however, because both proposals contain a potpourri of requests and demands that are no more than "chips" to be bargained away in the negotiating process.

Following the required sunshining of the proposals, the two negotiating teams meet and establish a calendar of negotiation sessions.

Nothing in the collective bargaining laws requires school district negotiations to be held in public. Typically, they are held in private at the request of the unions.

Good Faith Bargaining

The two negotiating teams are charged with the responsibility of bargaining in good faith. At the end of two or three months of negotiations, a tentative agreement is usually produced. Once this tentative agreement has been accepted by the teachers' association and adopted by the school board, the new contract is in force and the negotiation process ends.

Impasse

If the two teams fail to reach agreement, either side can ask the state-level labor relations board to declare an impasse.

Mediation

Following the declaration of impasse by the labor relations board, a mediator is assigned by the state to the negotiation process. The mediator attempts to counsel both parties and to suggest alternatives for breaking the impasse. Often, a mediator is able to clarify the real bottom-line issues and, in many cases, propose rational compromise packages that could not have been developed in the hostile arena of traditional adversarial negotiations.

Fact-Finding

If the mediation process is not successful, the next step is fact-finding. Although the name of this phase of negotiations suggests some sort of independent investigation, fact-finding is simply a courtroom-style hearing of the arguments. The "fact-finder" is a hearing officer or law judge who hears the cases presented by the negotiators for each side (often attorneys). Once the cases are presented and the witnesses cross-examined, the fact-finder closes the hearing and writes his or her "findings." The fact-finder's recommendations are not binding on the school board.

Post-Fact-Finding Negotiations

Once the fact-finder's report has been released, the two negotiating teams are again obliged to meet for post-fact-finding negotiations. The purpose of these negotiations is to explore whether the objective fact-finder has added any insights that might bring about a settlement.

Arbitration

In some states, the law provides for an arbitrator to settle the dispute in the event that the teachers' union and the school board cannot reach a final settlement. In most cases, the arbitrator's decision must be one of the two "last best offers." In other words, after hearing the evidence and considering the argument, the arbitrator will rule in favor of the union or in favor of the district. "Splitting the difference" is not permitted. Theoretically, this procedure motivates the two sides to bargain reasonably and in good faith before going to arbitration. Outrageous demands, presumably, would cause the arbitrator to rule in favor of the other team's last best offer.

CONCERTED ACTION

After the mediation and fact-finding processes are over, unions in states where strikes are permitted are entitled to withhold services. In some states where strikes are not expressly permitted, the courts have ruled that work stoppages are not illegal and thus cannot be stopped by court action. It is important to note, however, that strikes and slowdowns are never sanctioned by labor relations boards or courts before the entire negotiations process has been exhausted—including mediation and fact-finding—unless provoked by an unfair labor practice. Complaints against unions that strike prematurely are usually supported by the labor relations boards. The unions are subsequently subject to substantial penalties.

UNION SECURITY

Unions negotiate with employers for various means to strengthen their positions with the bargaining units they represent. One of three arrangements is usually sought: agency fees, payroll deduction, or maintenance of membership.

AGENCY FEE

The agency fee is most advantageous for the union. It requires that all employees in the bargaining unit either join the union and pay dues or pay a "fee" roughly equivalent to the dues. The purpose of the fee is to require all employees to pay a fair share of the union's cost of representing the employees. The Supreme Court has ruled that the employee's nonunion fee cannot be calculated to include the cost of the union's political activities (*Chicago Teachers Union v. Hudson,* 1986). Consequently, in many states, the required fee for employees who choose not to join the union is approximately 10 to 30 percent less than membership dues.

CONTRACT MANAGEMENT AND GRIEVANCE PROCEDURES

Commenting on the future of the United Auto Workers, one of the union's colorful outgoing presidents pointed out that union leaders don't build strong unions; company managers build strong unions. Whether the school district is involved with a progressive, cooperative labor relations model or a traditional adversarial model, the success of negotiations often lies in the hands of school administrators. In the past, this has meant equal and uniform application and implementation of the contracts at all sites and with all employees. The evolution of unionism in education, as well as the demand for more flexibility in school systems, now renders this expectation more difficult to deliver.

Decentralizing authority to empower faculty closest to the point of implementation requires that contract management and contracts also be decentralized to a certain degree. This requires a new way of thinking about school systems, unions, and managers. Attitudes on both sides of the table must change to make school reform possible. Exhibit 4.2 is a diagnostic test of attitudes prevalent in a district. A district typified by attitudes in column A (Industrial Unions) is forced to manage the contract in a highly uniform, centralized fashion. A district typified by attitudes in Column B (Professional Unions) will be able to afford greater flexibility at the site level.

Exhibit 4.2. A Diagnostic Test of Attitudes toward Union–Management Collaboration

(Circle the statements most typical of the attitudes in your district)

Industrial Unionism Attitudes	*Professional Unionism Attitudes*
1. Management viewed as adversaries	1. Management viewed as collaborator
2. Us vs. them (teachers vs. administrators)	2. We (educators)
3. Centralized control of the contract	3. Decentralized control of the contract
4. Separate union/management committees	4. Joint union–management committees
5. Protection of employment most important	5. Quality of teaching most important
6. Uniformity of work rules	6. Flexibility of work rules
7. Initial response is to attack management	7. Initial response is to attack the problem
8. Risk belongs to management, reward to employees	8. Risk and reward belong to both
9. Self-interest of employees is primary	9. Self-interest is balanced with public good
10. "Customer" is the union member	10. "Customer" is the student, profession, community, union member

---

ASSESSING A DISTRICT'S POTENTIAL FOR COLLABORATIVE LABOR RELATIONS

An analysis of district attitudes described in exhibit 4.2 would also be useful in determining whether to vigorously pursue the launch of collaborative labor relations or to spend more energy preparing for traditional positional bargaining. Chapter 5 explores preparation for collaboration; chapter 6 explores preparation for the traditional model.

5

Launching Collaborative Relations with the Teachers' Union

M oving from enemy to collaborator along the continuum described by Ken Parker in chapter 4 requires a readiness on the part of both the district leadership and the union leadership. The courtship between these two players requires maturity and experience as Koppich (1993) quite correctly points out. The new marriage of labor and management is built around three mutually reinforcing principles: the first amounts to "joint custody" of the reform efforts by the management and the union. The second is a necessary but dangerous and politically charged concept of union–management collaboration in the governance of the school district, and the third is a more noble and authentic concern for the interests of the public—the communities we serve. Both factions of the school district must own the system and be willing to collaborate for the greater good of the students in the community.

Unfortunately, many district and union leaders have achieved the necessary maturity, wisdom, and experience the hard way—by experiencing the pain and suffering of prolonged labor turmoil with its concomitant negative impact on community relations, teacher productivity, and job satisfaction. One superintendent who has observed numerous failed attempts at collaborative labor relations told me that the best chance for success occurs *after* the community, board members, administrators, and employees have all tasted the bitter fruits of a protracted war of rhetoric, strikes, and dirty tricks. It is frightening to think that the agony of strikes or prolonged labor strife must be endured before the scene can be set for the kind of collaboration Parker describes. But it may be naive to believe that wise people with noble spirits and honorable intentions can learn from the experience and research of others.

THE BASICS—DEALING WITH SALARIES AND CONTRACTS

Whether the readiness for collaborative labor relations is achieved through intellectual inquiry or through the school of hard knocks, willingness on both sides to relearn roles is critical. Union leaders must abandon the traditional "troop rallying" tactics that previously have been the basis of their power. In doing so, they risk loss of support by their constituents or by state and national union officials. On the other hand, the school board and administrators of the district must be willing to relinquish a certain amount of authority and control. To make it work, however, leaders on both sides must transcend petty politics and embrace a higher-order organizational philosophy that considers all human endeavor important.

Twenty-five years ago, when educational scholars and leaders were calling for cooperative labor relations, the big argument was greater job satisfaction and productivity among teachers. Today those arguments still apply. However, at stake now is the very existence of public schools. It is worth saying again: School districts and their unions must permanently discard the action–reaction, adversarial management models and climb aboard the bandwagon of organizational reform that is reshaping some of America's industries. Simply put, excellence in the school business ultimately is teachers teaching very well, and this fact demands a highly developed labor relations model.

Highly developed or not, a labor relations model has two distinct halves: the first is composed of the processes and procedures for negotiating the contract. The second is the administration of the contract. Naturally, the success of each of these two components depends, to a degree, upon the success of the other. That is, negotiations will be more difficult when the contract is administered poorly, resulting in a long list of employee grievances, and vice versa. If negotiations are long and hostile, the administration of the contract becomes more difficult. For a quality union–management relations model to succeed, it must stress *both* contract negotiation and contract administration.

Following is a discussion of four principles that directly address the barriers to the development of a collaborative labor relations model in a school district. The four principles are interdependent and, in my experience, must all be present for the model to succeed.

Principle #1: Get the Money off the Table

As I stated in chapter 1, the major complication in the union–management relationship is salary. Almost everything a school district does boils down to money. The first step in the development of a collaborative labor–management relationship is to adopt a method for establishing salaries and benefits that avoids the potentially explosive offer–counteroffer approach.

I've found that the most successful districts set salaries and benefits by adopting a set of criteria or a formula that very specifically defines salary and benefits adjustments. (See exhibit 5.1.) These are based on district income, cost of living, and other pertinent indices. In several districts, the ease of tying the teachers' annual salary hikes to the state's cost of living adjustment (COLA) resulted in a mistake similar to the one General Motors made when it tied raises to a national cost of living index. Codifying the statewide COLA in the contract created a rigidity that eventually caused the "formula" to fail. No single indicator is adequate to establish an equitable increase in salary. The key here is to be precise enough to avoid misunderstanding while at the same time protecting the interests of both parties. I've found that successful formulae have three features in common.

- *Salary goals.* The sizes of salaries for the unit members are defined in terms of comparisons with other districts in the county or state. In other words, the union and board establish where their salaries will rank among others paid in the profession. This is the definition of "paying the going wage." A good way to approach this is to identify a "benchmark" salary placement on the salary schedule, such as the highest regularly scheduled salary (not including super-anniversary increments). Naturally, pick one that is common to all the salary schedules of the districts in the comparison group you agree upon.

Picking the highest salary a teacher can make after ten to fifteen years in the district eliminates the possibility that other salaries on a schedule might be out of line and not representative of the entire schedule. And, it guarantees that the professional teacher who reaches the top of the schedule always earns a salary commensurate with the district's salary goals.

- *Total compensation concept.* When comparing salaries among comparison districts, ALL compensation must be included. This means the cost of medical and dental benefits, pro-rata retirement benefits, golden handshakes, master's degrees, and so forth. In other words, it is the total compensation an employee receives when he or she is assigned to a position on the salary schedule. A great deal of care must be taken when comparing salaries that all benefits and salary enhancements are included. Otherwise, true comparability cannot be achieved, and decisions to pay the "going rate" cannot be made based on these comparisons.

- *Forecasting mechanism for salary increases.* A method exists for forecasting the raises other districts in the comparison group eventually receive. It is unfair to ask employees to wait for other districts to settle their salary negotiations before granting a raise. Adjusting salaries to the benchmarks a year late means the salaries are always behind a year. Some of the very traditional districts might not settle for two or three years, resulting in skewed salary averages. Eventually, these districts always settle, resulting in huge "catch-up" raises. In states where the legislature sets the COLA for school districts each year, the task is easier. A formula based on the expected increase in funds can be established, which will probably reflect average raises across the state and in the comparison group used by your district. However, unforeseen variables, such as special state or federal grants to accomplish various political objectives, can distort the salary increases. For this reason, the forecasting mechanism must allow the district and union leaders the flexibility to modify the forecast based on extraordinary circumstances.

  Here is where it is essential that both union and district leaders fully understand the larger picture. Both parties benefit from very accurate predictions. If a prediction is too low and the salaries fall behind the comparison districts, then salaries must be boosted a larger amount the following year, causing a budget squeeze for the business manager. If predictions are too high, a lower raise the following year results, causing employees to question their union leadership.

Exhibit 5.1 presents an example of a formula actually in use today in a state where the legislature determines the COLA each year. Note that the

COLA is not mentioned in the formula. District and union leaders in this district wanted to avoid the rigidity that could lead to ultimate failure. Instead, the formula leaves the determination up to the union president and the superintendent—recognizing fully that the success of the process depends on the accuracy of their forecast. Both parties accept ownership of the final settlement and responsibility for explaining the results to their constituents. Note also that the "formula" does not prevent another small incremental adjustment in the event that certain aspects of the financial picture are not clear when the school year begins and employees expect their increases.

Exhibit 5.1 addresses the idea that all employee benefits should be increased by the same formula-based amount. Since this amount has a rational basis in district revenue increases, the concept usually works well and prevents the undesirable catch-up game.

Skeptics often ask, "What happens when the costs of fringe benefits go through the ceiling?" The answer to this lies in the concept of total compensation described above. When faced with the real costs of "nice" but not essential fringes, union leaders can help make decisions to reduce or cap benefits that represent the best mix of good salaries and good benefits for the employees. When these costs are irrationally deemed to be "outside" the scope of compensation, an unfair burden is placed on the district, which I believe will eventually result in failure of the formula.

What happens when the electrical bills and other utilities skyrocket? This variable is more difficult and requires more sophistication on the part of the union and district leaders. An unexpected financial burden imposed by the utility companies or by other real or political disasters amounts to a decrease in available funds. The formula in exhibit 5.1

Exhibit 5.1. A Formula for Salary Increases

Serendipity School District Certificated Master Contract

Certificated Salary Schedule Formula
In subsequent years, raises will be calculated to the following formula:
1. Projected mean salary increase for San Diego County Unified School Districts as determined jointly by the superintendent and the association president or representatives.
2. Plus (positive or negative) difference between prior years' negotiated salary increase and mean SDCUSD salary increase in order to maintain number four (4) position among the ten San Diego County Unified Districts. For comparison purposes, the top regularly scheduled salary (step 11, class VI for XYZ) will be used.

The District will apply the yearly percentage increases for all monetary benefits for certificated personnel (i.e., stipends, hourly rates, etc.).

would allow for this sort of crisis, especially if the comparison group districts were sufficiently alike and were experiencing the same problems. Over the years, however, most of these spiking costs even out and will not put a formula in jeopardy.

It is advisable for negotiators to consult with a district that has had successful experience using criteria applicable to their district and their state's financial scheme before entering into a formula agreement. Visits to other districts also provide opportunities for union and district leaders to extend their dialogue and build a foundation for collaboration. This foundation is most fragile at the beginning and can be destroyed easily by a blundering superintendent or a power-hungry union leader. Our profession has an ample supply of both types; consequently, there aren't many long-lasting examples of collaboration in existence. A thoughtful examination of exhibit 5.1 should convince you that trust is an essential ingredient of a collaborative labor relationship.

Once the question of salaries and benefits is resolved, many other issues "evaporate." The way is paved to eliminate the "we–they" mind-set characteristic of the industrial-style bargaining model. This is not to say there are no other important issues. Certainly academic freedom, transfer, discipline, and grievance procedures are of concern to teachers. However, for a number of reasons very basic to human beings, salaries and benefits have the greatest emotional impact. When unions no longer need big blue-chip trade-offs, collegial union–management teams become possible. School boards can concentrate on being good policymakers; teachers and administrators can concentrate on educating children. Consequently, a good deal of time and energy must be spent to accomplish this first step effectively. In fact, nothing can really be accomplished until this first step is solidly nailed down. As I point out in chapter 3, moving on to other aspects of developing a collaborative model before the salary and benefits issue has been settled can lead to disaster.

Since salaries and benefits are extremely important to virtually every person in the organization, this first step can make or break the effort to launch collaborative labor relations. Collaboration must not appear to union members to be capitulation. Nor must it assume an aspect of cohabitation between union officers and district administrators. If this happens, the arrangement will be short-lived, and the aftermath may create greater antagonism than existed before the experimentation began. Union leaders must continue to be perceived as taking care of business— handling bread-and-butter matters for the membership.

Principle #2: Put the Contract on the Shelf

Teachers, particularly union leaders, feel more comfortable if they have the protection of a standard master contract that includes all the traditional provisions. A strong contract actually helps create a climate of positive labor–management trust and relieves the concern that a future malevolent board and administration will take advantage of the union's trust. Establishment of this basic document allows the union leadership to forgo the annual language-negotiations ritual, providing a workable conflict resolution mechanism is put in place that allows the employee representatives to work out problems as they arise. This prevents the union from being "stung" by contract language (or lack of it) as times change. Instead, the leaders can spend their time planning and implementing reform.

Only when provisions of the contract become obsolete, or when circumstances require sound personnel policy to be written into the contract, is it necessary to negotiate changes. Even then, the deliberations assume a problem-solving format. "Escape clauses" allowing contract language to be suspended under certain circumstances must be added to eliminate the paralyzing effect on reform efforts that rigid and complicated work rules have had. The idea is to develop fair employment practices within a climate of trust. Union officials should no longer feel an urgency to make "progress" on the contract. However, all of this requires that a *satisfactory mechanism* for dealing with myriad employee concerns and grievances be established and operating effectively.

Principle #3: Develop a First-Class Employer–Employee Grievance and Communications Process

In order to establish a satisfactory mechanism for communicating with employees and dealing with their concerns, the district leadership must first accept the premise that employee organizations are not simply informal interest groups outside the official district structure, but rather are affiliate institutions parallel to the district's administration and lawfully sanctioned by the legislature. It does not take an expert to recognize that employee organizations should be included formally in the management scheme of the school district. Like the salary and benefits criteria for formulas, this can be done in a variety of ways, depending upon the size of the district and/or the district's customs and priorities.

Districts that have successfully developed collaborative relations with their employees often utilize formally constituted contract management councils that are similar to grievance councils used in the private sector. The councils are usually composed of the superintendent, a few administrators, the executive officers of the association, and some assorted representatives. Usually separate councils are organized for the certificated and classified staffs. These councils meet monthly (or more often if needed) to discuss any topic of concern to district employees. Conclusions are drawn, and decisions are made that result in proposals to the management team and governing board in the form of administrative procedures and board policies. Exhibit 5.2 displays a policy and administrative procedure establishing employee councils.

Exhibit 5.2. Employee Advisory Councils

Serendipity School District
Board Policy
Administration

ADMINISTRATIVE ORGANIZATION EMPLOYEE ADVISORY COUNCILS

The superintendent of the Serendipity Unified School District is encouraged to utilize all of the resources, both human and material, available to him/her for the purpose of effective and efficient operation of the school district in order to develop and maintain positive employer–employee relations, to provide an opportunity for all employees to contribute to the improvement of the district, to conduct negotiations, and to better implement the Employee Master Contracts; the superintendent shall establish employee advisory councils which will assist him/her with these tasks.

Serendipity School District
Administrative Procedures
Personnel

ADMINISTRATIVE ORGANIZATION EMPLOYEE ADVISORY COUNCIL CERTIFICATED/CLASSIFIED

The certificated Advisory Council (Kitchen Cabinet)

Membership

The council shall be composed of the executive board of the exclusive representative of the certificated bargaining unit, the personnel director, and the superintendent.

Purpose

The purpose of the council shall be (1) to effectively implement the SEA master contract, (2) to assist the district superintendent in developing and maintaining positive employer–employee relations, (3) to conduct negotiations and to provide a formal channel through which suggestions for improvement or other concerns of employees may be reviewed.

This council shall *not* replace the formal procedures established in district policies or employee agreements for the processing of employee concerns, neither shall it replace the regular organizational structure established for the development, administration, and operation of district programs. The intent will be for the council to help identify and resolve potential problems prior to the need for the utilization of any of the formal procedures established for this purpose. The council will meet with the superintendent once per month and on special occasions as agreed by the superintendent and the association president.

The benefit of this process is obvious. Instead of allowing situations to fester for months, awaiting the once-a-year or once-every-three-years contract negotiations, employee work-rule problems are confronted and resolved as they occur. The organization grows and changes with the times.

Principle #4: Establish Union-Managed Input Systems

The unions must join with the district leadership to clear the lines of communication. In one district, for example, the union employed elaborate communication devices at each of the school sites to collect employee concerns. The teachers' association had a suggestion box attached to the bulletin board in every staff lounge. Instructions on the box encouraged teachers to submit topics to the contract management council, which in their district had been dubbed the Kitchen Cabinet. Exhibit 5.3 gives an example of the forms that were located in every faculty room.

In stark contrast to the standard operating procedures employed by their industrial-style counterparts, unions participating in collaborative district governance play a significant role in clarifying district procedures and opening important lines of communication. No longer are they required to foster suspicion and fear among their constituents with misinterpretations of administrative actions. Instead, the majority of the concerns brought to the associations by employees are resolved informally, *by association representatives or leaders.* If a concern is the result of a misunderstanding, it is addressed simply by correcting the misunderstanding. At other times, union representatives will counsel employees to help them use the established system to solve their problems. In other words, the new professional union uses its resources and energy to help the system operate more effectively. In this role unions become a very valuable part of a system's governance and contribute measurably to its success.

Exhibit 5.3.   Serendipity School District Teacher Concern Survey

Submitted to: Kitchen Cabinet _____ Rep Council _____
Confidential: Yes/No

From:_____

Site:_____

Date:_____

Problem or concern:

6

✛

Preparing for Positional Bargaining with the Teachers' Union

A major disadvantage of formal industrial-style bargaining is the lockstep, legalistic calendar of procedures that govern the process. As noted in chapter 5, negotiations with employee unions rightfully should take place all year long. Bread-and-butter issues, of course, such as salaries, wages, retirement, leaves of absence, extra pay, and insurance, should be studied in depth shortly before the commencement of a formal negotiations session, and rightly should be settled once per year. However, negotiating non-salary related issues, such as teacher evaluations, transfers, extra duty, class size, student discipline, and faculty discipline on a once-a-year basis, or worse, on a once-every-three-years basis, is not good for the organization. It guarantees slow school district response to a rapidly changing environment. As I will point out later, this is an aggravating weakness of the industrial-style model. When a contract is "sewn up" for three years, it often prevents management from making decisions in the best interests of faculty and the school district.

One Midwestern superintendent described his experience with this dilemma. His school district had suffered a long period of student decline, resulting in many faculty layoffs, which, in turn, caused forced transfers of teachers from school to school to balance the staffs. In many cases, first grade teachers ended up teaching fourth grade, high school teachers teaching junior high, and social studies teachers teaching English. The district's contract gave administration enough flexibility to make the shifts as long as seniority was observed and the need to transfer was firmly established.

A few years later, a new baby boomlet reversed the declining enrollment trend and caused the district to begin rehiring. From every corner of the district came pleas from teachers to return to their former assignments, but the contract did not provide for automatic return. (And many of the principals were reluctant to take back the older teacher who was out of sight and out of mind and thereby displace a new faculty member. The superintendent also noted that a few of the district's new teachers were outperforming the displaced veterans, making the principal even more reluctant to displace the newcomer.) The district was in a tough spot. The union, of course, was willing to negotiate changes in the rules that would provide fair, evenhanded management of the displaced veterans. On the other hand, the superintendent was being advised by his chief negotiator that changing the rules now would be giving up a valuable "blue chip" that could be bargained at the table in the negotiations scheduled to open the following year.

This superintendent was feeling the weight of the archaic industrial-style bargaining model. He and the board were forced to save up their "chips" for the once-a-year or once-every-three-years adjustment of the work rules. In the meantime, the rigidity of this model causes the district to add bureaucracy in order to cope with the mismatches and grievances caused by an organization that responds grudgingly only once a year or so. For the people toiling within the organization, this may be the best argument of all for embracing a collaborative labor relations model.

When the union leaders in your district ignore your district's entreaties for collaborative labor relations and demand industrial-style negotiations—the minimum prescribed by your state's collective bargaining law—it is time for you to question their motives. Such a position on the union's part is often a clear signal that it intends to press for more than is in the best interests of the district as a whole. This may take the form of a self-serving union issue, such as agency fees or released time for the union president, or it can be a salary hike or benefits increase that would require cuts in the instructional program unacceptable to the board and even perhaps to the teachers. In this latter instance, hard-line unionists like to take the position, "They can afford it! It's up to them to come up with it." In these circumstances, collaborative, interest-based discussions could only result in a compromise position—a sign of weakness in the eyes of the hard-liners.

AN OUNCE OF PREVENTION—EARLY PLANNING FOR INDUSTRIAL-STYLE BARGAINING

Negotiations planning by your bargaining team must identify potential strike issues at the onset, anticipating the union's proposal and formulating strategies and tactics to compromise the strike issues. This means the school board must meet early on with the superintendent and bargaining team to orient trustees on the issues. Bringing the board along gradually so that each member understands the consequences of teacher proposals is vital. Surprising them with a crisis will not result in the kind of firm commitment needed to face a hostile union, no matter how well the issues are explained to them.

GETTING THE BOARD ON BOARD FOR POSITIONAL BARGAINING

The conduct of traditional industrial-style bilateral negotiations requires discipline and preparation on the part of the school board members. The success or failure of a school district to cope adequately with a strike begins with the governing board. I argue that school boards of the twenty-first century should embrace and advocate collaborative negotiations. However, I recognize that many board members are not willing to share their power and authority with rank-and-file teachers. I recognize, too, that some boards have attempted collaboration with the unions but have failed because of their inability to address the money issues effectively. Finally, I realize that it definitely takes two to tango when it comes to collaborative labor relations, and some union leaders simply will refuse. If these are the circumstances in your district, and a collective bargaining law exists in your state, then the board has no alternative than to prepare for traditional "hardball" bargaining, which may result in a strike.

Solid board consensus and support are two of the essential elements of a successful strike management plan. Whatever the strategy, there must be a solid majority in favor of it. If not, then you must work on an alternate strategy. The swing vote on a board who declares, "Well, go ahead and try it; I'll make up my mind when I see what happens" is inviting disaster. The board must be told that if it is going to accede to demands because of a strike, then accede before the strike and save the pain. Bluffing only works in poker, or more precisely, it may work in certain cases, but it's not worth the gamble. Whenever a strike action pays off, the unions will be even more likely to resort to this tactic in the future.

The key to the district's success at this point is to carry out the traditional model skillfully. This begins with a well-prepared board with no heads in the sand. Following are essential board activities.

Develop and Adopt an Approach to Bargaining

Early on, even *before* table bargaining begins, the board must conduct discussions of the collective bargaining process, including the possibility of impasse and strike. Many "what if" scenarios must be discussed and resolved. Board members must know how they will respond before bargaining begins to bog down. These discussions should include a review of the history of the district's labor relations, the current atmosphere, and the willingness of the board to withstand a strike. Tough questions should be asked. Board members will often be faced with a recall election or a drive headed by the teachers' union to unseat them at the next regular election. Many times these political retaliations are successful, especially if the district's strike management squashes the strike. Voters who have recently witnessed a strike will express their dismay by voting school board members out of office, regardless of this member's sympathy or performance. I once expressed to my poker group the injustice of this knee-jerk reaction on the part of the electorate. Without even pausing to reflect, one businessman and city councilman retorted, "There's no injustice. Something went wrong in the school district, and they're accountable! We'd vote the union out of office too if we had the chance." Board members who strive to hang on to their offices at all costs may be a serious liability when the going gets tough. Other frank assessments include the solidarity of the board. Will the board present a united front? Are board members split over the issues? Are board members willing to defer comments about negotiations and a strike to one district information officer? None of these questions stands alone as a litmus test for the board's successful management of negotiations or ultimately a strike, but they must be taken into consideration. A renegade board member or two does not mean the board's majority will fail. It simply makes it more difficult. Many district collective bargaining disasters include stories of ambitious board members who break rank to dabble in amateur mediation. The seasoned union pros use these incidents to support their claims that the board is unreasonable or under the thumb of a personalized demon; otherwise, why would one or two good-hearted souls try to defect? Following these frank discussions, the board should review point-by-point the district's strike plan (see appendix A) with particular attention to the approach embodied in the plan.

Develop Bottom-Line Positions

It's really up to the superintendent to hold the private discussions of the trade-offs and determine jointly with the board the bottom line—the point at which the board will suffer the turmoil of the strike rather than acquiesce. To be sure, fixing the bottom line is not a recommended practice when going into collaborative, interest-based problem-solving negotiations with conscientious union representatives. But, as I discuss in chapters 5, 10, and 11, the commitment to collaborate must be made before entering negotiations on the issues. Board members and district leaders must disabuse themselves of the idea that collaboration can emerge from the traditional negotiations shoot-out. Bottom lines are a necessary component of traditional positional bargaining. Asking what the board will plant its flag on is essential. What would the board deem to be a "fair" settlement? The answer to this question usually defines the administration's bargaining goals. The most significant "bottom lines" are usually salary or benefits issues. Since these are the issues that the union leaders can use most effectively to arouse the membership, negotiation strategies must be established that allow room for slight movement in these areas, even after regular talks have broken down and statutory procedures have taken over—impasse, mediation, fact-finding, and post-fact-finding bargaining.

Identify the Chief Negotiator

If this is a member of the human resources department, then he or she will double as the chair of the bargaining team. If a professional negotiator is hired, he or she will work "in consultation with the bargaining team."

Prepare the Board Members

The superintendent must support the board's efforts as follows:

- Orient the board to the collective bargaining process well ahead of the commencement of formal negotiations.
- Spend a closed study session reviewing the current contract and discussing the concerns of administrators.
- Inform the board of the union's anticipated positions and anticipated strategies.
- Request adopted formal direction.

In closed session the board must develop firm direction for the superintendent by

(1) Reviewing and adopting the district's initial proposal, along with the strategies for bargaining the proposal.

(2) Adopting the strike plan as outlined in chapter 7 (see sample strike plan in appendix A).

(3) Reviewing and endorsing an emergency procedures resolution to be adopted in the event of an emergency (see appendixes B, C, and D).

(4) Deciding on salaries for strike replacement substitute teachers. Twice the average sub pay in the area should be considered. The board should also consider authorizing a special in-service day for strike replacement substitute teacher applicants to defray the costs of emergency credentials and to encourage applications.

(5) Adopting positions regarding withholding of wages and benefits for striking teachers.

(6) Authorizing discipline of strikers or teachers participating in other illegal concerted actions against the district. These discussions should include legal counsel to avoid clear conflicts with state law or public employee relations board rulings. The discussion should also focus on letters warning temporary, probationary, and permanent teachers of the disciplinary action planned by the district. Part of this discussion should focus on whether the district follows through with the disciplinary action once the strike is over. I disagree with the conventional wisdom on this subject that emphasizes the reestablishment of a positive image for the educational community by reestablishing "business as usual" as soon as possible. I maintain that following through with actions pledged by the board and administration is essential for maintaining the credibility of the district and forcing faculty to rethink the notion that striking every five or ten years is "the way we do business in this district."

(7) Authorizing the district's attorneys to plan and carry out a campaign designed to thwart disruptive schemes planned by the union and to challenge the legality and constitutionality of actions that threaten the safety of students or impair their right to a public education.

(8) Establishing a tight communications system with the negotiations team in order to keep track of developments as they happen.

(9) Together with the superintendent, adopting a series of protocols for board members in dealing with teachers, the media, interested citizens, administrators, and other employees. The protocol should also address board member behavior during strikes, jammed board meetings, personal residence picketing, threaten-

ing phone calls, vandalism, and other typical union tactics during periods of labor conflict.

THE ALL-IMPORTANT PUBLIC INFORMATION FUNCTION

The next phase in traditional bargaining takes place at the table, but of equal importance is the behind-the-scenes support system. As early as possible, assign responsibility for public information and press relations. This person should be part of the bargaining team and should be provided the resources to do the job professionally. Of course, if the district has a public information officer, this is the person. If not, then a member of the bargaining team with a talent for writing and meeting the press should be identified. When the going gets rough, there will be no substitute for the superintendent or board president, but for the all-important months leading up to the rough going, the public information officer function is essential.

Remember, good, straightforward public information is *not* in the best interest of the union, since union demands at the table will often inflame anti-union sentiment in the community and among the faculty. This is the beginning of the "PR war" I discussed in the introduction. Bad press is equivalent to a "lost battle." So don't let the union talk you into "cooperatively managing the news." This is another example of straddling the fence that leads to disaster. As with all positional bargaining transactions with the union negotiators, a cool, civil, always polite, but arm's-length approach is best.

Be ready for accusations that your public information campaign will "torpedo" the negotiations. It won't.

Be ready for the union to threaten to start a paper war that distorts your offers and puts the district in a bad light. They'll do that anyway.

Be ready for union representatives to threaten to walk away from the table. They may, but it won't last long.

Establish this approach as *standard operating procedure* from the beginning. Report the bargaining sessions extensively, honestly, and objectively.

THE ADVANTAGE OF HIRING AN OUTSIDE NEGOTIATOR

Employing an outside negotiator is the best way for a district to conduct positional negotiations—provided the professional carries out his mission according to your plans. Find one who is cordial, coolly professional, articulate, and knowledgeable in educational collective bargaining laws and procedures. Winning for the district requires that the game be played tenaciously. The chief negotiator will be required to be firm and adamant and eventually unyielding.

Putting the superintendent, business manager, human resources director, or some other functionary in the school system in this position will interfere with the person's ability to carry out his professional tasks in the future. The professional negotiator should also be an attorney, preferably one associated with a law firm specializing in school labor relations. Make no mistake about it: When the union leaders insist upon industrial-style bargaining, they have defined your task, namely, to win for the board at the bargaining table—including a strike, if necessary.

By this time I hope I've convinced you that industrial-style positional bargaining is incompatible with the problem-solving processes at the core of any collaborative labor relations model. It is a mistake to mix them. To make collaboration work, the problem solving must be able to take place unfettered by the big money issue of salary and benefits. This is the issue that generates the heated emotions. This is the one that will upset a district's labor peace. The money issues cause unions to destroy the image of a district in the eyes of a community in order to put pressure on a political board. At times strikes cannot be avoided. If your union insists on positional bargaining, and if your district is large enough for the parent statewide union to care, then the possibility of a strike is real. And attempting to ward off a strike at all costs only makes matters worse. Surviving a strike requires teamwork and preparation. Preparing for strike survival begins with your initial planning for negotiations.

7

✝

Preparing for the Strike

Successful strike preparation is an integral part of planning for positional collective bargaining. The best advice I can give is don't wait until negotiations have fallen apart and impasse is imminent. Gearing up rapidly at this point startles the administration—the people who you count on to keep cool heads. Strike preparation from the beginning simply recognizes that this preparation is simply a normal part of positional bargaining.

Preparing the district well for an eventuality of this sort will probably be attacked in the union rhetoric as a "sign" that the board wants to encourage a strike. In truth, many teachers, suspicious of the board's motives, will believe this rhetoric. Others, more experienced in these matters, will understand why the district must begin preparations. On the positive side, all members of the organization will understand that the district is prepared for the worst—and this alone will make a strike a little less likely. This is especially true if yours is a suburban school district and the union in your state is gearing up to tackle a large district where bargaining specialists can be used more cost-effectively. Fighting a smaller but well-prepared district is often a gamble for the union leaders. They have much to lose by suffering a defeat at the hands of a small fry and not much to gain in prestige if they are successful.

THE STRIKE MANAGEMENT TEAM

A first step in preparing for positional bargaining that may include a strike is to organize the Strike Management Team (SMT). This committee should be composed of the superintendent, the district's legal counsel, the professional negotiator, and all of the chief line officers. Since keeping the schools open and maintaining order is a major part of strike management, the line and staff officers in the district assume great importance during this phase of positional bargaining. The SMT members should spend extensive time preparing themselves for carrying out their strategic functions. This is the group that will anticipate union tactics and devise countertactics. This is also the group that must support and protect the principals while leading them to perform their necessary functions. The possibility of strike and of pressure tactics by the union should be recognized from the onset. The SMT members must be the experts, and they must interface regularly with the school board. In the final analysis, whether or not you are able to effectively counter union attacks will depend upon whether the board adopts smart strategies. Board members will look to you, the professionals, to provide them with information about how to conduct the strike. If the board has hired a professional negotiator, that person can interface with the school district as a member of the SMT and help this team design sound recommendations for the school board. In this respect, unions are ahead of school boards and administrators at the beginning. Unions have seasoned specialists. They are ruthless, in the best sense of the word. That is, they recommend tactics without emotional attachment to the district. They are able to play the tit for tat game expertly, and they also recognize when a district is well prepared.

Union tacticians have the same challenge the SMT has. That is, once they've arrived at appropriate strategies, they must convince teacher leaders, just as the administration must convince the school board. The union pros, of course, have an advantage since they are dealing with a group made up entirely of teachers. In most cases, the board is not all management. Quite the contrary, in many cases these days, boards are made up of union advocates, teacher candidates, moms who would never believe their friendly neighborhood teachers would stoop to deceit, and, in all fairness, a goodly portion of straight-thinking citizens who want better schools. For the board, preparing for a strike begins with the preparations for positional bargaining described in chapter 6. Now, the board must focus on strike management. Exhibit 7.1 at the end of this chapter presents a checklist of preparation activities for the board.

THE STRIKE PLAN

Once you've convinced the board members and key administrators that strike preparation from the onset is a wise move, the next step is to gather together strike preparation resources. Most school administrator associations in states with collective bargaining laws for teachers can furnish you with a model strike preparation manual that contains all the fundamentals and is tailored to take into consideration the legal peculiarities of your state. I suggest you also contact associations in a couple of the big collective bargaining states (New York and California, for example) for additional tips. The Association of California School Administrators produces a strike preparation manual that contains everything from legal issues to checklists for board members and administrators on strike days. Manuals of this sort provide convenient materials that can be modified to fit the special needs of your district. Appendix A of this book contains an example of a strike plan used by a California school district to manage a strike.

PREPARING THE DISTRICT'S ADMINISTRATORS

Once your strike plan has been prepared and formally adopted by the board, your next step is to distribute it to the administrative staff and begin the task of systematically acquainting them with their duties and responsibilities. This is the time to open up the dialogue with them about the district's position. Presumably, you and the board would prefer a collaborative model, since you are the folks responsible to the citizenry for keeping the schools open and the faculty happy. If this is an incorrect assumption, I suggest you go back and reread chapters 1 and 2 of this book. The time you devote to helping every member of the administrative team understand the district's position and understand why thorough strike preparation is important during the initial stages of bargaining will be time well spent. As a point of departure, you might have all of them read this small book. Or if you really want to get into it, assign Fisher and Ury's

(1981) *Getting to Yes*, Lieberman's (1997) *The Teacher Unions*, and Kerchner and Koppich's (1997) *United Mind Workers*.

FOCUS ON WINNING

For the time being, you can assume that most of your administrators want only the basics: What are the issues? What are the sticking points? What is my role? From the very first meeting to begin the strike preparations, district leaders must make it crystal clear that the mission of the strike management team and the purpose of the strike preparation is to *win* the strike game if the union decides to use that tactic. You may be surprised that this will shock a majority of your administrative team. Most of them have been brainwashed with the idea that a strike is a "no-win" proposition. It is true that both sides of a strike sustain serious wounds, and the district as a whole always loses stature. But this is no excuse for the leadership of the district to shrink from the difficult tasks that will, in the long run, help the district to recover. During my data collection travels, I found this belief to be rampant among the districts that were most severely beaten by the unions. Administrators approached preparation for the difficult crisis with the feeling that a "victory" was impossible. This belief actually helps these people endure and accept their fate as they experience political and organizational injury. Since they believe their defeat was inevitable, none of them blame themselves in the slightest for the devastating losses in community support, staff pride, and the quest for excellence.

DEFINING VICTORY

Your first task is to define "victory." Each district's definition will be a little different, depending upon the circumstances, but the list of mission objectives usually includes:

- Keep the schools open and operating.
- Minimize the number of teachers participating in the strike.
- Neutralize the union's political attacks on the district.
- Inflict losses on the union's professionals through effective legal actions with the Public Employee Relations Board and the courts as well as an effective, multifaceted public relations campaign aimed at the union's underbelly.

More about how to accomplish these objectives will be presented in chapter 8, "Managing the Strike."

Victory doesn't mean the district won't be beat up. Victory means the union fell short of its goals in each of the areas addressed above and therefore would be much less likely to jump into a strike again. In fact, if the strike management is carried out in an even-handed, highly professional manner by all of the administrative team members, the perceived losses suffered by the union will push many of the straight-thinking rank and file to insist that a more rational approach to bargaining be adopted. In other words, the stage can be set for collaborative labor relations at another time in the future. At the very least, it will cool the ardor for concerted action. I am not suggesting that a strike is the best means to establish collaborative labor relations, but it is true that the men returning home from the Civil War were a lot less excited about war than the boys who left home to fight five or six years before. Likewise, teachers and administrators who have suffered a strike are a lot less excited about doing it again soon.

ORIENTING THE ADMINISTRATORS

The first task is to orient all administrators about what to expect during the strike. In most cases, friends and colleagues with whom valued professional relationships have been forged are on the picket line, singing strike songs directed at the district leaders and chanting the obligatory strike slogans. When the strike is over, the leaders must again take charge of the facilities and help begin the healing process. The entire management team, but especially site principals, must remain professionally aloof during the moments leading up to a strike and during the strike itself. At the same time, all leaders must make it clear to all teachers that they are professionally committed to the district's position. Above all, the administrators must remain poised. This means when friends and colleagues on the staff urge administrators to confess "what you really feel," they must with all sincerity announce that they don't condone a faculty strike. A reasonable administrator must, of course, recognize that there are honest differences between the union's position and the district's position. It is both reasonable and honest for administrators to express dismay about the circumstances and compassion for their colleagues caught in the jaws of a dilemma. The administrator remains a friend and colleague, but not an ally in these circumstances. Show compassion, but don't serve coffee to the picketers outside the school or district office. In the long run teachers won't respect a weak principal or other administrator who joins them in a labor dispute any more than they would respect hostile administrators who see the strike as a threat to their control. On either end of the spectrum, inappropriate actions help sustain the emotion necessary to keep a strike alive.

Moreover, either extreme could cause resentment among varying political polarities on the staff when the teachers return to work. An administrator's subsequent success in the district may hinge on whether or not professional poise can be maintained under fire.

It's important for all district leaders, including board members, to put strike activities in perspective. An energized crowd at a rally or at a board meeting, or even a small, energized group on a picket line, is still a mob. All of the principles of mob psychology apply. The most weak-kneed, nonaggressive member of an administrator's faculty may feel safe enough to shout an insult from the picket line. If the picketer is one for whom the administrator has a particularly low esteem, holding the temper is even more difficult—but absolutely essential.

All members of the district's leadership must remember the mob psychology at work. If picketers threaten, withdraw. If picketers attempt to engage in reasonable discussion about the issues, listen. Then the administrator must state unapologetically his or her support of the board's position. Once is probably enough. Above all, no arguments. When teachers are on a picket line, the time for rational argument and critical thinking has long passed.

During the period of time leading up to a strike as well as during the strike itself, the administrators in charge of every site or operational unit must play a critical role in communicating with faculty as well as students, parents, and other members of the community. Once again, the key is cool, confident, professional poise. The goal is to communicate the district's message to parents and community as well as staff without inflaming them. The parents and the community have a right to know that things are going badly at the bargaining table. They also have a right to know the issues. The administration's stance should demonstrate to parents that the schools are in good hands and that labor turmoil and strikes are just "one of those things" that happen when positional collective bargaining is practiced. Once again, in the communications role, each administrator must express alliance with the district's position as well as sympathy for the ordeal the teachers and families are facing.

After a strike is over, all administrators, but especially the site administrators, must resume a close working relationship with parents and community members in much the same way relationships are resumed with teachers. For this reason, superintendents, public information officers, and strike management coordinators must bear in mind the delicate political situation of site administrators and refrain from asking them to be part of the district's rhetorical assault team. Their task of keeping the school open is the most difficult. It shouldn't be made more difficult. Ask only that they refrain from undermining the district's positions. A simple statement of support is all that should be required.

Specific roles and duties for each district administrator are discussed in detail in chapter 9. Checklists of vital activities and duties are also provided to assist with the task of mobilizing the administrative team.

WATCH OUT FOR UNFAIR LABOR PRACTICES

The entire management team, including board members, should avoid discussions with teachers about what they would be willing to settle for. Often as not, these conversations become part of an unfair labor practice charge filed with the public employee relations board (PERB). Negotiations, after all, are supposed to happen only at the table and only between authorized negotiators. This is particularly important during the buildup before the strike since the union may need an unfair labor practice charge of some sort to justify a strike action with the PERB.

BREAKING THE CYCLE OF LABOR TURMOIL

One middle-sized district I studied had a history of several strikes during a ten-year period of time. Leading up to each strike, the school board would make bellicose statements challenging the teachers, but in each case they caved in and gave the teachers what they wanted in the end. The teacher attitudes were predictable. They were best expressed by one first grade teacher: "It's just something we have to do from time to time with this crazy board [or this crazy community]. Besides, we don't lose anything."

The teachers in this district were being conditioned to strike periodically, although this was the last thing the board and administrators had in mind. Personally, I don't believe in the efficacy of behaviorism as a management technique, but Hitler, among a long list of others, proved that behaviorism, when practiced on the masses, works. Teacher unions are infamous for using these practices to fire up the masses of teachers. The school administrator's challenge is to counter this mass psychology.

How can a school district effectively counter these activities in order to prevent repetition of the strike behavior in the future? First, make the strike a gamble instead of a sure thing. The teachers in the story above, in grand Pavlovian tradition, allowed themselves to be "prepared" each year by a talented, professional bargaining specialist. And each year they were rewarded—an experience with virtually no pain (other than natural friction among faculty members for and against the strike). This was combined with experienced, almost routine strike management by the administration. They had become, as a result, a very proficient, professional group able to manage every aspect of a strike with a high level of effectiveness. It was an irony that the same conditioning that created an easily led faculty also produced a magnificently professional cadre of strike managers.

In order to end this stimulus–response cycle, the board and administration had to hold the line on post-strike concessions. They made the strike an expensive proposition for the participants. They stood firm on the district's monetary offer and deducted salary and benefits during strike days. In addition, they "imposed" the board's last best offer, giving the process a sense of finality. That is, they adopted the last best offer and even awarded the striking teachers a small raise they had previously rejected. This, combined with the deductions of salary, sick leave, and benefits, injected a real chance of substantive loss for each teacher who decided to strike. The strike ended one day later.

Holding the line on salary and adopting the board's last best offer unilaterally forced the union to choose between returning to work without a settlement or extending the strike longer, making it even more expensive—a loss either way. This put the ball in the strike specialist's court and forced the union leaders to deal with flagging enthusiasm for the walkout. Since public school teacher strikes are not really true economic strikes in the classic private-sector sense, convincing teachers to sacrifice salary and benefits over an extended time for what amounts to a public relations stunt is a hard sell to say the least. More than anything else, this forces teachers to look more critically into the union's "fire up" rhetoric in future years to see if it is true, part true, or all false.

The idea of adopting unilaterally the board's last salary offer (if state law allows it) is worth discussing. Once teachers have been notified that the board's offer has been adopted and their salaries have been raised a certain percentage, two things are accomplished. First, union propaganda diminishing the size of the district's offer is neutralized. Second, teachers now recognize that they are striking for the difference between the district's offer and the union's last position. In the past I have been amazed that teachers perceive their strike activities as necessary to capture the entire amount demanded by the union when, in fact, the district is obliged by good faith bargaining to honor its last offer (often a fraction of a percentage from the union's demand). Union leaders and teachers use this whole amount to calculate their potential for lost income—convincing themselves that the raise will cover the lost days of wages. Adopting the raise unilaterally squelches this myth and helps them understand that it might be decades before they "break even," if ever.

COUNTERING HARASSMENT TACTICS

Preparing the district to cope with the union's harassing tactics is a task that takes the thinking of all key members of the SMT. What tactics should you prepare to counter? The truth is, there's no set pattern of action that the NEA or AFT prescribes.

"That's why it's so much fun," one veteran teacher leader confided, continuing with an animated description of an "earthquake drill" that he organized in his district. At a predetermined time one Monday morning, a large number of the teachers escorted their classes onto the lawns in front of the schools and discussed earthquake procedures. The activity was unannounced and surprised every administrator, many parents, and virtually everyone in the community—except the newspaper reporters, who had been given advance notice. The teacher leader grinned and chuckled, "We got their attention."

Later, this same teacher leader made a presentation at a board meeting dressed as the Easter bunny. Humorous, but the message was clear: You are dealing with a highly organized, well-disciplined faculty union.

THE TOP TWENTY-ONE TACTICS
THAT WORK WELL FOR TEACHER UNIONS

There are a few tactics, however, that are almost always employed—old standbys used by die-hard positional devotees. For years administrators have struggled with methods to counter these tactics, unfortunately with limited success. (That's probably the reason they are old standbys.) The following paragraphs discuss these strategies in enough details to alert your administrative team and board—at least to give them a flavor of what to expect. Also discussed are possible countertactics. I should also point out that the emergence of these tactics in your negotiations is often a strong signal that the leadership of the union is headed for a showdown probably resulting in a strike unless the district backs off on one or more of its bottom-line positions.

It is probably unnecessary to mention that not all unions will employ the strategies that follow. Many districts and their unions have achieved a mature bargaining relationship using the traditional model. At the same time, they have avoided the venom and animosity that wreaks havoc in the organization and with the community. It is sufficient to say that diligent preparation is an absolute necessity for entering all forms of collective bargaining. This includes thorough training preparation for exigencies resulting from significant differences of opinion (always a possibility) or a breakdown in the relationships among the individuals involved in the negotiations. Solid preparation includes a realistic understanding of hard-core union tactics, as well as the kinder, gentler type.

Most of the strategies and tactics I will discuss have been distributed to school district leaders and negotiators at one time or another at negotiation workshops or have been passed under wraps from superintendent to superintendent. I first ran into a document fifteen years ago whose preface claimed that the information had been obtained from another document "used by the NEA and their affiliates to control negotiations." I recently showed a similar document to a union official who laughed and added, "I've seen similar lists of strategies and tactics before, but it's nothing put out by NEA." However, he admitted that all of the strategies had at one time or another been used by union leaders to put political pressure on school boards. Studying the tactics in advance and considering various countermeasures will prevent district leaders from being surprised and help assure that they react rationally and effectively.

The list of strategies and tactics that follows is by no means comprehensive. However, these are the most common and are representative of the spectrum.

Strategy #1. As negotiations get underway, put a spin on the district's initial offer that puts the board in a bad light. Claim that the union's bargaining team was shocked, and that the board's positions reveal an insensitivity to teachers. Editorialize regularly about various aspects of the board's offer. Compare the salary increase with the cost of living index or what neighboring districts will "probably" receive. Conclude each communication with a promise to work diligently for the interests of the teachers no matter how long it takes. Emphasize unity with slogans like "Together We Can" or "United We Stand."

Some union leaders routinely begin negotiations using this strategy and continue throughout—even when talks are proceeding satisfactorily and settlement seems likely. And sometimes the administration is *really* bad and malignant—so the motives are not always clear. These leaders are taking a "just-in-case" position. The goal is to breed distrust and dissatisfaction in the school district so that "rallying the troops" will be less difficult later in the event that talks break down. It should be said that sometimes these actions are not tactics, per se. That is, they are honest statements made by distrustful people who lack confidence in their school district leaders.

Although this behavior does not necessarily signal an impending strike, it does indicate that the union leaders are willing to resort to concerted action and are laying the necessary groundwork. There is really no other reason to begin a propaganda campaign of this sort. The district must respond in a measured fashion.

The first step is to arrange a meeting between the superintendent and the union president or perhaps the two bargaining teams to discuss the information—a call for reason. If the slanted versions of negotiations continue, then the district must counter.

Unions love to point out that no one wins a paper war. Maybe. But one side most certainly can *lose*. Often, politically minded board members and superintendents don't want to create a public perception of unrest in the district by making public the possibility of disharmony at the bargaining table. Over the years I have learned to reject this notion. Every time I agreed to ignore misinformation, I have been stung. The district must counter calmly and rationally with articles in district newsletters and other normal house organs. If none exists, this is a good time to create them. The information contained in the articles should be carefully factual and must not contain loaded emotional words. On the other hand, it must be clear that this article is a response to the union's article and a clarification of facts. For example, when the union characterizes the board's initial salary offer as the board's final offer, explain the error. Comment on the bargaining process and assure the teachers that initial offer represents the *least* increase the board is prepared to give. Explain that only if one or more of the usual looming disasters materialize would the board stick with its initial offer. Your purpose is to calmly and rationally begin a long-term process of educating all of the teachers about the collective bargaining process so that they will have a better understanding of the forces that affect them.

When the union propaganda begins to personalize the conflict by discussing the personal fortunes or salaries of board members and administrators, criticize the practice of personalization, don't rebut with personalizations of your own. Most faculty are sophisticated enough to understand the unprofessional nature of this type of rhetoric. One faculty uprising over this strategy in recent history caused the local union leaders to ask the NEA's Uniserve Director to assign another bargaining specialist to the school district.

Managing public information is a difficult task, even when enormous resources are available. Indeed, the president of the United States, with a well-organized nationwide political party, has a difficult time of it. However, the task must be accomplished. Larger districts assign responsibility to a public information officer with a staff. Although very effective at times, expenditure of district funds to support this office is not always well understood by the public it is supposed to inform. Avoiding names like "public relations" or "public information officer" helps. "Assistant to the superintendent" is usually more palatable. Smaller districts must assign the public information function to another district officer as a part-time responsibility. In this case, advance planning, which will allow the officer to be released nearly full time during the heavy negotiations, is necessary. Very small districts could not afford even this small luxury, but hostile union activity in these districts is rare. Remember, whoever ends up with responsibility for public information must be provided with training and resources. Your state's local chapter of the National School Public Relations Association (NSPRA) is a good place to start. Make certain that this officer develops an appropriate public information plan that reaches out to parents, the media, and the general community, as well as special groups like senior citizens, real estate agents, and law enforcement. From the outset the officer should understand that the plan should take into consideration the eventuality of a collective bargaining deadlock and even a strike. Charge the officer with the responsibility for outreach to the media—for becoming a "source." This means the person must be accessible and earn the reputation of being impeccably honest. The Educational Research Service adds the following additional tips.

- *Try to avoid "No comment."* Explain exactly why you can't answer the question.
- *Speak in "sound bites."* Keep your message simple.
- *Assume you will be quoted*. Information obtained in "off the record" interviews will probably be made public later when the reporter gets confirmation from another source.
- *Avoid humor.* When a *Los Angeles Times* reporter began his interview by asking me how I went about approaching the teachers' union leaders to establish what eventually was an exemplary collaborative labor relations model, I quipped, "I told the board president I wanted to meet with the meanest son of a gun in the district." I thought I was establishing an informal atmosphere. The remark ended up as the lead line in his article the next morning.
- *Understand that you won't have the last word.* Don't lose your temper with reporters or editors or "punish" them by making yourself unavailable. If a story contains inaccurate information or an unfair slant, a courteous letter to the editor explaining the facts and attempting to clear up confusion is appropriate. If it's strictly a personal affront, it's probably best to ignore it. For example, when a newspaper article describes a superintendent's comments as "scolding" or "mean spirited," nothing can be accomplished by objecting to the depiction. A better idea would be to bring the matter up with the reporter in an informal setting to let him or her know the superintendent's feelings were hurt.

The key is this: A teachers' strike against a public school district is a public relations war, nothing else. A teachers' strike will not force a public school district into bankruptcy. It can only affect public sentiment about the school district, and, in particular, about the people running the school district. The PR war begins with the first misleading message to the unit members from the union leaders. District leaders must enter the war at this moment with measured, accurate information. The key is tit for tat— be certain the district's response is appropriate for the union's action.

Even so, the union will cry foul—accusing the district of taking a belligerent, "union-busting" stance. This must be anticipated and ignored. Use radio and television if the PR war continues to escalate. Tasteful, carefully designed ads done by a professional (not a school official) can be very effective, especially when aimed at the national unions.

With television, cost analysis is important. If your area has a local cable franchise that will target your message, the price may be right. Don't forget to use the district website to provide complete and up-to-date information on the negotiations. The idea is to be a worthy adversary in the industrial-style adversarial negotiations that include a strike to resolve an impasse. As I explained before, the public information campaigns, the slowdowns, the sick-outs, the information picketing, and the strike are all part of a PR war to put pressure on the public's representative school board members. The district must enter this war following the first shot from the union's cannon.

Strategy #2. Attack the board's negotiator. Professional negotiators hired to advise the board and conduct the negotiations are targets for a variety of attacks from the union. Most often, the union president or another spokesperson begins the attack early in the negotiations process by including criticisms of the negotiator in the union's regular presentation at the scheduled board meeting. Within weeks the complaints will grow to include a negotiator's bad temper, inappropriate sense of humor, rudeness, lack of punctuality, unwillingness to bring matters to closure, and so forth. At this point, the union may also deliver a written statement to the press outlining its "sincere concerns" about the competence of the board's negotiator. "If we could only sit down and talk with you people person to person, we could have these matters settled in no time." Or "If we could only sit down with old Charlie like we used to, we could have this settled in an afternoon."

The purpose of this strategy is to put the board at a further disadvantage in terms of expert advice. The teachers have very high-powered, competent bargaining specialists advising them closely. Without a professional to advise it, the board's disadvantage in the negotiation grows larger. What's more, as negotiations grow gradually more rancorous, the union leaders have a scapegoat to take the blame for the mounting hostilities.

The best defense against this strategy is to forewarn the board and the administrators as part of the orientation to the bargaining process. An unbiased observer might be suggested (for example, the mayor or the chairman of the ministerial association). This suggestion is usually met with strong opposition by the union, which claims that the district is trying to destroy the collective bargaining process by tampering with one of its fundamental components—secrecy. Probably the best bet is simply to ask for a short consensus report by the administrators on the negotiating team about their perceptions of the performance of the negotiator. Since the union's accusations are rarely, if ever, based entirely on fact, the board can report this at the board meeting in response to the next attack on the negotiator. The best tactic is to stay the course, maintain support of the negotiator, and take this tactic in stride with the others.

Strategy #3. Camouflage the salary and benefit demands. In order to capture the moral high ground in negotiations, union negotiators will claim that salary is not the issue. Instead they will point to poor working conditions, poor heating and air conditioning systems, inadequate supplies, inadequate staff development—in fact, anything except salary and benefits. In the private sector, this tactic would be patently absurd, but, as I explained before, public school union negotiations are purely PR wars—a strike being only one tactic in those wars. Claiming that the teachers are negotiating primarily for the welfare of students (for example, smaller classes, more supplies, higher quality services) carries a lot of favor with parents and the general community. The teacher unions cloak themselves in respectability as advocates for better schools—something we all favor. This tactic also steers public attention away from teacher salaries and benefits and quells the growing suspicion among the community that teacher compensation may already be too high.

Investigations of key issues in strikes around the nation have confirmed that salary or remuneration is virtually always number one on the list, followed by fringe benefits (Shreeve et al., 1990)—this in spite of the fact that the publicized issues were smaller classes, more respect, and so forth. This adds even greater weight to my proposition that a successful labor relations model must first of all get the money off the table before the scope of negotiations can be broadened.

The best way to cope with this strategy is to anticipate it and capture the high ground with similar motherhood and apple pie issues. After all, board members are keenly interested in improving education and providing better services for their school and their students. This strategy has two benefits: If the traditional bargaining relationship is mature, and the teacher representatives are reasonable, authentic improvements can be made in working conditions by allocating resources to these initiatives with the support of the union. On the other hand, if the traditional negotiations are moving toward militant confrontation, the board has adopted positions that will take the steam out of much of the PR war.

Strategy #4. Attack the superintendent. As negotiations begin to heat up and settlement seems unlikely, the union leaders will attack the chief school administrator in an attempt to undermine his or her credibility with the board and community. This may take the form of a recitation of griev-ances against the superintendent's management and personnel relations. If the union leaders are on a fast track to a strike, sensing recalcitrance on the part of board members, or the general lack of support for the superin-tendent on the part of some of the board members, a "vote of no confi-dence" may be organized and presented to the board. The major purpose of the tactic is to discredit the district's management, gather allies in the community, and put additional pressure on the school board members and superintendent. In other words, it is a PR war tactic. However, it also has the potential to split the board (one or more members withdrawing support for the superintendent and the board's negotiating strategies) or to goad the board into removing the superintendent from the leadership of the negotiations. Both threaten negative consequences down the road when the district is involved with mediation, fact-finding, or strike man-agement. The last thing the school board needs in these critical circum-stances is a wounded superintendent who has been undermined by board action.

The best countermeasure to this tactic is to discuss it fully and openly. The press, the faculty, the community, but especially the board members should be aware that a list of superintendents who have had no confi-dence votes by the union leaders during negotiations often resembles a who's who list of effective school leaders.

Strategy #5. Telephone campaign to badger board members. As tensions at the table mount and the community becomes more aware of the looming cri-sis in the school district, union leaders will recruit members of the com-munity, acquaintances of board members, and teacher activists to launch a telephone campaign aimed at persuading individual board members to jump ship "for the benefit of the children." This is especially effective since most board members are pro-teacher and have a high degree of pas-sion for children of the schools. Usually the campaigner can lead the board member into a discussion of other board members' positions and ideas and, more often than not, one of the board members will commit to helping break the deadlock.

Countering the possible destructive effects of this strategy begins with creating an atmosphere of trust on the board and allowing time during negotiations planning sessions to discuss feedback from teachers, com-munity leaders, and others who may have telephoned board members. This practice will quickly expose the telephone campaign strategy, and it may also provide grounds for filing an unfair practice charge with the PERB.

Strategy #6. File unfair practice charges with the PERB. At this point in ne-gotiations, a strike is becoming a real possibility. Union leaders will file a series of unfair practice charges with the PERB in order to establish the basis for a strike. In the absence of an unfair practice charge, the PERB could block the strike. Most of these unfair practice charges are thrown out at a hearing if they ever get that far. Some have substance. Most commonly, one of the principals in the district tries to "talk sense" to his teacher friends about the bargaining issues. When a building rep reports this to leadership, an unfair practice charge can be filed for circumventing the negotiating process. If it can be documented that this has happened in several schools across the district (as it often can), the union will claim a "conspiracy" to circumvent. Administrators should be alerted to these possibilities and avoid these practices as part of their ongoing training and briefings.

The board's response to the filing of unfair practice charges should be in keeping with its tit for tat approach to the PR war in general. The district's attorneys should draw up unfair practice charges relating to perceived job slowdowns, threats directed at students, and other unsavory labor practices that may have been undertaken. Like other actions taken by the board, this should be well publicized. This will immediately cause strident cries of outrage from the union leaders, but will tend to suppress vulgar and unsavory practices—a far more important goal in the long run. And it will at least cause some of your more serious teachers to pause and consider the approach of their union.

Strategy #7. Call for round-the-clock bargaining. As a precursor to more serious concerted activities, union leaders will demand at an open board meeting or with an open letter that the school board enter into marathon bargaining sessions designed to bring the protracted negotiations to a rapid conclusion. Again, the tactic is designed to escalate the PR war. Whether you and the board accept the proposal really depends on how successful you have been in putting your PR campaign together. Round-the-clock bargaining artificially creates the opportunity for a daily press release about where negotiations are going and what the various positions are. If you are the officer in your district in charge of public information, and you have established good relations with the media and are able to influence the reporters with releases, then it would probably be to your advantage to participate. You have an opportunity to tip the PR war in your direction. On the other hand, if your public information efforts are not going well, or if the officer or the superintendent do not do well in press conferences, then it would probably be to your advantage to turn down the round-the-clock bargaining proposal and attempt to expose the tactic as another PR ploy.

Strategy #8. Conduct informational pickets. In an effort to intensify the political pressure on the school board by bringing the bargaining issues to the front page of the newspaper as well as the evening news on TV, union leaders will organize informational picket lines in front of schools and the district administration building before and after school. This strategy is not only effective in terms of escalating the confrontation, it is also a litmus test for the union to judge the readiness of the staff to take concerted action. Most teachers feel humiliated when participating in a picket line. Consequently, a large number of volunteers for picketing is a good sign that the teachers are ready.

Strategy #9. Sympathy march. Whenever possible, union leaders try to create the impression that the general community is with the teachers and against the board of education and administration in the negotiations deadlock. To create this impression, the association will recruit non-teaching personnel, often spouses, relatives of teachers, neighbors, and small children, to continue the marching during school hours. The sign prominently declares the carrier to be a "parent" or "concerned citizen" who supports the teachers' cause.

Strategy #10. Jam the school board meetings. Since the press usually covers school board meetings, this venue is a natural for staging political demonstrations. It also is the perfect setting to stage attacks on the board's position, the superintendent's strike preparations, and other sensitive issues related to the negotiations. Usually forty or fifty teachers at a board meeting can cause "standing room only" conditions. With minimal coaching the group can create a circus-like atmosphere by cheering and applauding the union president's demands that the board treat the teachers with respect at the bargaining table. The remainder of the meeting can be effectively disrupted with occasional catcalls, boos, guffaws, and applause. Often union activists from other school districts who live in your district will address your board, posing as "parents" or "concerned citizens of the community." Activists from other unions are also recruited to participate in these demonstrations.

Coping with informational pickets and board meeting demonstrations is probably the most difficult tribulation for board members. Controlling board meetings is often difficult for the lay board president since the business of the district must be conducted. Often the best bet is to adjourn an unruly meeting to an adjacent secure room, inviting the press in conformance with your state's open meeting laws. This gives the union more rhetoric about the board "running," but it is probably less stressful in the long run. I have witnessed boards absorbing far more abuse than required by law because the members are reluctant to adjourn the meeting to a secure location. From a political point of view I can understand their reluctance. However, less tolerance of disruption is the wiser course. The superintendent and board president should plan for disruption during these times. That is, security should be beefed up with a good number of plain-clothes as well as uniformed police. And it's foolish to ignore the fact that the union demonstration is a mob—with all the irrational characteristics of a mob. Peaceful, rational educators can and do become violent animals under these circumstances. Planning should also include abbreviated agenda, suspension of oral reports to the board, and the imposition of strict speaker rules. An official time clock and a cutoff switch on the speaker podium microphone are standard equipment. The key here is to anticipate the union's activity and be prepared. At the same time, the district's public information operation must continue in high gear, developing press releases following every event. The releases must be scrupulously accurate and objective in their description of the union's activity but must always put forward as simply and as straightforwardly as possible a full description of the bargaining table issues and the board's position. The idea here is to use the attention stirred up by the union to give the board an opportunity to deliver its message. District leaders must constantly bear in mind that they are waging a PR war of their own and exploit every opportunity.

Strategy #11. Distribute propaganda leaflets. Distributing leaflets at shopping malls, PTA meetings, athletic events, etc., telling how unfair the board is and how poorly teachers are treated, can be a fairly effective activity. The purpose, of course, is to influence community political support for teachers and against the board. Usually the message on the leaflets is more argument than fact. Teachers from relatively well-paid districts will often prepare leaflets claiming they are the lowest-compensated in the region. Another favorite is to claim that the administrators of the district received an enormous pay hike while the teachers are being denied a simple cost of living adjustment. This activity can often be combined with advertising in the various media carrying a similar story.

Combating mass distribution of misinformation is more difficult than it would seem. Often the teacher distributing the leaflet in front of the supermarket is known by members of the community as a responsible, rational person. More than likely she believes the information on the leaflets. Why not? She hasn't spent time researching the salaries of surrounding school districts or the raises of the administrators. She believes what her building union representative tells her. The building rep, in turn, believes what the union's bargaining specialists are saying.

One approach to combating a misinformation campaign is to develop a carefully researched and documented fact sheet for distribution to the press and service clubs and for mailing home with the district's newsletters. The problem with this approach lies with the complexity of the truth and the incredible difficulty of transmitting the complicated facts to your community. Advertising executives as well as political demagogues have learned long ago that a simple "sound bite" repeated over and over is far more effective. Fact sheets should be developed for use by those people in the community who wish to carefully analyze the issues. But the district's interests will probably be best served with a couple of obtuse statements claiming the district simply has no money or proposing that the hefty salary increases being demanded would require draconian program cuts at all levels. This approach is more effective for two reasons: (1) It frames the issues strictly in economic terms with which all community members can identify, and (2) It avoids the rancor that all too often marks these kinds of disputes. Parents as well as interested community members are confronted with the single real issue: Do we want higher-paid teachers or higher-quality programs?

I became a confirmed proponent of the simple message years ago in a particularly difficult bargaining deadlock. As the teachers moved closer to the inevitable strike, I performed my part in the public information campaign by arranging speaking engagements with all of the service clubs in the three communities we served. Usually I passed out the district's official (and very sterile) fact sheet, which authoritatively documented the relative status of our teacher salaries, the various issues on the table, and so on. After more than a dozen of these appearances, I was convinced that the district's message was not getting across. Then I was interviewed by a television reporter who gave me a brief opportunity to explain that the district could not offer the services the community expected and grant the raises the teachers demanded. The next afternoon, as I was lining up for lunch at my Rotary Club, one of the Rotarians turned to me and stated, "I saw you on television last night. Now I know what you were talking about. You don't have enough money to pay the raises! I can understand that." From then on I was convinced that the members of the community want to know the *essence* of the conflict, not all of the gory details. Forcing the details, in fact, gives the appearance that the district is trying to cover something up.

Strategy #12. Stage a news conference. Called unilaterally, this strategy can put political pressure on the school board. Usually, the union will discuss its withdrawal of one or more demands that they claim should break the deadlock quickly. Often the chips they play are insignificant, and if the board is stuck on a major issue such as the salary increase, nothing changes—except that the board looks recalcitrant.

Experienced media personnel usually recognize a one-sided news conference of this sort and will not attend, but the education reporter for many newspapers is often a beginning reporter. The board and administration are free to use the same tactic; however, they risk having the media feel used. On the other hand, a news conference is the best way to break a legitimate major news story such as settlement of the impasse.

Strategy #13. Seek the support of other labor organizations. Employed at the right moment, this strategy will give the impression that organizations observing the negotiations in the school district have become convinced that the teachers' union's demands are fair and should be met by the school board. It carries weight with people whose political sentiments are in line with the various organizations. The endorsements are usually fairly automatic, and in some cases the unions will offer personnel in support of job actions. In the San Diego district strike, teamsters and other labor union members joined the ranks of teachers to jam the board meeting, and when the doors were locked, they beat on them, rendering the meeting inside difficult. Since these people had no connection with the district (and no crime was being committed) they felt free to add to the media show in support of one of their fellow labor organizations.

Strategy #14. Establish a crisis center. This highly visible strategy attracts reporters and gives the illusion that things are getting serious—that a strike might be near. Properly located and properly carried out, this strategy is a masterful, compelling public relations contrivance. But the center can also be put to use for informational picket sign construction and other concerted action planning activities.

The district leadership's best bet at this point is to stay the course with the public relations campaign, perhaps escalating it to radio or TV if these are available and reasonable. In addition, regular briefings should be held for all administrative team members assigned responsibilities to manage a strike. Other strike operations that we will discuss later should also be put into high gear.

Strategy #15. Organize a slowdown. This action, like many of the others described before, is a page right out of the industrial sector handbook. However, in the school setting it really is not very effective. The best thing the district leadership can do is do nothing. Administrators are best advised to cancel their department chair meetings, faculty meetings, and other functions outside of the classroom that might give the school's union "red hots" a forum. This job action has the potential to backfire since it draws attention to the length of the teacher's contract day and other job conditions that can be seen as out of line with the norm in the private sector. Moreover, informing the community that a slowdown means no special help to struggling students or meetings with interested parents does not build support among parents—the most critical audience in the public relations war. I have always wondered why savvy bargaining specialists for the union would allow this kind of action to take place. It almost always scores a point or two for the district in the PR war.

Even though a work slowdown is a minor nuisance at worst, the district's attorneys should immediately file an unfair practice charge with the PERB, including a request for an injunction on future slowdowns. The PERB may be reluctant to respond quickly, but the action alerts the PERB staff that a potentially serious problem exists in your district. Taking action at this time helps clarify lines of communication and establish emergency contacts. The PERB may be a district's best friend when confronted with unethical job actions by an antagonistic or ill-advised union.

Strategy #16. Use personal leave days. The idea here is to disrupt school by lining up as many faculty as possible to use their personal leave day on the same day. Union leaders will try to convince the teachers that it is legal and results in no financial loss—a painless way to show the board that the teachers are organized and ready to strike.

Contrary to this advice, job actions of this sort are unfair practices since your state's collective bargaining procedures laid out in law have not been culminated. This action will definitely disrupt school, and it should be anticipated in your strike plan. Principals need to be ready to take this sort of activity in stride. If administrators catch wind of the plan before it happens (and they almost always do) the district's attorneys should approach the PERB for an emergency injunction against the action.

Strategy #17. Stage a sick-out. Like the personal day caper, a sick-out is appealing to teachers because there will be no financial consequences. The district's human resources division, in collaboration with the principals, must assure that contract provisions relating to sick leave are strictly observed. In some cases, teachers can be docked if they cannot produce a physician's note. But in my experience, this is more trouble for the administration than it is for the teachers, most of whom simply drop by their family doctor's office and ask the nurse to write a note. The key, again, is preparation. Principals should be ready with large group activities to take the job action in stride. In the likely event that the administration has advance notice, preparation can be even more complete. The district's attorneys should also file an unfair practice charge with the PERB and request an emergency injunction.

Strategy #18. Call for boycotts. Last-ditch efforts to bring strong pressure to bear on school board members can be engineered by calling for boycotts of the businesses of the board members. Another variation of this is to boycott not only the businesses of the board members but also the businesses of anyone who supports the board members. In my experience, this tactic does not have an appreciable impact. What's more, it has the potential for backfiring on the teachers by making the individual school board members victims and arousing support for the board where none existed before.

Strategy #19. Organize pickets at the homes of board members and the superintendent. Having their homes picketed has a personal impact on each of the members and the superintendent. It also affects spouses, children, and neighbors. Although individual board members react differently (some ignore the picketers; others walk out to chat with them), all that I spoke with agreed that they felt the privacy of their homes had been violated. District leaders must keep in mind that these small groups of picketers are not always harmless. Although only four or five in number, they are still vulnerable to mob psychology. For this reason, districts must provide strong, around-the-clock security guards for the homes of board members and top administrators when negotiations reach this point. Many of the collective bargaining states may recognize this as a necessary cost and will reimburse the district for this, along with the other costs of collective bargaining.

Strategy #20. Request that the whole board meet with the union leaders. Union leaders will implore, "We're so close. If we could only get everyone together we could settle this in no time." Wrong. Nothing can be accomplished and much can be undone. The request, probably issued publicly at a board meeting, is plainly and simply another volley in the public relations war. Union leaders figure that if the board turns them down it's a point for them. If the board accepts, they can orchestrate a session designed to divide the board or to move it off its reasonable final positions. The union has nothing to lose. The board has everything to lose.

Strategy #21. Threaten strike. At this final stage the union leadership begins leaking information about an impending strike. The union newsletter may report that the union's strike committee has requested the strike vote. A subsequent article may announce that the executive committee voted to take a strike vote. Finally, union leaders conduct a vote; the vote is held at only one school in the district, which tends to limit voting to the more active union members of the district. The ballot calls for authorization for the committee to call a strike.

Short of a strike, the strike threat is the most powerful pressure tactic the union has in its bag of tricks. If the board is going to cave in, my advice is that this is the time to do it. There certainly is no point in taking the brunt of a strike and then backing away from your bottom line. The grief of a strike is not worth it if in the end you simply reinforce the union's belief that strikes are necessary to achieve settlement in your district. Allowing the strike to be "successful" in the eyes of the teachers' union members is a surefire way to encourage another in the future.

The twenty-one strategies discussed above by no means constitute a complete list. I mentioned earlier the "earthquake drill" pulled off by creative union leaders in Southern California. (A tornado drill would be more appropriate in the Midwest.) Calls for a blue-ribbon panel or the local ministerial association to mediate the dispute is another ploy. The purpose for discussing strategies is to underscore the necessity of district preparation. All of the strategies discussed have been used from time to time by unions in their efforts to control negotiations.

Some may feel I have exaggerated. Believe me, I have not. In fact, I purposely did not include such strategies as death threats, physical abuse, or vandalism—mainly because I don't think they are officially sanctioned by union leadership, although they nearly always occur to some extent in a strike situation. However, acts like the ones described above happen regularly as a part of the buildup to a strike. Others may feel I am accusing the union of immoral or unethical activities to further its own ends. I am not. I fully understand Goethe's observation that "Conscience is the virtue of observers and not of agents of action." Union organizers, bargaining specialists, and strike specialists are agents of action who make things happen. They are cheered by the people whose ends they promote and reviled by those whose ends are thwarted. The union's means, when they are used against us, are viewed by us as unethical or immoral, while *our* means, of course, are rooted in the highest of our culture's values. Later I will discuss examples of strategies the school board can use to discourage strikes or render them unsuccessful. These strategies include attacking the unions politically at their weakest points and forcing their members to consider the short-range and long-range financial costs of participation in the job action. From the union's point of view, these strategies are dirty tricks, and thus immoral. From the school board's perspective, they are strong, forthright actions aimed at neutralizing an adversary.

I have pointed out throughout this discourse that a teachers' strike and its prelude is a public relations war. And in war, the end justifies almost any means. In World War II, arch anticommunist Winston Churchill was attacked for his support of Stalin and the Soviet Communists. Churchill replied that the purpose of the war was to destroy Hitler and quipped, "If Hitler invaded hell, I would at least make a favorable reference to the Devil in the House of Commons." Teacher unions certainly cannot be compared to Stalin's Communist regime, and few school superintendents measure up to Winston Churchill. However, the passions generated by a teachers' strike are similar, and the human responses described by Sir Winston are clearly observable.

Winston Churchill also pointed out that weakness invites aggression. If the district is saddled with an adversarial union, lack of preparation on the district's part will encourage a strike. Likewise, statements from the district or from board members and administrators that indicate the district is afraid of a strike will also embolden the union perpetrators. The first step in warding off a strike is to prepare the district to combat a strike effectively. No one doubts that all-out aggression by the Soviet Union during the Cold War was stymied by the preparedness of the allies. Most folks in America who lived through those perilous times agree that the best way to prevent the war we didn't want was to be well prepared to fight it. Frustrated board members and superintendents who are dedicated to collaborative approaches to labor relations are confronted with an uncomfortable dilemma: "How can I reconcile my dedication to cooperative labor relations with aggressive antistrike initiatives?" My advice is keep the faith and never give up trying. But above all, don't fall in the trap of neglecting to prepare the district to defend itself as a "goodwill gesture" to a recalcitrant union. The results will be disastrous. And you will deserve everything that happens.

Exhibit 7.1.   Checklist for Board Members

(The checklist presented here is provided courtesy of the California Association of School Administrators and is contained in the association's publication entitled *Strike Manual*.)

____ 1. **Adopt an Emergency Procedures Resolution.** One of the most important policies to combat a strike is an emergency procedures resolution. Such a resolution does three things: (1) it signals potential strikers that the board will take the strike seriously; (2) it plugs any loopholes the district may have left in its current practices; and (3) it sets the pay rate for strike replacements.

Before adopting such a resolution, the board should seek specific legal advice from its attorney. A number of PERB cases have challenged the adoption of such policies on the grounds that they are unlawful unilateral adoptions of a negotiable matter. For example, in *Rio Hondo Community College District* (1983), the school board, anticipating a strike, passed an emergency resolution. Reviewing the legality of the resolution, PERB found that the district could probably pass a resolution declaring its intent to continue to provide educational services by: (1) hiring replacement faculty; (2) hiring security guards; (3) initiating appropriate legal action to prevent disruption of district activities; and (4) refusing to pay strikers for time not worked, including fringe benefits. PERB found unlawful, however, that portion of the resolution which unilaterally changed existing board policies by requiring prior approval for certain types of leaves, thereby rejecting the "business necessity" defense asserted by the district.

____ 2. **Assess the Employee Organization's Ability to Withstand a Strike.** The following questions should be considered and answered with the assistance of the district superintendent:

____ a. Does the union leadership really want a strike?
____ b. Does the union membership really want a strike?

____ c. What percentage of the unit are union members?

____ d. Does the union have an agency shop clause?

____ e. What internal union politics and specific potential power struggles exist?

____ f. Does the union pay strike benefits? If yes, how much, and when do payments begin?

____ g. When was the last time the employees got paychecks?

____ h. How long can strikers be expected to hold out in spite of installment payments, living expenses, etc.?

____ i. What promises has the union made to its membership?

____ j. Does the union have a "war chest"? If yes, how big is it?

____ k. Will the state or national organization support the strike financially?

____ l. What percentage of employees will go out on strike?

____ m. Will other unions honor the picket line? If yes, which ones, and what are the consequences?

____ n. Does the union have a public relations specialist? Will the state or national organization supply one?

____ o. Does the local media support the union's position?

____ p. Does the union have the ability to stop the delivery of educational services?

____ q. Do union negotiators/representatives control the membership, or does the membership control the negotiators/representatives?

____ 3. **Assess the Strengths/Weaknesses of the District to Withstand a Strike.**

Determine:

____ a. Is the board united or is it split on the bargaining issues?

____ b. Is the board willing to take a strike? If yes, will it remain firm throughout the strike?

____ c. How much community pressure will be put on the district and individual board members?

____ d. What is the likelihood of a recall election in response to the board's position?

____ e. Is the management team prepared to take a strike?

____ f. How many days after the strike starts will the district hold to its prestrike offer?

____ g. How many days will the district go before accepting the employee organization proposal?

____ h. Is the district able to replace strikers so as to maintain educational services?

____ i. Does the district have a formal ongoing public relations program?

____ j. Does the local media support the district's position?

____ k. Will students attend school during the strike? How many?

____ l. What are the district's chances of winning?

____ 4. **Pre-Agree on One District Communicator.** The board, the administration, and the district's negotiator need to be protected from interference from media and outsiders. The only effective way to do this is to have a prestrike agreement by the board that in the event of a strike there will only be one outside communicator. If the board adopts such a practice and then imposes it, the district will eliminate much of the divisiveness and wasted time created by outsiders.

____ 5. **Pre-Agree on One District Negotiator.** There can be only one negotiator in a district at a time. Unfortunately, in a strike, everyone tries to be a negotiator. In one district, a local minister convinced the board president that if the board made a better offer, a large number of teachers who had been talking to him would cross the line. He was also successful in convincing the board to make the offer. When the teachers didn't come back, the minister said he was sorry. Of course, the board's final settlement was that much higher. If the board agrees that all proposals and counterproposals must be funneled through the negotiator, the process will resolve itself much more quickly.

___ 6. **Pre-Agree on One Mediator.** In most strikes, multiple "mediators" make themselves available. Mediation can be a beneficial process, but only if conducted by a professional who knows what he is doing. State law provides for a PERB-appointed mediator from the State Conciliation Service. Any other mediator is superfluous. The board must pre-agree to use only one mediator to work between the parties.

___ 7. **Adopt Salaries for Strike Replacements.** The Board of Education should adopt attractive salaries to encourage potential temporary employees to cross the picket line. For example, a salary of twice the regular sub pay is reasonable. The employer can "save" money, even though teacher replacement salaries seem generous.

___ 8. **Establish Policies with Regard to Strikers and Union.** Prior to the strike, the board must determine what its policies will be with regard to strikers and their union. Items to be addressed include:

    ___ a. Payment of wages

    ___ b. Health coverage continuation

    ___ c. Life and disability policy coverage

    ___ d. Vacation time and pay

    ___ e. Sick leave

    ___ f. Allowing strikers to perform extra duty assignments

    ___ g. Credit for service during strike period

    ___ h. Disciplinary action

    ___ i. Authorization to legal counsel to seek injunctive relief

    ___ j. Filing of unfair practice charges or action for breach of contract

___ 9. **Review Effectiveness of Resolution and Procedures.** Direct the superintendents to evaluate the effectiveness of the emergency resolutions and procedures in effect during the emergency and make recommendations for revisions as needed.

___ 10. **Keep Apprised of Developments.** Maintain close contact with your administration, your negotiator and legal counsel to keep fully apprised of problems as they arise during pendency of the strike.

___ 11. **Plan for Post-Strike Problems.**

___ 12. **Review State Laws Regarding Public Comment Portion of Board Meeting.** One tactic used by employee organizations, especially if impasse is declared in negotiations, is crowding school board meetings and monopolizing the public comment portion of the meeting. Unless otherwise authorized by law, school board meetings in most states must be open to the public. Further, each regular school board meeting agenda usually must provide for an opportunity for the public to address the school board members on items of interest to the public that are within the jurisdiction of the school board. Since public employees are also members of the public and the subject of employee relations is within the jurisdiction of the board, school district employees must be accorded the right to address the board on such issues, particularly since the employees have a vital interest in the proceedings of the board. *City of Madison. Joint School District v. Wisconsin Employment Relations Commission,* 429 U.S. 167, 175 (1976). Even minority or dissenting views must be heard.

To permit one side of a debatable public question to have a monopoly in expressing its views to the government is the antithesis of constitutional guarantees. Whatever its duties as an employer, when the board sits in public meetings to conduct public business and hear the views of citizens, it may not be required to discriminate between speakers on the basis of their employment or the content of their speech.

The board is not required to allow each speaker an unlimited opportunity to speak. To do so would be an unreasonable burden on the board and would prevent much of the work of the board from getting done. Under law, the board is authorized to promulgate reasonable regulations to permit public comment, including regulations limiting the total amount of time allocated for public testimony on particular issues and for each individual speaker. In the absence of such regulations, it appears that it is within the authority of the board president to limit the discussion on a particular topic to a reasonable extent. The preferable course of action is, however, to promulgate or update regulations to limit public comment pursuant to state law.

8

✛

Managing the Strike

When discussing teacher strikes, district and union leaders love to announce in somber tones, "In a school district strike, no one wins." Nonsense. Whenever a strike happens in a school district, one side *always* comes out ahead. In my book this is a win. As I pointed out in chapter 7, school district leaders who prepare their administrative staffs to fight a losing battle will most surely lose. Similarly, those who prepare their teams to win will achieve more satisfactory long-term benefits to the district and for the students, parents, teachers, and administrators involved. To accomplish this the board and administration should define exactly what the administration must accomplish to "win" the strike. After that the Strike Management Team (SMT) must design winning strategies for strike management.

I don't mean to imply that certain strategies will result in a resounding declaration of victory by the school district leaders or public employers. This almost never happens (the air controllers strike during the Reagan presidency is one of the few exceptions). Usually all strikes end with a union declaration of victory—even when the strike has been crushed with no appreciable gain in salary or working conditions. This is simply standard operating procedure for unions, which attempt to justify their decisions and salvage the loyalty of their members. Saddam Hussein used the same tactics when he declared victory over the United States in the Gulf War in the "mother of all battles." After all, he had prevented the United States from capturing Baghdad, and his administration retained its firm grasp on the country's government.

This last volley by the union in the public relations war against the district always goes unanswered. School districts have nothing to gain by rubbing the noses of striking teachers in the dirt. Information about the extent of their losses will not lessen their loyalty to their union. Instead, the animosity teachers feel toward their "enemies," the district leaders, will be piqued and will turn to a more lasting hatred. This hatred, in turn, will inspire even more aggressive job actions in the future, and the district's primary strike management goal will be thwarted— namely, to suppress future strikes by causing the participating faculty discomfort, expense, and most of all a feeling that strikes are futile and counterproductive.

No amount of hooting and hollering over an empty victory by union leaders can disguise the bitterness of defeat felt by the teachers who put their faith in union leaders. Eventually most of the faculty will understand, and the result will be a reluctance to participate in job actions in the future. Even the most ardent flag wavers will not deny today that our country took a beating in Vietnam. The result in the years since has been a profound reluctance on the part of the American citizenry to commit to prolonged military engagements with a high-casualty price tag. Managing a school district's strike with the clear goal of winning will make future strikes less likely and will help pave the way to "a better way of doing business." The following paragraphs will elaborate on the objectives for winning the strike game outlined in chapter 7, along with approaches to the PR war, which reaches its zenith during the strike.

TACTICS AND STRATEGIES THAT WORK WELL FOR THE SCHOOL BOARD AND ADMINISTRATION

Strategic Objective #1: Keep the schools open. Closing the schools doesn't make sense because it means locking out faculty members who are supportive of the district's leadership and who would cross the picket lines. In addition, state laws usually require that the school days be made up at the end of the year, resulting in no financial loss to the strikers. Careful planning for keeping the schools open is the heart of a well-designed strike management plan. At the onset, district leaders must recognize that services in the schools will be significantly curbed, but extensive plans covering a myriad of contingencies must be developed, and the administrative team must be ready to carry them out.

- **Round up subs**. The human resources division must work closely with site administrators to develop plans for providing large numbers of substitute teachers. This division must develop strategies for recruiting large numbers of subs, while the site administrator must develop strategies for dealing with students in the absence of adequate numbers of teachers. Recruitment of substitute teachers for strike replacements has been most successful in districts when the process began at the first sign of impasse. One district, experienced in strike management, began recruiting eligible substitute teachers at the first sign of deadlock. The state law provided for the emergency credentialing of persons with at least ninety units of college work for the purpose of substitute teaching. The district cast a wide net that included students at nearby colleges. Although by law the district could not pay for the credential fees for the recruited students, all recruits were guaranteed a one-day paid training session at a rate of pay more than twice the cost of the credentials. The result: the district was ready with an abundance of subs when the teachers went on strike.
- **Pay strikebreakers well**. Other strategies include raising the substitute teacher pay during the period of the strike to make the positions more attractive. Instructing the subs to report to a central location, then transporting them to the schools is another good practice that helps shield the teachers from derisive comments and catcalls from the picket lines. The difficulties faced by substitute teachers during a strike are enormous. Exhibit 8.1 ("From the 'Scab's' Point of View") contains the testimonial of strike subs during two strikes.

    Assuring the regular subs that they will have top priority for substitute employment when the strike is over is important to counteract union claims that they will not be rehired. If substitute teachers are part of the bargaining unit, they may be less anxious to work during the strike, even for the increased pay. Informing them of the policy giving priority to strike replacements may increase the number of subs willing to serve during the strike.

Exhibit 8.1. From the "Scab's" Point of View

Oak Tree Unified School District

My first time crossing the picket line I was in college. I heard about the strike through a friend who knew some administrators of the district. We thought we could make some good money, so we agreed to skip classes to teach for the day. I had no idea about the politics behind the strike, nor had I ever known of anyone involved in one. My friend warned me that the striking teachers might not be that nice to us because we were considered "scabs." I had never heard the term, but I was not worried. We set off for Oak Tree excited to see what was in store for us as teachers.

When we entered the parking lot, a group of people with picket signs had gathered and began shouting at us, "Scabs! Scabs!" I asked my friend who those people were, and when she told me they were the *teachers*, I was shocked! Why were they acting like such idiots? Things got worse when we went into the teachers' lounge where the other *substitutes* had gathered. On the wall hung a picture of the superintendent with concentric circles superimposed on it like a dartboard; someone had colored a "Hitler" mustache under his nose. A couple of the subs approached us, and we talked nervously about leaving school and facing the mob in the parking lot again.

I do not recall if any of the contracted teachers had crossed the picket line to teach; nor do I remember discussing the event with anyone except my friend, so I do not have much feeling about the individual reactions of the subs. I do, however, remember the subs were quiet and a little nervous about the whole situation. We all wondered if any children would show up for school. As it turned out, few did come to school, and we ended up combining the classes and watching *Gone with the Wind* for most of the day.

The day proved to be quite a lesson for me on the dynamics of a strike. I would have never expected that teachers, respected members of the community, could yell, taunt, and motion in such an animalistic manner. Maybe that is why I decided not to become a teacher after all!

San Diego

When the teachers of the San Diego Unified School District went on strike, I was in school yet again. This time, I knew what to expect, and I braced myself and my roommate for the worst. We both needed the money, so we figured it wouldn't be that bad. This one was almost worse. We could not even get in the parking lot of Bethune Elementary because of the teacher blockade. They stood across the only entrance into the lot shaking their picket signs at us and shouting, "Shame on you," "Scabs," "You're only hurting the children." My roommate slowly crept her car forward until the teachers were forced to part to avoid getting hit. As we drove through, one of the teachers whacked her sign down on the windshield of the car. It scared the heck out of me, and unfortunately, enraged my friend. She jumped out of the car, and I followed as she ran up to the teacher and started asking her what the hell she was thinking. The teacher started screaming at her until one of the other ones pulled her away. Great start.

Once inside, the Vice Principal gathered all the subs in the teachers' lounge to tell us about the day. We reported what had happened, and the Principal agreed to monitor our cars during the day and to clear the way when it was time for us to leave school. *(cont.)*

(cont.)

The subs incredulously discussed the greeting we received, and one teacher who had crossed the picket line identified the teacher who had hit my friend's car. The teacher said she was most likely going to be ostracized once the strike was over, but she did not care. She supported the demands of the teachers, but not the methods for getting those demands met.

The Vice Principal had all sorts of worksheets and activities for us to do with the children in anticipation that the teachers did not leave lesson plans. In fact, the teachers had left us a letter as each sub discovered upon entering their room. The letter, entitled, *Ode to a Scab* was a scathing description of a "scab," comparing one to the scourge of the earth. Once again, the irrational statements made in this letter frightened me—who is teaching our kids? Only a completely delusional person could believe that scabs were "of the devil" as the letter claimed. This time, however, I just laughed it off and proceeded to teach my class. The day went quite well, except the poor kids were very confused.

At recreation time, some of the children went running up to the fence to see their teachers as they picketed on the sidewalk in front of the school. Watching the children talking to their teachers through the wire fence seemed eerie and at the same time sad. I could tell some of the teachers really just wanted to be back with their kids, and the kids didn't really understand why they didn't come back.

We ended up subbing throughout the strike, and while the morale inside the school continued to be high, fewer teachers showed up to picket each day. Beyond the one militant member who had attacked our car that day, very few said anything directly to my roommate and me as we came and went. They seemed tired and sad. I felt bad for them and hoped for the end of the strike. Meanwhile, I tried to reassure the kids that their teacher would be back soon and that they were all right. Some kids wrote cards for the teacher, some for me. I think the uncertainty of who would be in the classroom was really hard for the third graders. At the end of every day they would all hug me and say they hoped to see me the next day, then got confused when we went outside and they saw the teacher there on the sidewalk.

If there was another strike in the district, I would cross the picket line again. Even though it is not the popular thing to do, I would rather have someone such as me with some substitute teaching experience who cares about kids watching over the teachers' kids while they do what they feel they have to do.

- **Scout your union and prepare for their best tricks.** Training sessions with site administrators should include discussions of the many problems they may face on strike days. These "what if" scenarios should include all the tactics the unions around you have used in the past. If your union has conducted strikes in the past, plans should focus on tactics that were most successful for them during the last strike. Administrators should be ready for all eventualities. For example, as a worst case scenario you might propose to your elementary principals, "What if school is about to begin in fifteen minutes and *nobody* but you and a couple of faithful classified staff members shows up?" Or more likely, "What if you and only five or six district strike replacements are on site to deal with your five hundred students?" Being prepared for these scenarios on each campus is the essence of good strike management.

- **Prepare for the worst**. Depending on the facilities available, the principals can plan large group activities on the playground, in the cafeterias, or in the gymnasium. I would hope that good strike replacement planning by the human resources division would prevent these difficult scenarios from happening. But good strike planning also means developing site administrators who are mentally prepared for just about anything. District administrators and volunteer administrators from other districts should be ready on strike day to help out in the event one of the two scenarios described above occurs.

Strategic Objective #2: Minimize teacher participation in the strike. Throughout the labor deadlock, information that clearly defines the district's positions and their rationale should be aimed at the teaching staff. Although it is clearly an unfair labor practice to negotiate with teachers, nothing in law requires the teachers to be kept in the dark about the district's position.

- **Inform teachers of consequences**. As soon as the union mentions strike, or if a strike authorization vote is sought, a letter from the district informing teachers of the district's planned reaction to a walkout is in order. This will provoke a response from the union, probably the subject of a flyer in every teacher's box claiming that the district is threatening them and claiming that their union will protect them. Ignore the reaction. The letter from the district is mandatory. It not only informs the rank and file that a price will be paid for their walkout (something they may not know based on past experience with the district), and it puts union leaders on alert that their tactics will be vigorously opposed. At the very least, this will cause some serious introspection by rational leaders in the union's hierarchy. Letters should inform all the teachers that strikers will lose a full day's pay for every day on strike. Moreover, they should be informed that payment of their various benefits will be also suspended. This latter advice should be accompanied with a provision for the teachers to pay for their benefits while on strike.
- **Express the board's disapproval of striking**. Other messages in the letter should be entered with the advice of the district's attorney. It is fair, for example, to indicate that the board of education does not approve of a strike as a means of exerting pressure on the bargaining

process. The letter may also comment that the board feels that striking is an unethical and unprofessional act. The wisdom of threatening to suspend teachers or to invoke further disciplinary action on strikers depends on the status of collective bargaining law in your state. Informing teachers that their participation in a walkout will be memorialized in their permanent records and, providing striking is not clearly a protected activity in your state, that appropriate disciplinary action will be considered has a chilling effect on the faculty's willingness to strike—exactly what you are trying to accomplish. I believe this is dangerous, however, if you don't plan to follow through. After all, the purpose of these antistrike measures is to break the Pavlovian cycle of job action leading to district acquiescence. This means you must carry out the district's announced reaction to a strike. This is the only way the district will effectively counteract the union's "no harm" message delivered to the faculty in an effort to rally them to strike in the future. Obviously, if strikes are protected in your state by law or court ruling, then threats to discipline strikers would be foolish.

Strategic Objective #3: End the strike without a rousing "win." In the public sector, a strike is a PR gimmick. No one in the union leadership believes the district will collapse financially as a result of its walkout. The district leaders must understand that the strike will end in a week or so (rarely more than four weeks). The rule of thumb is to divide the raise sought by the daily wage of an average teacher. The result is a good ballpark guess about the number of days a faculty can be expected to stay out. Teachers, like any group of human beings, can get fired up to a certain degree by union rhetoric. They can be truly angered by cruel, callous comments made by board members or the superintendent (some true, some fictitious). However, they aren't fools. They know they have good jobs. They like to compare themselves with doctors, lawyers, and scientists, but most recognize they have not obtained the education or certification necessary to qualify in a higher-paying marketplace. Further, none of them have been fired summarily or have contracted black lung disease as a result of intolerable, exploitive management practices. They are simply doing what union leaders say is "smart" in order to raise their salaries and maximize the return on their investment. You can't blame them for trying, especially if it has worked in the past and the union leaders assure them that the district will, once again, cave into their demands. If nothing else, adding a price to the strike activities causes rational teachers to do a reality check. In the long run this is probably good for all of us once in a while.

Strategic Objective #4: Concentrate on the PR war. From the first shot out of the cannon (meaning the first time the union circulates a negotiations update flyer with *distorted* information) the district must put its public information campaign into high gear.

- **Emphasize the money**. To begin with, the message should focus on the finances of the district and the costs of various employee-related benefits. Teacher unions claim they rarely strike "just for the money," and in rare cases this may be true. But serious investigations nationwide consistently place salaries and fringe benefits at the top of the list of key issues in strikes (McDonnell and Pascal, 1988; Bacharach, Bamberger, and Conley, 1990). I believe that after all the dust has cleared, including the accusation of overloaded classes and top-down management, the key issue in any district is salary. I also assume that given unlimited means, most districts would be paying their teachers at least a little more money. So the convincing argument, after all is said and done, must be founded on whether the district can afford to pay the additional salary. One of the most heated and complicated strikes of the last half century was the 1992 Detroit teachers' strike, where angry union leaders accused the district of everything from union busting (the well-publicized site empowerment proposal) to racism. The marathon strike, which lasted nearly four weeks, featured interventions by numerous factions in the community, including the clergy, chamber of commerce, and various other community leaders. The impasse was resolved in a startlingly short time by the Wayne County executive's office when the county offered to serve as the bonding agent so that the Detroit schools could borrow against delinquent taxes *to pay for a higher wage demand.* After all the whooping and hollering (and four weeks of strike) it came down to money. In my view, this is not surprising. Money is seen as an indicator of how the district values its employees. Nothing is more emotional. If a district is holding the line on a salary increase, it must be crystal clear that the district lacks the money to offer more. This rationale for the district's salary position is easily understood by the faculty (if not believed), as well as the community. The longer you maintain this position, the more believable it becomes. The PR campaign must concentrate on getting this message across to all stakeholders in the district, and it must begin at the first sign of hostility at the table by the union.
- **Focus on relative salaries of the district's teachers**. A second PR campaign theme should involve the relative salaries of the district's teachers. The information must be honest, straightforward, and should not portray your teachers as overpaid; however, total compensation comparisons of your district with other districts in your area are legitimate and serve to assuage the feelings of your

teachers, who may be misled by union propagandists telling them the district doesn't care enough to pay a decent salary. These comparisons, combined with the district's financial position, create the best bet for general community acceptance of the district's position. If these statistics tell a good story, then you should run with it. If, on the other hand, your teachers don't make a comparable salary, then you should work to remedy that deficiency. There is no clever labor practice that can cover for a district's failure to pay the going rate for its teachers. Districts that underpay their teachers pay for it in low quality performance, high turnover, union troubles, or all of the above.

- **Focus on the union's weak spots**. Beyond the two fundamentals, the district's ability to pay and the teachers' comparative salaries, the PR campaign is most effective focusing on the union's vulnerabilities. At the top of the list are the high cost of union dues and the union's dubious record of advancing the profession. Attacking the high cost of union membership is especially effective in districts with required agency fees or closed shop status. All members are required to pay a hefty chunk of their salary to belong to the union and to support national causes in which they have little sympathy or interest. Moreover, the NEA's and the AFT's reputations nationwide for improving the salaries and working conditions of teachers have been lackluster at best. As I discussed in the introduction, strong tenure laws and other important teacher protections were already part of the law in most states before the NEA became a union. Legislation was influenced by the large educational associations that formerly included administrators and represented "the voice of education." These organizations were popular with the rank-and-file citizens and were able to cajole legislatures into enacting extraordinary protections for teachers. Little progress has been made in the legislatures since the advent of the NEA's conversion to industrial-style unionism. Even more disheartening to teachers is the fact that in dollars adjusted for inflation, teachers have gained almost nothing in salary during the last thirty years—hardly a resounding endorsement of hardball collective bargaining. (See the discussion of teachers' salaries in chapter 2, "Unfulfilled Promises to Teachers.") Other areas where the union is vulnerable include high salaries for union officials (more than three thousand make six-digit salaries) and efforts to block school reform (the Detroit strike was a prime example). These latter issues are not key. They are simply targets of opportunity. For a handbook on the extent of the AFT's and the NEA's corruption and vulnerabilities written by an ex-official of the NEA, read Myron Lieberman's (1997) *The Teacher Unions*.

- **Implement the last best offer**. A union can only call a strike when all collective bargaining procedures required by your state's collective bargaining laws have been exhausted. A premature strike in violation of these protocols usually results in intervention by the state's PERB board—a real loss for the union leadership. However, once all the processes have been exhausted and a strike is definitely possible, the district should consider implementing its last best offer unilaterally. This tactic demonstrates vividly to the rank and file the *real* monetary stakes of a strike. Sample arithmetic usually shows them the financial folly of even a short walkout. This is a tactic employed by one of the districts I studied that won its teachers' strike. That is, the teachers came back to work after a very brief walkout with no concessions from the district.

Strategic Objective #5: Put the lawyers to work. In many states, costs directly related to collective bargaining activities are reimbursed. But whether reimbursed or not, an aggressive legal offense pays off. The attorneys can play a significant role in training your administrators to watch for unfair labor practices. Work-to-rule actions, sick-outs, back-to-school night boycotts, and other unsavory union practices during the bargaining process should be filed as unfair labor practices with the PERB and injunctions against future actions of this sort requested. The attorneys can also review the behavior of the union during the last few bargaining sessions or the last strike and request that these activities be enjoined also. Whenever a teachers' union activity results in the abridgement of a student's right to an education, the action should be challenged by a complaint to the PERB or in superior or federal court. Likewise, whenever student safety is involved, or whenever administrators are put into a position where student safety is compromised, charges should be filed. In other words, *every* questionable tactic by the union should be courageously confronted.

   In one district, aggressive legal offense resulted in injunctions against "rolling strikes." The idea behind rolling strikes was to catch the administrators off guard. Teachers would wait across the street on any given day. Then, when the first bell rang, they would either walk off the job or onto campus. Under these circumstances, administrators would not know whether or not to hire subs. If the teachers walked onto campus and the administrators hired subs, the district would be forced to pay substantial sums for services not needed. If, on the other hand, the district failed to hire enough subs, students would be left unsupervised and perhaps in physical danger. The tactic was designed to complicate the administration's duties by exposing the district to a lawsuit if a student was injured or killed because of a lack of supervision. The unions ceased this tactic only when ordered to do so by the court—the result of a district's aggressive attorney. Keeping the legal pressure on union leaders helps prevent them from committing unethical or illegal acts and helps keep some of the more "creative" union soldiers under control.

Strategic Objective #6: Organize and train the district's best. When organizing the strike management team, select the best of the high-ranking school administrators to coordinate strike day activities, including site planning, security planning, legal support, public information support, and strike day operations. Above all, select courageous people who will remain firm in their loyalty and who are not afraid to confront head-on the unknowns in a strike action. Avoid administrators with a reputation for "bending in the wind." Teacher pressure, and often parent pressure, will be extreme. Putting malleable, "other-directed" administrators in charge of anything is a big mistake. Instead, choose the strongest, most loyal, most self-assured, "inner-directed" leaders. Putting these people in charge of site administrators with firmly assigned accountability will give the district the best chance of success on strike days. Courageous, aggressive leaders will help inspire the same kind of courage necessary to carry out the very difficult site leadership functions.

Strategic Objective #7: Protect the principals. The site principals make or break a district's strike management effort. This is not to say that other key functions are not important. Certainly the human resources department and its strike replacement substitute organization is critical, and from the beginning I have emphasized the public information functions. Likewise, the emergency operations leadership, including the district's security functions and the board's role, are all important. But the rubber hits the roads at the site where the principal is in charge. These frontline leaders are the keys to the successful implementation of the district strike management plan. At the same time, they must be the key leaders in the school system once the strike is over. They are put in the position of mending fences with teachers who struck over district positions that the principals did not necessarily formulate. I believe a critical strategy of a successful strike management plan takes into consideration the aftermath of a strike. When a strike is over, and they are all relatively short-lived in public education, the district must pick up where it left off and accomplish its important mission of educating our youth. This means the authority and influence of the principals cannot be diminished by the strike. The district must protect its frontline administrators.

- **Train the principals well**. First, protect them by training them well, by schooling them in proper and improper approaches to striking picketers, teacher appeals, and so forth.

- **No dirty work**. Second, the principals should be relieved of "dirty work." Naturally, when they observe illegal activities, they are ethically and legally bound to confront the situation. Likewise, if students or substitute teachers are harassed, they must intervene. But beyond these expected responses, the principals should be relieved to keep the school open. They should not be armed with cameras to take photographs of striking staff, nor should they be required to write up strikers for post-strike discipline.

9

The Roles and Duties
of the Administration

The superintendent occupies a unique position in the school district, especially during labor unrest and strike. He or she works directly with the political governance of the school district and is the primary source of orientation and training for that entity. In addition, the superintendent is the chief executive officer of the district and is responsible for all administrative functions including carrying out negotiations processes. Although not directly involved with the administration of any of the myriad functions of a school district, the superintendent is usually more knowledgeable than any one person in the school district regarding all functions. Moreover, in the normal course of school district operations, as well as the crisis circumstances addressed in the district's emergency strike resolution, the superintendent has command and control of people and resources necessary to make a district-wide strategy work.

THE SUPERINTENDENT'S ROLE

The superintendent is responsible for organization and communication among the critical components of the district's collective bargaining and strike management operations. Following are operations the superintendent must coordinate. A superintendent's checklist with critical activities is included as exhibit 9.1 at the end of this chapter. Also included, as exhibit 9.2, is an auxiliary coordinator checklist. Superintendents in larger districts will want to appoint this special position, usually from the ranks of the classified managers. Superintendents in smaller districts may have to divide these duties among other management personnel.

Before the Strike

1. Organize the Strike Management Team (SMT) and the negotiating team and recommend to the governing board the appointment of a chief negotiator. As I have said before, I prefer an outsider, preferably an attorney with connections to a legal firm specializing in school labor relations. This provides the district with up-to-date expertise and keeps its regular administrators out of the line of fire.
2. Serve as liaison between negotiating team and the school board. Direct contact between the chief negotiator and the school board is necessary and desirable. However, it is crucial that the board understand that the negotiator works with the superintendent and the joint mission of the negotiator and superintendent is to communicate adequately with the board and receive board direction. I'm making this point for a simple reason: The board's chief negotiator should not control board strategy at the table. Rather, the strategy should be founded in the broader interests of the educational organization. Professional negotiators are available in assisting the board superintendent to conduct its negotiations business correctly and legally. But the nuances of understanding the school district and its educational operations are the domain of the superintendent and, in the final analysis, the superintendent's direction must prevail. In short, allowing the chief negotiator to take over negotiation strategies is usually a mistake.
3. Design a public information operation, assign responsibilities and resources, and initiate the processes.
4. Develop a strike plan and organize the Strike Management Team (SMT) as follows (see chapter 7, "Preparing for the Strike"):
   a. The superintendent—acts as chair and coordinator of the committee activities.
   b. Assistant superintendents (or directors in some cases)—the line administrators in charge of school operations.
   c. The business manager—the person in charge of business operations, auxiliary services, and budget.
   d. The director (or assistant superintendent) of human resources— plays a primary role in developing an adequate pool of strike replacement substitute teachers.
   e. The public information officer—plays a critical role in the "PR war" aspect of a strike.
   f. The district's chief negotiator—acts as spokesman and negotiator with the union during the period of time leading up to a strike and during the strike.
   g. The district's attorney—provides legal advice for the strike management deliberations (in some cases, this person is also the chief negotiator).

5. Maintain stepped-up liaison with community organizations, parents, and the general public. A smart move during the negotiations process is to schedule presentations at breakfast and luncheon meetings of various service organizations in the community. Assigning liaison responsibilities to other top administrators in the district as well as board members is also a smart move. People in the community who become aware of the issues during the more rational period preceding the strike are less likely to be influenced by distorted rhetoric; the greater their numbers, the better. These organizations can also be the source of moral support in times of crisis. On the day following a particularly rancorous three-day teachers' strike, accompanied by a barrage of orchestrated phone calls designed to convince me that I had no support in the community, I attended the meeting of the local Rotary Club, where I was given a spontaneous standing ovation. Needless to say, it was exactly what I needed at that moment.

6. Coordinate training of all components of the strike management plan. Providing enough orientation and training so that administrators are not flustered by strike activities on the first few days makes life easier for them. Equally important, it bolsters the confidence of the parents and community that the schools are in good hands and will remain open.

During the Strike

1. The superintendent's first responsibility, once a strike has been deemed imminent, is to call an emergency closed meeting of the governing board and adopt a resolution to effect the emergency strike procedures. Usually the resolution is accompanied by a delegation of broad authority to the superintendent to take actions necessary to implement the strike management plan as well as a declaration to the employees and community of its intent to keep the schools open, hire security guards, dock striker pay, and initiate appropriate legal action to prevent disruption of the district's programs.

2. The next step is to initiate daily meetings of the SMT. These meetings will usually take place early in the morning and again at the end of day in order to assure high levels of communication and coordination. Initial meetings will focus on preparedness in each of the strike management operational areas. During the actual strike, the focus will be on problems developing in these areas.

3. After the strike, the SMT will spearhead the rebuilding process. The superintendent will coordinate the post-strike procedures with the SMT.

THE HUMAN RESOURCES ADMINISTRATOR'S ROLE

Since a primary objective of the strike management plan is to keep the schools open, the director (or assistant superintendent) of human resources shoulders the major responsibility of ensuring that strike replacement substitute teachers are available to staff the schools during the strike. This task is made even more difficult if the classified staff union also strikes. Providing adequate staff for schools during strikes is probably the most important operational support function provided by the district. Consequently, plans for rounding up staff must be made well in advance. The main elements of this plan are presented below, and a helpful human resources administrator checklist is included as exhibit 9.3 at the end of this chapter along with sample forms and letters (exhibits 9.4–9.6).

Before the Strike

1. Since staffing is the prime concern, the first task is to figure out who will be on board to help manage the students during the strike. Instructional aides and other paraprofessionals can be used under the direction of a certified teacher or administrator to help reduce the number of certified strike replacement substitute teachers needed. At the same time, estimates should be made of the loyalties of other employees, i.e., secretaries, custodians, cafeteria workers, bus drivers, clerks, and other noninstructional personnel. This is the time you should take a hard look at the history of the district's teacher walkouts by school. Even in districts with reputedly pugnacious union leadership, the culture of one or more schools may reject the industrial-type pressure tactics and refuse to participate in a walkout.

   Temporary teachers, probationary teachers, and part-time teachers aspiring to be full-time teachers also feel more vulnerable in walkout situations because their jobs are less secure than permanent, tenured teachers. Union leaders have been known to "excuse" these teachers from participation in an attempt to appear "understanding" or "humane" to the membership. Even if not excused, the peer pressure to strike is less intensely focused on these more vulnerable personnel, especially if the board has formally communicated its disdain for teacher walkouts and threatened disciplinary action.

2. Once these estimates have been made, the human resources administrator, in collaboration with the other members of the strike management team, can develop an emergency staffing plan. The plan should focus primarily on staffing the classrooms and supervising the students. This means many nonessential services may be sus-

pended during the period of strike. Remember, teacher strikes are always short-term affairs usually over in five or six days and rarely lasting over four weeks. The strike plan should fully utilize all management employees to be certain all students are supervised. The strike management plan should take into consideration management personnel who do not have direct responsibilities for sites. Each of these should be assigned special strike duties.

3. Next, develop an extensive strike replacement substitute list. This task begins with a careful screening of the district's regular substitute list. As negotiations begin to heat up, time should be set aside to contact each substitute on the district's list to discuss service during a strike. Many subs will be reluctant, fearing the reprisals of the staff after the strike is over or fearing the discomfort of moving through teachers' picket lines to their classroom assignments. Districts that arrange to have substitutes bussed onto the campuses may alleviate part of this fear. Other subs may be emboldened by the higher daily substitute pay that should be established by the board prior to contacting the sub list.

Another valuable source of strike replacement substitutes can be found in the substitute lists of surrounding school districts. These substitutes will be attracted by the higher substitute salary and are often less reluctant to serve at a school where they are unknown to the faculty. The substitutes on these lists should be contacted in the same manner you contacted the subs on your own district's list.

As the strike draws near, advertise for subs in local newspapers, as well as on the radio, covering a wide area around the district. Subs have been known to travel seventy or eighty miles to earn the higher strike wage. Since these long-distance substitutes have no connection with the community, they feel much less reluctant to serve. The ads, by the way, should clearly stipulate that the positions are strike replacement substitutes. Frequently, regular teachers from nearby districts will take several days of sick leave or personal leave to substitute in another district, especially another district in another county where they are not likely to be recognized as full-time teachers. This certainly is not the intent of advertising in other counties. I mention it simply to point out the higher degree of "safety" that out-of-the-area teachers feel.

Finally, the human resources administrator should scour the community for willing volunteers. Community colleges and colleges in the area are a source of instructional aides or strike replacement substitute teachers. One district contacted fraternities and sororities at a nearby large university, producing a large number of qualified personnel with no compunction whatsoever about crossing picket lines.

At this point in the strike replacement substitute recruitment campaign the director of human resources should establish simple procedures in the grand strategy for processing the strike replacement personnel so that all state laws governing emergency credentialing and classified staff hiring are strictly observed. Under ordinary circumstances, the process may be complex. The more the district can simplify it and make it worthwhile for the strike replacement prospects, the more successful the campaign will be. Setting aside a special day and organizing staff in a "assembly line" works well. All the processes, including health tests, fingerprinting, and so forth, should be part of the assembly line. At the end of the line the applicant should leave with the proper certification, a map of the district, and a potential assignment. As I mentioned previously, guaranteeing the replacements at least a half-day's pay for orientation and training will usually offset any costs they might encounter for state credentialing fees and encourage potential subs to apply.

4. Assist site principals and area coordinators in developing site strike plans. In this way, the human resources administrator is intimately familiar with the needs of each of the sites and can coordinate with the area coordinators to deliver needed personnel on the first day of the strike. If bus transportation will be used to transport strike replacements onto campuses, the transportation chief must be an integral part of these team discussions. Recruitment of parent and community volunteers is usually better accomplished by the site principals, who have far more extensive contact with parents. Many of these people have teaching credentials that can qualify them to perform as strike replacement substitutes.

During the Strike

1. The prime objective of the human resources administrator is to oversee the implementation of the strike replacement substitute operations. As soon as notification of an impending strike is given, the human resources administrator must kick off the strike replacement assignment plan. Notifying subs can be done in a variety of ways. Smaller districts may wish to call the subs from the central office using a half dozen or more sub callers instead of the usual one. Other larger districts have had success assigning subs to schools in advance and giving the principal the responsibility for contacting the subs once the strike notification has been received. The decentralized model has the advantage of putting the substitute into contact with the principal, vice principal, or secretary of the school where the strike replacement assignment will take place. This allows local site

personnel to pass on any special information about parking or about where to catch the bus if busing is part of the district's plan. The site personnel can also brief the sub on the circumstances and alleviate some of the fear and trepidation.

2. The human resources administrator is also responsible for establishing accounting processes for the principals. This is the paperwork function that accompanies any strike action. This includes collection of prestrike estimates of the number of striking teachers as well as a system for taking attendance of all employees and delivering the information to the superintendent's office for use by the SMT. If additional strike replacement substitutes are needed, the director of human resources should step up the advertisement for replacements, widening the targeted areas. The local site managers will agree that it is far better to have too many people on the campus than too few—especially at the elementary and middle school levels. High school students can be supervised adequately with fewer personnel and, typically, student absenteeism is highest by far in the secondary schools, precluding the need for large numbers of strike replacements. High school principals should take this into consideration when planning for a strike. After the first day of the strike, they should trim back their replacement staff to reflect the lowered number of students.

Business managers tell me that if striking teachers are properly docked salary and benefits and strike replacement substitutes properly assigned, the district usually "makes money" during a strike. This frees up funds for other necessary expenditures in the expensive public relations war.

THE PUBLIC INFORMATION OFFICER'S ROLE

Since a teachers' strike is one aspect of a public relations war, the public information function of a district is crucial. Throughout the country, school districts are uniformly weak in organizing their efforts to communicate with their various publics. In times of budget crisis, the public information personnel are the first on the cut list. "How can we justify a PR director and office staff when we are cutting back the music program and other essential services to children?" Few argue that at times like these, the public information officer (PIO) may be the most important position in the school district's administration. Helping the public to understand the functioning of its school district results in rational voter response at the polls and strong public support for solutions to problems. But unfortunately, the public information office is viewed suspiciously by most of the district's stakeholders—the people who would most benefit from the public information officer's work. Americans see the public information function in a school district as "a propaganda mill," and in a sense, it is.

The question is whether it makes sense for a district to have a first-class PR operation when it decides to engage the teachers' union in a PR war. The answer is an unqualified *yes*. Public school districts are political organizations operating within communities. Districts that choose to operate without public information offices in times of labor peace merely flirt with fickle public opinion. Districts that enter traditional collective bargaining without the benefit of a clearly defined public information function are courting disaster.

The number of personnel involved in the public information function depends on the size of the district. In very small school systems serving small, close communities the function can be entirely assumed by the superintendent, who keeps contact with most of the community leaders through participation in various community public service activities and through direct contact with the community's press. In communities such as these, communications between the school district leadership and the community are less apt to become befuddled. Consequently, labor unrest resulting from poor communications is less likely. Moreover, less effort is necessary to reach all stakeholders. As communities grow larger and more disconnected, school district communication with stakeholders becomes more difficult, and ironically, it becomes more important. The public information officer's duties are discussed below. A public information officer's checklist (exhibit 9.7) and samples of press releases and letters are presented (exhibits 9.8–9.14) at the end of this chapter.

Before the Strike

An effective public information program should begin long before negotiations are deadlocked. In fact, it must be an ongoing function of the school district during periods between negotiations. Astute school leaders will use these times to get ahead of the game by solidifying community support, which becomes more important during difficult contract negotiations and becomes a primary goal of strike managers during a strike.

It is difficult to outline a canned program for public information during the period leading up to a strike. However, all the "basics" of the advertising and public relations industries apply.

1. First, the audiences must be identified. In the public school setting this means all of the employees (teachers as well as all of the noncertificated employees), parents, students, the business community, senior citizens, the various special interest groups, and, last but not

least, the media. The public information officer must sort out these audiences and devise the best strategies to reach each of them.

2. Second, a plan must be developed. A yearly calendar of events with assigned responsibilities for processes, procedures, and products must be established. In a very small district, this will be accomplished by the superintendent and his secretary or one of the talented clerks in the superintendent's office. As districts grow larger, more personnel time will be allocated to the function. In middle-sized districts and larger suburban school districts, a small staff of one or two people should be allocated to the function and regular formal communications devices institutionalized. These include:

   - Regular district newsletters
   - Staff newsletters
   - Periodic press releases on school district operations
   - A district speaker's bureau for communication with community groups
   - Radio and television programs and reports
   - Special press conferences for newsworthy events

Clearly, the public information officer must be close to the superintendent and board in order to perform the function properly. One of the most important tasks is to make certain that everybody in the school system is reading from the same page—that the school district delivers consistent messages about the issues of the day. This becomes even more important during labor conflict and strikes.

3. Third, the critical relationships in the community must be cultivated. The person responsible for the public information function must reach out to establish a working relationship with each of the reporters covering the school district. Since the turnover for educational reporters is high, this can become what seems like a never-ending task of orienting one rookie reporter after another. But it is worth the effort. Inviting reporters regularly for lunch or breakfast pays off. The same applies to newspaper and television news personnel, but they are usually harder to contact. Besides, unless a school burns down, they usually take their cue about schools from the newspapers.

   Dealing with reporters is an art. Hiring a public information officer with newspaper reporter experience is usually a plus for this reason. Reporters, however, like to talk to superintendents and principals to get their information "firsthand," or at least to make it seem like it's firsthand. This means that most of the site administrators and district officials are vulnerable to being questioned by reporters. This is especially true if the school district's public information policy is to encourage open access by the press to the district. This is a smart way to do business except during the period immediately preceding the strike and during a strike. During a strike, the necessity for clear, consistent communication is so monumentally critical that the district's source of information must be carefully centralized. In a typical district, the public information officer and/or the superintendent must be the *only* person(s) to speak on behalf of the district. All other members of the district's leadership are instructed to defer questions to the public information officer/superintendent.

4. These same sort of relationships must be established with law enforcement agencies and the various city and county governments. Again, the key is outreach. The public information officer, along with the superintendent, must reach out and establish liaison with the various city managers, police chiefs, fire chiefs, recreation directors, and other vital functionaries of the local community and its government.

5. Not to be overlooked in the effort to establish firm relationships within the community are the various service clubs, including the parent–teacher organizations, the rotary clubs, Kiwanis Clubs, Junior Chambers of Commerce, Chambers of Commerce, League of Women Voters, veterans groups, senior citizens groups, and so forth. During periods of normalcy, these groups are great channels for disseminating the good news about the school district. During deadlocked labor negotiations and strikes, they are the school district's best bet for neutralizing the union's PR offensive.

6. Finally, a comprehensive plan for public information during negotiations, including a strike, must be in place from the beginning. Public information protocols are included as part of the district's strike plan, but the public information officer's planning is much more extensive. Plans for direct letters to parents, taxpayers, students, employees, service clubs, local governments, police, fire, must all be readied (see exhibits 9.12 and 9.13 at the end of this chapter). Mailing lists must be prepared. Emergency personnel must be organized. In addition, a whirlwind of fact sheets, negotiations, summaries, and reports of board meeting activities must be facilitated. The only way this will happen effectively is through careful public information planning in advance with proper allocation of resources and delegation of responsibilities. Effective planning will enable the public information officer to concentrate on immediate, high-profile communication tasks such as radio "chats" with the stakeholders and regular press conferences.

During the Strike

Although day-to-day communication with parents and children during a strike is usually the primary responsibility of the site administrators, taped phone messages answering the questions of myriad parent phone calls are the responsibility of the PIO. Likewise, the establishment and advertisement of a community/parent hotline with up-to-the-hour information about the status of the strike in the schools is also the PIO's job. Samples of phone messages can be found in exhibit 9.10 at the end of this chapter, along with sample news releases and sample letters to various stakeholders (exhibits 9.11–9.14). As negotiations begin to bog down, the PIO must provide for training the district leadership, including the board members, in effective communication with the media and the public. The key is to remain calm, polite, and rational and refer the questions to the PIO. This, of course, is easier said than done. Parents, reporters, teachers, and community leaders desire to engage administrators at all levels by asking them to respond to various issues and concerns. Training site principals and other administrators to listen politely, consider the comments thoughtfully, and refer questions to the PIO's strike information center greatly relieves the pressure on site administrators and supports what I consider to be an important strategy—keeping the site administrators out of the line of fire in a strike.

THE PRINCIPAL'S ROLE

The district leadership must do what it can to prevent principals from becoming the victims of a strike. In many school district labor disputes, principals are saddled with the weary burden of enforcing policies they didn't make, then stuck with the task of mending fences with teachers involved in strikes over these policies. Principals who try to avoid the reality of a strike by joining strikers on the picket line or by providing coffee and doughnuts to picketers find it doesn't work. The principal loses respect in the eyes of the teachers, who see the actions as a sign of a weak, even disloyal member of the management team. The administrator is put in a further squeeze when a similar opinion is generated among his or her administrative team colleagues. On the other hand, a principal who becomes emotionally involved in the issues of the strike and subsequently tries to threaten or punish striking teachers also loses. The responsibility of the district leadership is to prevent either of these two scenarios from happening. The principal's role is discussed below. A principal's checklist is included at the end of this chapter as exhibit 9.15, along with helpful forms and materials for preparing to keep the school open during a strike.

Before the Strike

I am convinced that organizing strike management to protect the site administrators is a critical part of surviving a strike. This boils down to three strategies.

1. Provide the principals with superior training. Even before the first sign of trouble, bring the site administrators together and orient them thoroughly to the issues, including the possible sticking points of the negotiations. Distribute the strike manual, orient them to the possibilities of difficult labor negotiations, and instruct them to prepare an initial site strike plan in conformance with the district's plan. Emphasize the principal's responsibility to keep a professional image at all times. Remind them that any possible concerted action, including a strike, is not a personal attack on them. Include in these initial orientations the necessity for them to plant themselves squarely on the side of the district, yet maintain an understanding and compassionate attitude toward their teachers. Provide plenty of time to discuss this. In the final analysis, a principal, like it or not, is seen as a part of the district management. It is especially important in periods of labor unrest that the principal's actions are seen as exemplifying the highest standards of leadership—and this does not include "being one of the guys" during a strike. On the other hand, the principal's opportunity to show compassion and provide counseling to teachers who are struggling to make it through the highly emotional event should be emphasized. Training should provide opportunities for principals with strike experience to share their insights. This may mean bringing in an exemplary administrator from another district. Opportunities to share stories should be provided. Lots of "what ifs" should be part of the training. What if an anonymous picketer swears at you as you try to escort your strike substitutes onto campus? What if a striker challenges you physically? What if strikers refuse to move from the driveway? What if an unidentified striker throws something at you? More difficult, sometimes, is a plea by teachers to "talk sense with them." Principals must be trained to listen, show compassion for the concerns, indicate a willingness to consider those concerns, and walk away without committing or without becoming embroiled in "ad hoc negotiations." Remember, the employees really can't make a serious mistake. This privilege is reserved for administrators.

   Using the district's professional negotiator to help provide planned training for the administrators is smart. State and national administrators' associations are also sources of assistance with labor unrest, including preparation for difficult negotiations and strikes. The Association of California School Administrators (ACSA), for example, provides professional expertise for this purpose. The ACSA also produces a comprehensive document entitled *Strike Manual*, which is a wonderful resource and can serve as a model for a strike manual as well as a text for an administrator strike management training program. Most of the strike management forms in this book came from this ACSA publication.

2. Provide each site administrator with an abundance of necessary personnel and resources. The principal's primary mission is to keep the schools operating. This requires strike substitutes. Establishing a system that guarantees an abundance of strike substitutes is the first step in supporting a principal with personnel and resources. In addition, the principal should be provided with sufficient uniformed and plainclothes security to handle almost any hostile physical activity by striking teachers. In some cases, this means giving the principal more security than he or she requests, since many principals dismiss the notion that members of their faculties could be subject to the forces of mob psychology. Principals should also be provided with operating mobile communications devices linked to district communications. If the district does not have a system of this sort, get one. It's worth every cent the first time the district has a toxic spill or a serious bus accident or a kidnapping. Strikes are a public relations war, and public relations is communication. Anything in the school district that enhances communication is usually worth the expenditure.

3. Make site administrator concerns the first priorities in negotiations. Listen to the major concerns of site administrators and demand contract reform consistent with their greatest concerns. If lack of time for teacher meetings to organize the school's curriculum is a barrier to the site administrator's efforts to improve instruction, demand concessions to accomplish this task—and be armed with the consensus of the principals. More important, avoid at all costs the practice of further limiting the site administrator's authority in the final moments of the strike in order to get settlement. Selling site administrators down the river to stop the strike is a sad commentary on our central office leadership. It happens far too often. One district, in order to maintain a facade of labor peace, signed off on a union demand that all principal decisions were subject to review and reversal by an "impartial panel" composed of parents, union representatives, and district administrators.

Moves of this type are, in the words of one administrators' association official, "felony stupid." First, teacher strikes will end without such historic concessions. The one-year strikes and one-month strikes that occur in the private sector are unheard of in public education, and such unreasonable demands would never attract widespread support in the PR war being waged in the community. Moreover, the rank-and-file teachers, usually less nervous about administrators than the union leaders are, would not rally around the idea of a blanket "neutering" of site administrators.

Solid district administrative support for site administrators is key to their effective performance in the volatile strike situation. Principals, in short, must feel secure in the idea that the district administration exists to support the operations of the local school principal.

A principal's first task in preparing for his role in strike management is to develop a sound site strike plan. Developing instructions for this task is a responsibility of the district and should take place during the early orientation.

During the Strike—The Site Strike Plan

Developing the local site plan early in the game is a good exercise for the site principals. Thinking through each of the contingencies helps them develop confidence that they will be able to accomplish the mission of keeping their schools open. The plan is grounded in the district strike plan and should draw heavily from the "what if" sessions conducted during the administrative orientation to traditional bargaining and strikes. During this initial planning, thinking, and visualization stage, I liked to use a "zero-based" approach. That is, I asked myself, "What is the absolute minimum quantity of faculty and personnel necessary to keep the school open and operating?" Then, using the district's strike plan as a guide (see emergency procedures manual in appendix A), and using the "what ifs" gleaned from the orientation sessions, I would begin the process of planning for every contingency, every eventuality. Later experience with live strikes has convinced me beyond the shadow of a doubt that the three keys to successful strike management are preparation, preparation, and more preparation. The following paragraphs discuss the basics of site strike plan preparation.

1. First, the principal must establish a plan for staffing the school. This means anticipating the number of staff members on strike and establishing emergency assignments for noncertificated employees, coadministrators, parent volunteers, student teachers, classroom aides, and strike replacement substitutes. Collective bargaining in school districts around the nation is mature enough now that many districts have history to draw on. This usually helps in estimating the staffing needs. As

a rule of thumb, high school teachers have a greater tendency to strike than junior high; junior high, a greater chance than elementary. On the other hand, as I mentioned before, the problems in staffing the high schools are usually less severe since most of the students decide the strike is a good reason to play hooky. Absenteeism of 90 percent at high schools is not uncommon. The junior highs and middle schools are another situation altogether. Many of the faculty tend to be more subject-oriented than elementary teachers, and they like to identify with the far more subject-oriented high school faculties. Consequently, a higher proportion of middle school and junior high school teachers strike, but the students are far less likely to skip school. The student-oriented elementary teacher is the most likely to cross the line on strike day. However, because of the greater vulnerability of the students, the site administrator must take extensive precautions to be certain that adequate personnel are available on campus to supervise, protect, and control the children.

Whether or not a large proportion of the staff strikes at an elementary school depends upon the strength and the reputation and credibility of the school site's union representative. More than half of the elementary teachers I spoke with wished the labor turmoil would "go away." As a group they are not highly political, and many are second-income earners in affluent families. When it's time to strike, teachers talk among themselves and make decisions for themselves. If the elementary staff includes two or three well-regarded colleagues who are "true believer" unionists and have been convinced that it is a sacred duty to participate in the work stoppage, then the mass of teachers will usually follow along and stay home. On the other hand, if the school site lacks this cadre, or if the cadre is not composed of well-respected, competent colleagues, the bulk of the teachers will not feel peer pressure to walk. It is not unusual in a strike to observe vast differences among schools in the percentage of teachers participating in the strike activity.

The intensity of the issue also plays a part in the likelihood of staff walking out; however, this is usually a lesser consideration than the other political dynamics I mentioned. By the time a strike rolls around, the union leaders have enough intense issues cooked up to start a third world war. Most teachers are relatively immune to these political firestorms, and only endorse them vehemently *after* they have decided to participate in the work stoppage—as a justification primarily to themselves and others close to them. Assuming that most of the teachers will strike is the best bet for most principals when preparing for a strike. He or she then can only be pleasantly surprised when a few or most of them cross the line.

2. Second, the principal must have emergency lesson plans available to distribute to strike replacement substitutes. This is an area where the district office can help if it has an instructional services division. If not, principals can get together and write their own. But having an adequate supply of simple, easy-to-carry-out emergency plans is essential. After all, the first day of the strike is the worst and least predictable. At the end of the first day, plans can be made in a meeting with the substitute faculty to carry on the following day with meaningful instruction. As soon as the strike is announced, principals should plan to request immediately the teacher's current lesson plans. These can be placed in the strike replacement substitute's folder to be used by the substitute for orientation to the instructional program. Emergency lesson plans should be kept in a special secure location along with other strike preparations (plans, supplies, class lists, keys, and so forth).

Folders for every teacher at the site must be prepared well in advance and stored in the secure location along with the other strike preparation materials. The "strike replacement substitute folder" should contain all the necessary information a substitute needs in the *most concise* form possible. It should contain the emergency lesson plan and (if possible) a copy of the striking teachers' most recent lesson plans obtained from the teacher as soon as the strike was announced. The folder should also contain a class list and instructions regarding attendance accounting. Next, the folder should contain a page of reference information—phone numbers and email addresses for administrators and the district's human resources office. For good measure, the principal should add a school brochure.

Other helpful items to place in the sub folders are

- School map
- List of all students
- Name of regular teacher
- Seating chart (if appropriate)
- List of teachers and their schedules and assignments
- List of department chairpersons
- Bell schedule
- First aid procedures plan
- Location of faculty restrooms
- Yard duty schedule
- Recess/lunch periods
- List of children with special needs
- Location of teacher's manuals
- List of support personnel such as school doctor, school nurse, office personnel, and plant manager

- Fire drill plan with maps of school plant
- Plan for civil defense procedures
- List of special films that can be made available to the local school from the instructional communications media branch during a period of emergency
- Library schedule
- Log of all television programs presented by the district

3. Next, the principals must make certain that the school has a protected cache of emergency supplies. Striking teachers will often padlock their closets or remove needed supplies such as projector bulbs, light bulbs, and textbooks. AV equipment is especially valuable in cases where classes must be combined until substitutes arrive or in the event that adequate numbers of strike replacement substitutes are not available. These emergency strike supplies should be stored in a secure location along with lesson plans, strike lists, class lists, strike plans, and other strike preparation materials. The key is to have on hand the essentials to get school moving under almost any circumstance.

4. Finally, the principal must analyze the school plant with regard to possibilities for disruption. Developing a plan for the security of students attending school as well as the faculty and the buildings is the next priority. Analyze the site to determine the number of day and night security personnel needed to keep the building safe from vandalism and allow the students and staff secure and peaceful access to the campus. This includes provisions to safeguard the automobiles of all staff members and faculty who chose not to strike, but especially those of the strike replacement substitutes (if the district does not provide central transportation to the sites). The campus should be reviewed carefully for vulnerabilities: phone lines that can be cut, restrooms that can be plugged up, student record files that can be vandalized. When school is not in session, care must be taken to lock all the entrances to the campus. During school hours, only one or two gates should be open for access and these attended by security personnel. Striking teachers should not be allowed on campus during the strike period for any reason—even for a drink of water, to use the telephone, or to use the restrooms. Principals should coordinate with district officials to develop a district-wide notice to striking teachers ordering them to remain off campuses.

Since the campus will be operating in a markedly different manner during the strike period, plans must be made for strike replacement substitutes entering the campus, as well as the normal traffic resulting from parents and students arriving and leaving.

Keeping the campus free of potentially paralyzing vandalism begins the instant a strike is announced. Whenever this occurs, the
principal must move immediately to provide security for the buildings and equipment. More often than not, aggravating tricks like
squirting airplane glue into all of the door locks happen before the
administration has had time to establish security. Phone lines can
be cut, sewer lines plugged, water lines disrupted, and millions of
dollars of taxpayer property destroyed by union zealots bent on preventing administrators from accomplishing their mission to keep the
schools open.

Sadly, some of the principals whose schools have been hardest hit
were those who claimed, "My faculty would never do this sort of
thing to me." Whenever this comment is made to me, I remind the
principal making the statement that the teachers are not acting
against the principal personally, but against a system they have been
told is their enemy. In addition, the teachers responsible for the vandalism are not necessarily the teachers at the school vandalized. Principals cannot depend upon their assessments of faculty loyalty to determine whether prompt action is required. The best course of action
is to be well prepared, then activate the plan for campus security at
the first sign of a strike. A final word about planning: the critical part
of site strike planning is careful communication with the district
strike management team. Everything undertaken at the site should
be consistent with the district's overall plan and should have the as-
surance of district support—from the number of strike replacement
substitutes to the extra personnel required for security to the extra resources needed to prepare for the first day.

THE ATTORNEY'S ROLE (LEGAL COORDINATOR)

The district's attorney has a critical role to play in every phase of traditional industrial-style collective bargaining. The outcome of labor negotiations including a strike can be impacted significantly by the quality of
the legal work undertaken. I wholeheartedly support the practice of con-
tracting a professional negotiator who is affiliated with a law firm specializing in school district labor relations. The close relationship between
legal work and human resources in the negotiations process makes this
connection a natural. Smaller districts should pursue the possibility of
forming a consortium to contract with the most competent school district
collective bargaining specialists available. During the initial planning
phases, as well as the final preparations leading to successful strike management, the district's negotiating team, and later, the strike management

team, will depend heavily on the district's attorneys for advice and support. For example, the attorneys will be involved in

- analyzing the contract,
- preparing the district's initial offer, and
- analyzing the union's initial proposal.

Before the Strike

In the strike plan preparation, the district's attorney is responsible for drafting the emergency procedures resolutions as well as developing plans for training administrators in legal aspects of strike management, including gathering information to support unfair labor practice charges against the unions. In most cases, the attorneys are not employees of the district. Rather, they have consultant status. Consequently, to render their services most effectively, a "legal coordinator" is a valuable assignment to consider for the strike management team. A "Checklist for Legal Coordinator" is included as exhibit 9.24 at the end of this chapter.

At every step of the way, good legal services are vital. These services and advice are also important as the district moves toward greater collaboration with its unions. The next chapter explores this possibility.

ADMINISTRATOR CHECKLISTS
AND SAMPLE STRIKE MANAGEMENT DOCUMENTS

The checklists and documents presented here are provided courtesy of the Association of California School Administrators and are contained in the association's publication entitled *Strike Manual*.

Exhibit 9.1. Checklist for the Superintendent

___ 1. **Notify Board of Education.** The superintendent should notify the board of trustees of the strike and keep the board apprised of the strike situation as it progresses. Provide them with a copy of the ACSA *Strike Manual.*

___ 2. **Organize Strike Management Committee.** The strike management committee ideally should consist of the following individuals:

    ___ a. Superintendent

    ___ b. Legal Coordinator

    ___ c. Communications Coordinator

    ___ d. Auxiliary Services Coordinator—The Auxiliary Services Coordinator is responsible for the areas of food service, transportation, and security. The Superintendent, along with the Auxiliary Services Coordinator, should appoint, if possible, one individual to each of those three areas who will in turn report to the Auxiliary Services Coordinator.

    ___ e. Staffing Coordinator

    ___ f. Area Administrators—Area Administrators have the responsibility of seeing that every school in their area has a strike plan which is complete and operational and assisting school site administrators in the administration of their strike plans. Area Administrators act as liaisons between the school site administrator and the strike management committee and act as the site administrator's principal contact when problems arise. The number of Area Administrators will depend upon the size and needs of the district.

The superintendent may also wish to appoint one individual to the strike management committee who would be responsible for coordinating the committee's activities and for reporting directly to the superintendent.

In all but the very largest districts, the strike management committee should be headed by the superintendent. In small districts, the superintendent, out of necessity, may have to assign more than one of the positions listed above to a single individual. For example, the strike committee may be comprised of the superintendent and two board members. While board members should normally not be involved in daily administration of the strike, in a small district there may be no other alternative. A small district faced with a strike should request outside help. The Association of California School Administrators, for example, provides trained consultants who can help the district plan its campaign. Some county superintendents have services available for districts as well. In some cases, districts should consider hiring attorneys or consultants to handle the strike planning and implementation.

In very large districts it may be necessary to divide the responsibilities of one position among several individuals. Each district should make such determinations based on their needs and the resources available to them.

A room should be designated as the strike management committee meeting room. The room should be large enough to accommodate all members of the committee for long periods of time. Equipment and supplies should include a chalkboard, two telephones (one listed and one unlisted), paper, pencils, radios, television, copy machine, etc. Clerical staff and other support personnel should be readily available. The strike management committee must have the resources at its disposal to respond to the emergency with quick decisions.

___ 3. **Letters to Employees.** Prior to the strike and with the assistance of the communications coordinator, the superintendent should send a letter to employees after receiving the union's notice of their intent to strike indicating that:

    ___ a. The district is committed to keeping the schools operating;

    ___ b. Work is available for those who wish to work;

    ___ c. Striking employees will not be paid for the periods of time they are striking and not working; and

    ___ d. Striking workers are ineligible to receive unemployment insurance benefits while on strike.

___ 4. **Consult Legal Counsel.** The superintendent should immediately check with legal counsel as to the desirability of securing an injunction or other relief through the Public Employees Relations Board or the courts. The superintendent should also work closely with legal counsel before a strike to review collective bargaining agreements and board policies.

___ 5. **Call Meetings of Strike Management Committee.** The superintendent should call a meeting of the strike management committee as soon as its composition has been designated and a strike is deemed imminent. At the initial meeting of the committee, the extent of the strike should be analyzed and district strike plans put into operation. The following issues are suggestions of those topics that should be considered:

    ___ a. Student welfare

    ___ b. Transportation

    ___ c. Food service

    ___ d. Building safety and maintenance (custodians)

    ___ e. Supplies

    ___ f. Mail

    ___ g. Substitutes

    ___ h. Emergency instruction

    ___ i. Public and staff communications

    ___ j. Liaison with police and fire departments

    ___ k. Parental contacts

    ___ l. Calendaring of needed meetings

    ___ m. Conditions under which schools would be closed

    ___ n. Security

    ___ o. Minimum days

    ___ p. Contingency plans for bus drivers, custodians, cafeteria maintenance, secretarial staff

During a strike, the strike management committee will usually hold a meeting early each morning. The committee will meet off and on throughout the day as needed to deal with problems. At the end of the day, the committee should meet again to review the day's events and make plans for the next day. It is not uncommon for members of the strike management committee to work twelve to eighteen hours a day throughout the duration of the strike.

___ 6. **Maintain Communication.** Maintain close and daily contact with board members and members of the strike management committee throughout the strike. Keep apprised of all developments and offer guidance and assistance where possible.

___ 7. **Letter to Administrators.** At conclusion of the strike, superintendent should inform the administrators in the district office and at the various sites that they should work to make the transition as smooth as possible and caution against discriminating against strikers by, for example, giving letters of appreciation to nonstrikers. [See chapter 10 for further post-strike considerations.]

Exhibit 9.2.   Checklist for the Auxiliary Services Coordinator

___ 1. **Check with Emergency Personnel.** Consult with emergency personnel and advise them of the need for substitute personnel. Coordinate plans.

___ 2. **Maintain Close Communication with Principals.** Keep in daily contact with your school principals and assist them in any way possible. Identify with the principal those services that are essential and those that can be temporarily suspended.

___ 3. **Develop Plan for Continuation of Food Service.**

    ___ a. Is it possible to contract with a neighboring district or food service company to provide lunches?

    ___ b. Consider providing sack lunches or "pre-packs" for the duration of the strike.

    ___ c. Provide extra trash cans for the increased volume of packaging materials.

    ___ d. Work with communications coordinator to have students bring bag lunches.

    ___ e. Provide alternative site for food deliveries if outside vendors will not cross picket lines, or change delivery times to before or after picket lines are established.

    ___ f. Consider providing group IV portions rather than attempting to adjust portions to age/grade group. Accurate distribution and content records should be kept in order to facilitate completion of the reimbursement claim form for the State Department of Education.

___ 4. **Assess Transportation Needs.**

    ___ a. Consider the advantages of providing safe car storage and bus transportation for replacement and non-striking employees.

    ___ b. If the environment is very hostile, consider police escorts for bus drivers or substitute drivers.

    ___ c. Provide round-the-clock security for the bus storage area.

    ___ d. Provide for frequent safety inspections of all buses.

    ___ e. Prior to the strike, develop list of substitute drivers with names, addresses, and telephone numbers. Work with staffing coordinator and pre-estimate as accurately as possible the number of substitutes that will be needed. Consider substitute drivers from neighboring districts.

    ___ f. If bus drivers strike, consider elimination of all non-mandated student transportation.

    ___ g. If bus drivers strike, consider contracting with a private transportation company.

    ___ h. If bus drivers strike, consider providing limited small-group transportation, unless prohibited by law.

    ___ i. If bus drivers strike, work with communications coordinator to notify parents. Consider radio announcements to meet immediate needs.

    ___ j. If bus drivers strike, consider organizing parents to form carpools.

    ___ k. Make contingency plans to provide transportation for student activities, or cancel them.

___ 5. **Develop Security Plan.**

    ___ a. Meet with local law enforcement and review in detail the services they will provide in the event of a strike. Find out what limitations they have in responding to calls for assistance. (Remember that most police officers are organized and represented by unions. The sympathies of the average police officer may be with the strikers. A number of school districts have found local police departments of little help. It's best to pin the police officials down to a commitment before the strike.)

___ b. Consider the possibility of hiring an outside security firm to provide temporary protection. Get a list of firms that provide security services during strikes. Check out their references. Find out not only cost but also the lead-time required by the company to field personnel.

___ c. Plan and develop strike surveillance activities and locations for placement of photographers for best surveillance coverage to document all "incidents." Many private sector employers now use videotape equipment. Some security firms provide this service, although it is expensive.

___ d. Review ingress and egress to all schools and buildings. Determine in advance which doors and gates will be used. As a general rule, the number of points of ingress and egress should be limited.

___ e. Review night lighting for each building. Burning the lights all night will increase the cost of electricity but may prevent expensive vandalism.

___ f. Review ingress and egress to grounds and parking lots. Determine which gates will be opened and the hours they will be opened.

___ g. Consider posting guards at strategic gates to insure that only authorized people are admitted to school district property.

___ h. Develop a system to make sure all gates, doors, and windows are locked at the end of the workday.

___ i. Consider paying someone to spend the night at each school site. Some districts have used custodians and other classified employees as night watchpersons during teacher strikes.

___ j. Determine in advance whether strikers will be allowed to enter school grounds or buildings to get a drink of water, use restrooms, etc. Most labor relations and security experts strongly recommend that strikers not be allowed on school property.

___ k. Prepare a system for the identification of personnel authorized to enter school property. Coded passes have been used with success.

___ l. Provide for the security of files and records. Unattended offices should be locked. One bottle of ink or a match can do a lot of damage to vital records.

___ m. Provide for the security of private automobiles of non-strikers. Consider having non-strikers report to a central location and using buses to take them to their site. This makes it easier to guard automobiles and prevent costly damage.

___ n. Arrange for a centralized, specially keyed storage area at each school site for audio-visual equipment and instructional supplies. Provide a checkout system for equipment and supplies prior to release to replacement teachers.

___ o. Develop procedure for false fire and burglar alarms.

___ p. Provide plans to operate buildings under emergency power.

___ q. Prepare a plan for strikers to turn in keys.

___ r. Make a list of locksmiths, electricians, carpenters, and plumbers in the area, including telephone numbers, and submit to principals.

___ s. Have numbers of emergency telephone and utilities repair personnel available.

___ t. Have number available for 24-hour towing service to remove cars used to block access to district sites.

___ u. Provide duplicate keys for classrooms, school sites, etc.

___ v. Develop, in cooperation with principals, a procedure for:
   ___ (1) Awareness of valves for water, gas, electricity
   ___ (2) Opening and closing of buildings

Exhibit 9.3.   Checklist for the Director of Human Resources

___ 1. **Determine Which Services Can Be Discontinued.** Which services can be discontinued and still allow the district to maintain essential education programs? Develop a list.

___ 2. **Communicate and Assist Area Coordinators and Principals.** Work closely with the area coordinators and principals. Assist them in developing a strike plan. Know their needs.

___ 3. **Determine If There Will Be Non-Striking Employees Performing Nonessential Services.** Are there any legal or contractual prohibitions against finding them other duties? Non-striking employees performing nonessential services should be assigned to perform essential services wherever possible. In some cases, there may be a problem if the non-striking employees have sympathy with the strikers. Other employees may refuse to change jobs during a strike. In other situations, employees crossing the picket line may be threatened if they replace strikers. Thus, great care must be taken in trying to get non-striking employees to perform other than their normal duties. Performance of any work other than normal work should be completely voluntary, and the district may not discharge or otherwise discipline an employee who refuses to perform "strike work" unless given that right by the collective bargaining agreement.

___ 4. **Determine If There Will Be Management Employees Available to Perform Essential Services.** If yes, prepare a strike assignment for each management person. The district has greater flexibility in using management employees to replace strikers. Those management employees performing nonessential services should be given a strike assignment aimed at maintaining essential programs. Management employees who earn at least $250 per week can perform any amount of nonexempt work during the strike without becoming subject to the Fair Labor Standards Act overtime provisions. *Marshall v. Western Union Tel. Co.,* 621 F2d 1246 (3d Cir. 1980). Management personnel generally are exempt from the overtime provisions of the Fair Labor Standards Act.

___ 5. **Establish a List of Parent and Community Volunteers.** Determine whether they will provide services during a strike, their availability, and the jobs they can perform. Many parents have teaching credentials that can be quickly registered with the Regional or County Office of Education. Retired certificated managers and teachers will often volunteer their services if asked. Other volunteers who can be of help are secretaries, locksmiths, nurses, police officers, and plumbers. Having responsible adults available to help in classrooms as aides and for playground supervision is a great help.

___ 6. **Instructional Aides.** Develop a plan for using instructional aides to reduce the number of substitutes needed. By combining classes and using instructional aides, the district will be able to reduce the number of substitute teachers needed to maintain educational services during a teacher strike. When using instructional aides to stretch the teaching staff, it is important to make sure that only certificated employees give direct instruction to the students. The aides monitor and provide practice, using activities designed by certificated personnel. If well organized, this technique will make it possible to cover several classes with one certificated replacement teacher.

___ 7. **Salaries for Strike Replacements.** Make sure the Board of Education has adopted attractive salaries for strike replacements.

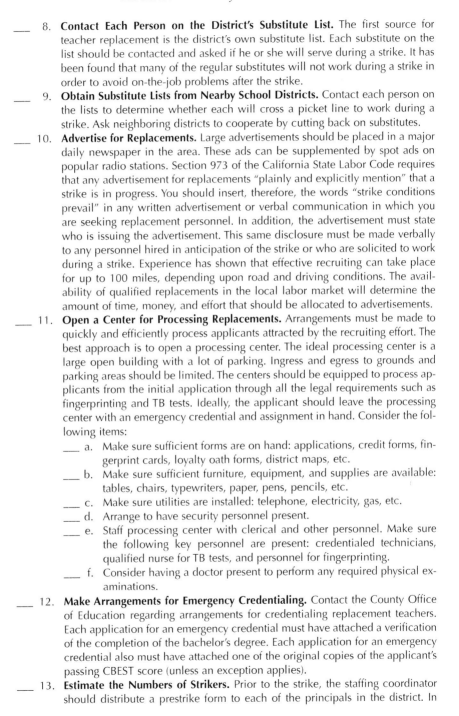

___ 8. **Contact Each Person on the District's Substitute List.** The first source for teacher replacement is the district's own substitute list. Each substitute on the list should be contacted and asked if he or she will serve during a strike. It has been found that many of the regular substitutes will not work during a strike in order to avoid on-the-job problems after the strike.

___ 9. **Obtain Substitute Lists from Nearby School Districts.** Contact each person on the lists to determine whether each will cross a picket line to work during a strike. Ask neighboring districts to cooperate by cutting back on substitutes.

___ 10. **Advertise for Replacements.** Large advertisements should be placed in a major daily newspaper in the area. These ads can be supplemented by spot ads on popular radio stations. Section 973 of the California State Labor Code requires that any advertisement for replacements "plainly and explicitly mention" that a strike is in progress. You should insert, therefore, the words "strike conditions prevail" in any written advertisement or verbal communication in which you are seeking replacement personnel. In addition, the advertisement must state who is issuing the advertisement. This same disclosure must be made verbally to any personnel hired in anticipation of the strike or who are solicited to work during a strike. Experience has shown that effective recruiting can take place for up to 100 miles, depending upon road and driving conditions. The availability of qualified replacements in the local labor market will determine the amount of time, money, and effort that should be allocated to advertisements.

___ 11. **Open a Center for Processing Replacements.** Arrangements must be made to quickly and efficiently process applicants attracted by the recruiting effort. The best approach is to open a processing center. The ideal processing center is a large open building with a lot of parking. Ingress and egress to grounds and parking areas should be limited. The centers should be equipped to process applicants from the initial application through all the legal requirements such as fingerprinting and TB tests. Ideally, the applicant should leave the processing center with an emergency credential and assignment in hand. Consider the following items:

    ___ a. Make sure sufficient forms are on hand: applications, credit forms, fingerprint cards, loyalty oath forms, district maps, etc.

    ___ b. Make sure sufficient furniture, equipment, and supplies are available: tables, chairs, typewriters, paper, pens, pencils, etc.

    ___ c. Make sure utilities are installed: telephone, electricity, gas, etc.

    ___ d. Arrange to have security personnel present.

    ___ e. Staff processing center with clerical and other personnel. Make sure the following key personnel are present: credentialed technicians, qualified nurse for TB tests, and personnel for fingerprinting.

    ___ f. Consider having a doctor present to perform any required physical examinations.

___ 12. **Make Arrangements for Emergency Credentialing.** Contact the County Office of Education regarding arrangements for credentialing replacement teachers. Each application for an emergency credential must have attached a verification of the completion of the bachelor's degree. Each application for an emergency credential also must have attached one of the original copies of the applicant's passing CBEST score (unless an exception applies).

___ 13. **Estimate the Numbers of Strikers.** Prior to the strike, the staffing coordinator should distribute a prestrike form to each of the principals in the district. In

Exhibit 9.3.   Checklist for the Director of Human Resources (*Continued*)

estimating the number of replacements needed, the principal should be advised not to directly question the employees as to whether they plan to participate in the strike. Such questioning could constitute an unfair labor practice.

___ 14. **Develop a System for Attendance Accounting for All Employees during a Strike.** Receive morning status reports from site administrators. Give information as soon as possible to the auxiliary services coordinator. Morning status reports should include the principal's estimate of the number of substitutes needed.

___ 15. **Determine Degree of Cooperation from Other Employees.** In the case of a strike by certificated employees, determine the degree of cooperation the district will receive from classified employees. Consider:

   ___ a. Transportation employees
   ___ b. Food service employees
   ___ c. Maintenance and custodial workers
   ___ d. Gardeners
   ___ e. Delivery people
   ___ f. Secretarial staff
   ___ g. Instructional aides
   ___ h. Clerk/payroll, personnel processing, curriculum employees, etc.

Exhibit 9.4.   Sample Advertisement for Replacements

SERENDIPITY CITY
UNIFIED SCHOOL DISTRICT is seeking qualified
REPLACEMENT AND SUBSTITUTE TEACHERS

Strike Conditions Prevail

If you have a valid California credential or a baccalaureate degree, you may qualify to serve as a replacement teacher in grades kindergarten through 12. No previous teaching experience is necessary.

The school district will pay for the first day of service and for each subsequent day during the emergency.

To Apply, Go To:

    1540 Tranquility Avenue, Serendipity, California.

    Take No. 1 Tranquility Off-Ramp to "A" Street;

    Then go right on Old School Road.

Applicants MUST BRING transcripts showing date of bachelor's degree.

Interested persons may apply between the hours of:

    6:00 a.m. and 4:30 p.m. daily beginning September 12.

    Secured parking will be available for applicants and replacement employees.

Exhibit 9.5. Prestrike Survey

School: _____

Area: _____

_____ _____
(Signature of Reporting Administrator)   (Title)

Date of Report: _____

Instructional Hours: *Start* _____   *End* _____

LEVEL (Check one)
____ Elementary
____ Secondary
____ Community Adult
____ Special Education
____ R.O.C.P.
____ Other _____
                    (Specify)

Exhibit 9.6.　Estimate Number

Staff Groups	Total Allot.	Pres.	Absent	Subs.	Reg.	Comments
I. CERTIFICATED						
Teachers, Regular Classroom						
Teacher, Non-Classroom						
Librarians						
Nurses						
Other(s):						
1.						
2.						
3.						
4.						
II. CLASSIFIED						
Secretary/Office Manager						
Clerical						
Custodians						
Cafeteria Manager						
Cafeteria Workers						
Security						
Transportation						
Educ. Aides						
Noon-Duty Aides						
Teacher Assistants						
Volunteers						
Other(s):						
1.						
2.						
3.						
4.						

SPECIAL REMARKS:

_____

_____

_____

_____

Exhibit 9.7.   Checklist for the Public Information Officer

___ 1. **Define Your Audience.** The district needs to identify:
  ___ a. The audience it wishes to address.
  ___ b. The most effective means to reach that audience.
  This is the area in which a district most needs a professional public relations person. If a district does not have its own public relations officer, it should consider hiring a consultant. Some county offices or adjacent districts will loan a communications expert. The ACSA Communications Office can help advise you on your crisis communications program and can help you find ongoing assistance.

___ 2. **Designate a District Spokesperson.** As noted above, the district spokesperson need not be the same individual as the communications coordinator. This will depend on various factors such as the size of the district and the speaking skills of the individuals being considered for the position.

___ 3. **Establish a Media Center.** It is essential that the district set aside an area for members of the press, radio, and television. This room should consist of at least a pressroom with outgoing phone lines, coffee, background material, and the latest press releases. The district public relations director should have an office close by.

  The purpose of the media center is to provide a place where the press can get credible material from the district. In addition, the center will give the district a place to discover what information the press is interested in and what information is being put out by the employee organization.

  Care should be taken as to the location of the media center. Do not place it where reporters can compromise security or confidentiality.

___ 4. **Develop a List of Contacts.** Develop a list of each newspaper, radio, and television station read or heard in your district including:
  ___ a. Name
  ___ b. Phone number
  ___ c. Deadlines for press releases, deadlines for press conferences, deadlines for nighttime television news coverage.

___ 5. **Establish a Liaison with Police, Fire, and News Media.**

___ 6. **Develop a List of Organizations.** Develop a complete list of organizations for continued communications throughout the strike, i.e., the PTA, Jaycees, Rotary Club, etc.

___ 7. **Prepare District Information Packet.** Few if any of the media people involved in covering the strike will have any experience with school districts. They will expect the district to provide that information. These packets should include:
  ___ a. A district overview (history, enrollment, budget size, area served, board member identification, date of election, term expiration, administrator identification, switchboard hours, district map, and anything that may be useful to people researching the district).
  ___ b. An explanation of substitute teacher qualifications, the process used to register them, and the district person who can respond to questions about them.
  ___ c. An attendance summary showing the format to be used in daily accounting of students and teachers during the strike. (This will differ from regular accounting because rotating or part-time staff may be assigned full time. Additionally, substitutes and returned regular staff should be designated. Daily attendance figures are newsworthy and important. Accounting must be explained to avoid misconceptions or deliberate misrepresentation of the numbers of students and regular teachers out and those returning.)

___ d. A history of the current negotiations, including the board's position, meetings held to date, impasse history, issues, past news clippings, and anything else that would help a reporter or community member who has not been following the process to understand what's happening.

___ e. Samples of letters the district has sent to parents, staff members, and community leaders to substantiate the district's candor, consistency, and efforts to communicate to all concerned audiences.

___ f. Communications center information (hours to be open, contact person, briefing schedules, attendance reporting procedures and schedules, incident report recording process and availability).

___ 8. **Select Communications Channels.** The district has to consider its most effective communication channels. Many of the most effective channels are the least costly. For example, one district found that by sending administrators out to local organizations such as Rotary to give talks, it could communicate credibly with 90 percent of the business leaders in the community. The cost to the district was minimal.

Besides the normal media communication devices, the district should consider other ways to communicate more effectively with the public. [See exhibit 9.8.]

___ 9. **Meet with Media Prior to Strike.** Meet with the reporters, editors, and/or news directors of your local media to provide them with a detailed understanding of the situation. Information communicated to media should include the:

___ a. True strike issues

___ b. District's last proposal

___ c. Board's position on the issues and its reasons for that position

___ d. Employee association's position on the issues

___ e. Board's position on the legality of the strike

___ f. Possibility of disciplinary action against strikers

___ 10. **Contact Principals and Other Administrators.** Discuss with principals and other members of the management team their role in the public information plan and in dealing with the media. Have principals relay all questions to the communications center rather than making off-the-cuff statements about the situation to reporters. Only *one* person should be the "news giver" rather than many.

___ 11. **Prepare Communications.**

___ a. Prestrike communications:

___ (1) Phone taped message advising that schools will be open in the event of a work stoppage. Install a taped telephone message system and widely publicize the number [exhibit 9.10, sample 1].

___ (2) News release regarding impasse [exhibit 9.11, sample 1].

___ (3) Letter to parents [exhibit 9.12].

___ (4) Letter to employees [exhibit 9.13].

___ (5) Regular communications to site administrators advising them of the last development.

___ b. Communications during strike:

___ (1) Phone taped message advising that schools will remain open and other important messages [exhibit 9.10, sample 2].

___ (2) News release on status of strike [exhibit 9.11, sample 2].

___ (3) Letter to parents [exhibit 9.12].

___ 12. **Determine the Normal Attendance at Each School.**

___ 13. **Distribute Daily Reporting Forms to All Principals.**

Exhibit 9.8.   Communication Channels

___ Direct letters to parents, taxpayers
___ Regular newsletters
___ Principal's meetings
___ District administrator's meetings
___ District administrator speeches to community groups
___ PTA
___ Community and service groups
___ School advisory councils
___ Reports on negotiations at board meetings
___ Press releases (radio, TV, newspapers)
___ Community telephone "hotline" center
___ Negotiations summaries
___ Regular radio reports on condition of schools by school spokesperson
___ Board meeting remarks

Employees
___ Negotiation summaries
___ Fact sheets
___ Review meetings with principals
___ Principal meetings with employees
___ Informal communication with employees
___ Distribution of meeting minutes to principal
___ Telephone "hotline" reports
___ Direct letter to employees
___ Employee handbook
___ TV, radio "chats"

Exhibit 9.9. Suggestions for Effective Communication with the Public

1. Develop a public relations strategy before negotiations break down.
2. Establish early contact with local newspapers and radio and TV stations. Create a phone list of names and numbers to call when a news release must be published.
3. Do not over-editorialize or engage in excessive propaganda.
4. Be sure to keep all relevant individuals informed of district positions and rationale— includes the public, teachers, district administration, and site-level administration.
5. Do not "bargain around" the union.
6. Avoid, if possible, communicating only as a response to union communications. Be willing to take the initiative in making public statements.
7. All statements should be carefully thought out and reviewed prior to issuance. A union representative is always willing to go further than a district representative in these discussions. The district representative may say something that is not in the best interest of the district. The district representative should politely state that he/she has heard the concerns of the speaker and will take them into consideration but will not respond to them immediately.
8. Take special care to avoid undermining the authority of the collective bargaining representative with whom you are negotiating. Early announcements of available resources disproportionately increase union expectations.
9. Be sure that all potential communications are reviewed by several individuals prior to issuance.

Exhibit 9.10.   Phone Tape Messages

SAMPLE 1—Before-Strike Phone Tape Message

This is the Sunnyside Union School District information line, Monday morning, September 3rd. Schools will be open on Friday, September 7th, in the event of a teacher work stoppage. Sunnyside Union School District officials and leaders of the Sunnyside Education Association are meeting daily in efforts to avert a threatened strike. Proceedings are conducted under the direction of Juan Brown, state mediator.

District officials have announced that if a strike occurs, schools will be open. All class, bus, and cafeteria schedules will be in operation as usual.

Classrooms will be staffed by qualified teachers. In accordance with board of education policies, all grading and homework procedures will be in effect.

Negotiations will continue until a final settlement is reached.

Please continue to call this number for up-to-date, accurate information 24 hours a day.

SAMPLE 2—First Morning of Strike Phone Tape Message

This is the Sunnyside Union School District information line, Friday morning, September 7th. Schools will operate this morning although leaders of the Sunnyside Education Association have called a strike. All schools in the district are open and operating with qualified teachers in the classrooms. The school will attempt to provide a normal instructional program, and all work completed by students will be counted.

Parents are urged to send students to their school. All services, including transportation and food, will continue.

Schools are looking for college graduates to teach and for volunteers. If you are interested in helping your principal, please phone your school.

Please continue to call this number for up-to-date, accurate information 24 hours a day.

Exhibit 9.11.   Sample News Releases

Sample News Release on Impasse

Sunnyside Union School District
July 1, 20____

For further information, call Charlie Brown, 765-4321

FOR IMMEDIATE RELEASE

Impasse has been declared in negotiations between representatives of the Sunnyside Board of Education and the Sunnyside Education Association (SEA).

After holding 10 negotiation sessions that lasted for approximately 60 hours, both sides declared impasse last night (June 30) saying they could not reach agreement on economic issues. This paves the way for a state appointed mediator to help both sides reach a mutually acceptable settlement.

Negotiators representing the Sunnyside Board of Education and the Sunnyside Education Association (SEA) had reached tentative agreements on a number of issues, including school calendar, leave policy, safety conditions, a grievance policy, and class size.

"At this point, the school board is ready to take the next step outlined in the Rodda Act," said Charlie Brown, district spokesperson. "The law calls for mediation with a neutral party. We want to try all possible ways to reach agreement."

The latest teachers' union salary proposal was for a 12 percent cost of living increase on the salary schedule. The district countered with 4 percent. *(Also mention any substantial fringe benefits in contest.)*

"If the district accepted the total package the union had last placed on the table, it would cost us $1 million," Brown said. "The salary schedule and fringe benefits offered by the board are comparable to those in neighboring districts. The board has made a fair offer considering its other responsibilities to the students, parents, and taxpayers."

Sample News Release When Strike Is Imminent

Sunnyside Union School District
August 5, 20____

For further information, call Charlie Brown, 765-4321

FOR IMMEDIATE RELEASE

Schools will be open tomorrow with qualified teachers in the classrooms as a teacher strike enters its first day in the Sunnyside Union School District.

Talks have broken off between the Sunnyside Board of Education and the Sunnyside Education Association (SEA) over a contract for the 200 district teachers. Both mediation and fact-finding failed to bring about a settlement.

"The Board of Education is committed to maintaining a quality education program for our 5,000 students," said Charlie Brown, district spokesperson. "We will attempt to have qualified substitute teachers in all classrooms tomorrow. If the strike continues, the district will improve its operation on a daily basis."

Schools will operate on a minimum schedule tomorrow with classes starting at 9:00 a.m. and running until 12:20 p.m. Brown emphasized that all student work completed during this time will count toward graduation or grade advancement.

The latest offer made by the board to the SEA, exclusive representative for the 200 district teachers, includes a 4 percent increase on the salary schedule and further discussion

Exhibit 9.11.   Sample News Releases (*Continued*)

on increased costs of the present health and welfare schedule, as well as longevity and advanced education.

"This is a very fair offer to the employees," said Charlie Brown, district spokesperson. "It would mean that the average teacher salary in this district would be $35,000, or $3,500 a month for the 10-month school year."

Brown indicated that the proposed salary schedule offered by the school board is very comparable to salaries in neighboring school districts.

"Our average teacher salary is the second best among the 10 elementary school districts in this county," he explained. "This is the best the board can do while still being fair with classified employees, students, and the taxpayers."

Brown explained that the union is demanding a 12 percent increase on the salary schedule. He encouraged parents to phone the district information line, 555-1234, for accurate, up-to-date information 24 hours a day.

Exhibit 9.12. Sample Letter to Parents

Dear Parents:

As you have likely heard by now, the Sunnyside Education Association (SEA) has called upon its members to withdraw their services from the district. The board of education has made an honest effort to be fair to the employees. The board has offered the SEA a 4 percent salary package. With other fringe benefits, including the increased costs of health insurance as well as mandated costs, the district's total offer is more than 9 percent.

The board of education feels that it has made a very fair offer and that this is the best it can do, considering the other demands upon the district's budget. The board will not cut into the budget to an extent that will force it to damage the instructional program for students.

The board is committed to keeping the schools operating and to continue providing a quality program for the district's 5,000 students. Your help is requested. Please encourage your youngsters to attend their normal classes. There will be qualified teachers in the classrooms. Students will receive meaningful instruction. Please have them bring a bag lunch and beverage to school.* Please organize carpools when necessary. All the work students do during this period will be counted toward graduation or grade advancement at the end of the year.

It is hoped that this withdrawal of services to the district will be brief. The board is confident that the majority of the employees in this district will soon be back working with the students. If you have any questions, please phone 555-1234 to receive an accurate, up-to-date message available 24 hours a day.

In order to keep your schools operating at full efficiency, many of your friends and neighbors have volunteered to help. If you will help at a school, please phone 555-1234, extension 30 or 35, or phone your school principal.

* To be stated only if food services are affected by the strike.

Exhibit 9.13.   Sample Letter to Employees

Dear _____:

   The district has been notified by the Sunnyside Education Association that a strike has
been called for _____date_____. The district's last salary proposal to the SEA was for
a 5 percent cost of living increase on the salary schedule.

   In the event of a work stoppage, the district is committed to keeping the schools operating and to continuing to provide a quality program of education for its 5,000 students.
Work will be available for those employees who wish to work, and the district will take
all appropriate measure to ensure the safety of its students and of employees who choose
to cross picket lines.

   Striking employees should be aware that they will not be entitled to receive wages for
any period of time that they are striking and not working. They are also ineligible under
California law to receive unemployment insurance benefits while out on strike. *(Mention
other insurance benefits—health, dental, etc.)*

   The district welcomes the support of all those who wish to offer their assistance and cooperation during this difficult period and is hopeful that a speedy resolution of the contract dispute will be forthcoming.

Sincerely,

Superintendent of Schools

Exhibit 9.14. Sample Letter to Employees for Use in Sick-Out

Dear _____:

We have heard that the association may request teachers to engage in a "sick-out" or other work stoppage to support its bargaining demands.

The teachers' contract *requires all employees to verify the specific reason for their absences.* Under the contract, sick leave may be used *ONLY* for your own illness or injury, a medical or dental appointment, or medical disability as verified by a licensed medical advisor (Article _____ Section _____). If you claim sick leave, you must sign the regular district absence report verifying your illness or accident under penalty of perjury in order to receive sick pay.*

If you make a personal decision to withhold your services as a teacher, whether by means of a "sick-out" or other work stoppage, you should not expect to be paid for not working.**

If you choose to strike, you will not be paid, you will lose State Retirement service credit, and you will be ineligible for unemployment insurance benefits. Should a strike extend, you may continue your health and welfare insurance by submitting the monthly premium payments for the month of _____ to the district office. Sick leave and other benefits do not accrue during a strike.***

If the association calls for any kind of work stoppage, the district will keep the schools open and will take appropriate measures to ensure the safety of its students and employees who choose to work.

Sincerely,

Superintendent of Schools

---

* This paragraph should be modified to conform to your district's relevant collective bargaining agreement.

** You may add that because of the threat of a sick-out, a doctor's excuse will be required for any request to use sick leave.

*** Omit this paragraph if dealing with a sick-out only.

Exhibit 9.15.   Checklist for Principals

___ 1. **Prestrike Preparations**

___ a. *Develop a school strike plan.* Obtain the district's strike plan, and with the assistance of your area coordinator, develop a school strike plan that conforms to the general guidelines and requirement of the district plan. The local school strike plan must interface with the planning at the district level, and it should follow the same general format. It is essential, therefore, that the principal obtain the district plan well before any strike.

___ b. *Anticipate staffing needs.* Prior to the strike, estimate as accurately as possible the number of employees that you anticipate will strike. Be realistic. Fill out prestrike survey form and submit to the personnel office and to the staffing coordinator. The principal should not directly question the employees as to whether they plan to participate in the strike. Such questioning could be held to constitute threatening or coercive conduct that interferes with or restrains employees in the exercise of their rights under the Educational Employment Relations Act. Experience shows more people than the principal estimates will go out on strike.

___ c. *Develop a plan for security.* One of the priority items of concern in the local school plan must be security measures for buildings and grounds for the staff who report to work and the pupils themselves. Work with the auxiliary services coordinator and the individual, if any, assigned to district security when developing your plan. The district may already have security procedures in place which adequately address some of the matters listed below and which merely need to be incorporated into your individual school's plan. Be sure to:

___ (1) Review ingress and egress to all schools and buildings. Determine in advance which doors and gates will be used. As a general rule, the number of points of ingress and egress should be strictly limited.

___ (2) Review night lighting for each building. Burning the lights all night will increase the cost of electricity but may prevent expensive vandalism.

___ (3) Review ingress and egress to grounds and parking lots. Determine which gates will be open and the hours they will be open.

___ (4) Consider posting guards at gates to ensure that only authorized people are admitted to school district property.

___ (5) Develop a system to make sure all gates, doors, and windows are locked at the end of the workday. Making one person responsible is the simplest method.

___ (6) Advise the district's security coordinator if you believe there is a need to pay an individual to spend the night at the school site. Some districts have used custodians and other classified employees as night watchpersons during strikes.

___ (7) The district should determine in advance whether strikers will be allowed to enter school grounds or buildings to get a drink of water, use restrooms, etc. Most labor relations and security experts strongly recommend that strikers not be allowed on school property.

    ___ (8) Prepare a system for the identification of personnel authorized to enter school property. Coded passes have been used with success.

    ___ (9) Provide security for files and records. Unattended offices should be locked.

    ___ (10) Provide for the security of private automobiles of non-strikers.

    ___ (11) Arrange for a centralized, specially keyed storage area at the school site for audio-visual equipment and instructional supplies. Have extra bulbs, lenses, etc.

___ d. *Develop a plan for key control.* Make sure you have a duplicate set of keys for each classroom. When a strike is called, require turn-in of keys by all staff.

___ e. *Develop a traffic control plan.* Determine in advance where buses will be unloaded.

___ f. *Become familiar with all building operations.* Learn the location of all utility shut-offs. A map should be made part of your plan with simple directions for checking utilities and turning them on and off. Attach this map to your strike plan. Include:

    ___ (1) Gas

    ___ (2) Electricity

    ___ (3) Water

    ___ (4) Sprinkler

    ___ (5) Furnace

    ___ (6) Secondary valves for each building

    ___ (7) Key or wrench to operate valve

    ___ (8) Fire alarm switches

___ g. *Establish a communication system.* Establish a communication system for your school. Along with the communications coordinator and area coordinator, develop sample letters to go home to parents and print sets of mailing labels. Prepare an alternative communication system (neighbors' telephones, two-way radios, courier system, automated calling systems). Maintain a directory of all key phone numbers, including:

    ___ (1) Police

    ___ (2) Fire

    ___ (3) District office

    ___ (4) Press

    ___ (5) Parents

___ h. *Prepare assignment folders.* Prepare an assignment folder for each class assignment. Information contained in this folder could include:

    ___ (1) Bell schedule

    ___ (2) Yard duty schedule

    ___ (3) Recess periods

    ___ (4) School map

    ___ (5) Fire drill instructions

    ___ (6) Name of regular classroom teacher

    ___ (7) Attendance rosters

    ___ (8) List of children who need special attention, medication, etc.

    ___ (9) School rules

    ___ (10) Attendance-keeping procedures

Exhibit 9.15.   Checklist for Principals (*Continued*)

   ___ (11) Special duties

   ___ (12) Location of teacher's manuals and any other information that would normally be necessary for a substitute teacher to have.

___ i. *Have lesson plans available.* Consider having pre-prepared lesson plans for various grade levels and/or special subject areas that would be useful for the first day of a strike. The district's instructional services department should assist you with this. When you are alerted that a strike is to be called, request and pick up the current lesson plans from each teacher. Non-striking personnel will find these lessons valuable in preparing instructional plans or in implementing the teachers' planned instructions.

___ j. *Check supplies.* Know how to replace and make sure that you have a supply of:

   ___ (1) Projection bulbs and lenses

   ___ (2) Phonograph equipment

   ___ (3) Textbooks

   ___ (4) Chalk

   ___ (5) Light bulbs and switches

   ___ (6) Alternate keys for rooms, desks, closets

   ___ (7) Other classroom supplies, i.e., paper, pencils, etc.

___ k. *Maintain student records and class lists.* Maintain an accurate and up-to-date set of class lists in a safe location. Maintenance of these lists will be important should the district desire to mail reports or communications to parents or need a set of telephone numbers that may be called. Obtain student records upon notice of a strike. Personally pick up all attendance records, registers, or any other materials which record student attendance through that date. Maintain these records in a place under your control, and do not let unauthorized persons have access to them. These are vitally important.

___ l. *Develop a pupil supervision plan.* Have a previously developed plan to ensure pupil supervision during noon and recess. You may wish to consider eliminating or reducing the time normally spent.

___ m. *Maintain a list of possible substitutes.* This list should include names of:

   ___ (1) Community members who possess credentials and substitutes

   ___ (2) Volunteer aides

   ___ (3) Noon-duty supervisors

   ___ (4) Retired teachers

   ___ (5) Secretarial substitutes

___ n. *Inform students and parents that there will be normal bus transportation unless they are advised otherwise.*

___ 2. **During the Strike**

___ a. *Open school early.* Principals should be at the school site at least one-half hour early to monitor the situation and make necessary preparations.

___ b. *Orient substitutes.* Be prepared to pass out substitute folders, lesson plans, and take substitutes to classroom.

___ c. *Assemble children.* Children should be assembled in a central place at the beginning of the school day so available staff can be assigned.

___ d. *Schedule group activities.* Group activities should be scheduled for children who cannot be accommodated in the classroom. Establish, if necessary, a period-by-period program of group activities. This program should provide for physical education activities both outside and inside the gymnasiums, for movies and music activities in large group instruction rooms, particularly in junior high schools, and for reading and study in the libraries and similar group activities in the cafeteria. Areas where activities can take place include:

  ___ (1) Yards
  ___ (2) Auditoriums
  ___ (3) Library
  ___ (4) Gymnasium
  ___ (5) Cafeteria

___ e. *Determine staffing needs.*

  ___ (1) Instruct all personnel to report to their regularly assigned work stations.
  ___ (2) Physically inspect each teaching work station to determine the number of substitutes needed.
  ___ (3) Fill all staffing needs without regard to student attendance. (Do not combine classes unless absolutely necessary.)

___ f. *Advise the district of your personnel needs.* Your area administrator and the staffing coordinator must be made aware of your needs and will assist you in obtaining replacement personnel. Complete the school report form daily.

___ g. *Prioritize classes.* Determine which classes are most essential. Give priority to 6th, 9th, and 12th graders. Implement alternatives planned for short day, combined classes, large group instruction, etc.

___ h. *Schedule faculty meetings.* A critical consideration is providing for necessary communication with non-striking staff members. One of the most effective vehicles for such communication is faculty meetings held at the close of each day during the strike. An agenda for such meetings can be planned in advance and should include such topics as the following:

  ___ (1) A review of the events of the day
  ___ (2) Plans for the following day, to include classes in session, directions to students without classes, exact designation of holding areas, hours of school, etc.
  ___ (3) Role of parents in assisting on campus
  ___ (4) Number of substitute teachers available for assistance on the following day
  ___ (5) Class coverage, including combination of classes
  ___ (6) Supervision and security measures
  ___ (7) Attendance and accounting procedures
  ___ (8) Availability of counseling and guidance services
  ___ (9) Operation of the cafeteria
  ___ (10) Announcements to be made to pupils the following day, including procedures to enable them to go directly home if the school is closed, availability of lunches, bus transportation, etc.

Exhibit 9.15.   Checklist for Principals (*Continued*)

     ___ (11) A status report on the situation in the rest of the district

     ___ (12) Status of negotiations and the district's position

___ i. *Tighten security on release of children during the day.*

___ j. *If necessary, advise parents of need to provide alternate transportation.*

___ k. *Visit classrooms at least once daily.* Give moral support to substitutes, answer questions, and allay fears of pupils.

___ l. *Prepare school report forms.* Prepare daily status report and forward to district.

___ m. *Prepare dismissal procedures.*

___ n. *Consider preparing newsletter to parents.* Consider periodic newsletter to parents keeping them apprised of the situation and assuring them that quality instruction is being provided for their children.

___ o. *Monitor and document activities of strikers.* The principal plays a critical function in obtaining information regarding the activities of strikers that can be used in court, possibly to obtain an injunction. The principal should take note of:

     ___ (1) Number of picketers

     ___ (2) Contents of picket signs

     ___ (3) Any illegal union/striker activity. Each of these should be thoroughly documented on an incident report. Contact the district immediately upon observing or obtaining knowledge of any illegal strike activity, including mass picketing.

___ p. *Know how to deal with the news media.* Caution teachers on duty not to make statements to reporters but to refer them to the principal. Give only factual information; don't make conjectures. Before speaking with any member of the news media, principals should first contact the communications coordinator for specific approval to speak to the media and for approval of the contents of any such communication.

___ q. *Advise students not to approach or speak with picketers.*

___ r. *Require daily turn-in of:*

     ___ (1) Keys

     ___ (2) Roll book

     ___ (3) Lesson plans

     ___ (4) Teacher editions of tests

     ___ (5) Seating charts

     ___ (6) Attendance cards

___ s. *Collect and report attendance figures.* School principals must collect and report attendance figures to the district office by a specific time each day. Prepare forms and instructions for simplified attendance procedure.

___ t. *Cancel/curtail extracurricular activities.* Assess your resources and cancel those extracurricular activities that you cannot reasonably expect to provide. Parents should be advised when activities will be canceled.

___ 3. **Post-Strike Considerations.** The post-strike period may be the most challenging problem a principal will face in his or her professional career. The following are suggestions for handling a post-strike situation:

___ a. *Be professional.* At some time during the strike, you will probably be mad at everyone—striking teachers, board members, central administration, etc. The first day after the strike be courteous and professional. Do not hold a faculty meeting unless for purely administrative details. Emotions may still be high. Give the situation some time.

___ b. *Avoid reprisals.* Work for a school atmosphere that will not be conducive to reprisals as a result of the strike.

___ c. *Be alert.* Be alert to situations that might lead to grievances, and try to forestall their occurrences. Also be alert to any situation in which the students may be subjected to brainwashing from either striking or non-striking teachers after the strike has settled.

___ d. *Avoid demonstrations of gratitude to non-strikers.* Demonstrations of gratitude such as flowers, luncheons by school administration, PTA, or community groups for non-striking teachers should be avoided. The principal should not discuss strike incidents or display undue friendliness or animosity towards strikers. Avoid the appearance of favoritism toward non-strikers. In one recent case, the district was held to have unlawfully issued letters of commendation to teachers who did not participate in the teachers' strike. This action was held to constitute discrimination against those teachers who engaged in protected strike activity.

___ e. *Provide special instruction where possible.* Consider providing tutoring or special instructors for pupils, particularly for those taking college preparatory classes, to make up work missed during a strike.

___ f. *Anticipate that:*

    ___ (1) Strikers will refuse to accept marks given pupils by substitutes for work done.

    ___ (2) Strikers will refuse to accept made-up work turned in.

    ___ (3) Substitutes lack supplies, so many supplies will be missing.

    ___ (4) There will be personal antagonism between teachers with the atmosphere being charged for some period of time following the strike. You will be most effective if during this period you:

        ___ (a) Talk to everyone.

        ___ (b) Stress service to pupils.

        ___ (c) Avoid the "he is the striker" syndrome.

    ___ (5) Pupils will object to make-up time and extra work.

    ___ (6) Teachers who have worked every day will have varying degrees of resentment toward make-up procedures that permit teachers who have been on strike to receive pay for services not rendered according to their regular contract.

___ g. *Work with the union and teachers to implement the new contract.* Work with teachers' organization leadership and individual teachers to implement the new contract whenever it is ratified. Also, work with teachers who have little, if any, sympathy with the organization's leadership or with its agreement.

Exhibit 9.16.   Elementary Check-In List

Welcome to _____ **School.**

Principal: _____

Assistant Principal: _____

Office Manager: _____

Clerk Typist: _____

Nurse: _____

You are substituting for: _____

Grade: _____   Room: _____

Yard Duty: _____

Room Partner: _____

Recess: _____

Lunch: _____

Additional Information:

_____

_____

Your Name: _____

_____

Exhibit 9.17.　Secondary Check-In List

Welcome to _____ **School.**

Principal: _____

Assistant Principals: _____

Nurse: _____

Counselors: _____

Department Chairperson: _____

You are substituting for: _____

Grade: _____　　Subject: _____　　Period: _____

Grade: _____　　Subject: _____　　Period: _____

Grade: _____　　Subject: _____　　Period: _____

Grade: _____　　Subject: _____　　Period: _____

Grade: _____　　Subject: _____　　Period: _____

Grade: _____　　Subject: _____　　Period: _____

Lunch: _____

Additional Information:

_____

_____

Your Name: _____

_____

Exhibit 9.18.   Typical Daily Faculty Meeting Agenda during Strike

1. Review events of day
2. Plan for the next day
3. Role of parents
4. Substitutes
5. Class coverage schedule
6. Security
7. Attendance accounting
8. Cafeteria
9. Bus transportation
10. District status report
11. Negotiations progress
12. Ideas/suggestions/problems

Exhibit 9.19.   School Report

DATE: _____   TIME: _____

SCHOOL: _____

Person Reporting: _____   Position: _____

Principal Present: Yes _____   No _____

All other administrators present: Yes _____   No _____

Number of faculty present: _____

Number of substitutes present: _____

Number of teachers from other schools present: _____

Substitutes still needed to serve students in school today: _____

Head custodian present: Yes _____   No _____

School secretary present: Yes _____   No _____

Number of other clerical staff absent: _____

Number of food service staff absent: _____

Pickets: Yes _____   No _____   Approximate Number: _____

Approximate number of students absent: _____

If your school receives bus students, did all buses arrive?   Yes _____   No _____

Additional information or requests for special assistance:

_____

_____

_____

Exhibit 9.20.   Incident Report

Your Name: _____   School: _____
Date of occurrence: _____   Time: _____
Location of incident: _____
Explain in detail what you saw. (Give names of persons involved.)

_____

_____

_____

_____

What statements did you hear and who made the statements?

_____

_____

_____

Where did this occur?

_____

_____

_____

_____

Who else saw or heard this incident? (Name and school location/department.)

_____

_____

_____

Do you have any documentation that supports your report? Yes _____ No _____ (Please
attach to this report.)

                                    _____
                                                              Signature

Exhibit 9.21.   Illegal Union/Striker Activity

1. Preventing non-striking employees, students, or suppliers from entering or leaving the school site.
2. Interfering with employees, students, or suppliers while they are driving between district property and their homes/businesses.
3. Bumping, jostling, or hitting a non-striker going through a picket line.
4. Causing damage to a vehicle or property going through a picket line.
5. Blocking access to school property with automobiles, railroad ties, etc., or by forming a human chain across the entranceway.
6. Carrying sticks, clubs, chains, guns, or piling bricks near the picket line for the use of pickets.
7. Threatening bodily harm to a non-striking employee at work crossing the picket line, at home, or anywhere.
8. Carrying out threats or assaults and batteries against non-striking employees, students, parents, or suppliers.
9. Attacking district property or a non-striker's real or personal property.
10. Threatening a non-striker with the loss of his or her job if the union wins the strike.
11. Threatening or insisting that a non-striker's seniority can be canceled.

Exhibit 9.22. Tips for Principals in a Strike Situation

Do not attempt to talk employees into coming to work if a strike occurs or before a strike occurs. If a striker calls you at work or at home and wants your advice on what to do (come to work or not), *tell him this and only this* (also try to have somebody pick up the phone as a witness—strikers sometimes don't tell the truth about what you say):

> "Charlie, I appreciate your call and concern. We will be keeping the schools open, and you are welcome to come back. You have a right to come to work, and you have a right to strike. It's your decision to make. Naturally, we would like to see you back to work, but the decision is yours to make. That's about all I can tell you. If you need more information, you'll have to call Jack Juanson at the district office. Sorry, I can't say any more to you, but the law restricts me quite a bit. Thanks for calling. Bye."

Do not promise an employee anything to get him to come back to work.

Do not threaten an employee in any way trying to get him to come back to work. For example, you can't threaten employees that you'll fire them if they decide to strike.

Do not "bad mouth" the union. This can get the district into a position of being accused that it is "undermining" the union (an unfair labor practice). You should always seek and follow the advice of attorneys before acting on your own.

Do not make private deals with your employees. As long as the union remains the certified bargaining representative, the district can only bargain with the union and cannot negotiate directly with employees.

Do not get trapped into meeting with striking employees—even if they request it. This is very dangerous because it can look like you are going to bargain with them. Also, you have the potential of multiple witnesses who may not tell the truth about what you did or did not say.

Do not interrogate employees about anything relating to the union—stick only to on-the-job needs when you must question them.

Do not interfere with strikers or pickets when you come in contact with them. Don't lose your temper if they hassle you—that may be exactly what they want to accomplish. If you overreact, they may be able to charge the district and you personally with an "unfair labor practice." Avoid talking to them for the same reason—even if they are your friends. You may be accused of something you didn't say. It is permissible to listen to what they say, but always try to have a witness of your own with you so they can't say you said something you did not.

Exhibit 9.23.　Preconcerted Activity Survey

School: _____

Date completed: _____

Normal school starting time: _____

Normal school ending time: _____

The following information is your best guess as to how your staff might react during a "concerted activity." The names and numbers you provide will help us in planning. All we are asking for is an estimate. The actual conditions of a "strike" or "concerted activity" will have a significant impact on how your staff will react. **Your input will be kept confidential.**

1. If there should be a teachers' strike, how many of your employees do you think would stay off the job?

	Present Allocation	# Who Probably Will Stay Out
Classroom Teachers		
Kindergarten	_____	_____
1–3	_____	_____
4–6	_____	_____
7–8	_____	_____
Non-Classroom Teachers		
Resource Teachers	_____	_____
Other	_____	_____
Other	_____	_____
Other	_____	_____
Classified Staff		
Secretary	_____	_____
Health Clerk	_____	_____
Library Aide	_____	_____
Aides	_____	_____
Food Service	_____	_____
Custodian	_____	_____

2. Are there some specific substitute teachers you would like to have during a strike? What are their names? _____

_____

_____

_____

3. Are there some specific substitute teachers you would not like to have during a strike?_____

_____

Are there any unique circumstances regarding subs at your school the Staffing Coordinator should be aware of (e.g., union officers, staff members with strong anti-union opinion, in an emergency situation ability to group classes due to arrangement of walls, very active parent support/volunteer group)?_____

Exhibit 9.23.   Preconcerted Activity Survey (*Continued*)

_____

_____

_____

Is there a key person in your community, PTA, or Home and School Club we could contact for assistance with volunteers?

Name: _____

Address: _____

_____

Phone: _____

What are the names, addresses and phone numbers of your usual volunteers? Do you guess that any of these volunteers would be particularly supportive or nonsupportive during a strike?

| | Nonsupportive |
Name/Address/Phone	/ Supportive
_____	_____
_____	_____
_____	_____
_____	_____

Comments:

_____

_____

_____

_____

_____

_____

4. Are there any people in your community who have a credential or qualify for an emergency credential?

Name	Phone	Address
_____	_____	_____
_____	_____	_____
_____	_____	_____
_____	_____	_____

Thank you for your help. We all hope we never have to use this information, but if we do, it is better to be well prepared. Remember, this survey is not to be shared with any employee other than the school administrator. **Do not ask a teacher or staff member if they would cross a picket line.**

Exhibit 9.24.   Checklist for the Legal Coordinator

___   1. **Prepare Emergency Procedures Resolution.** Prepare emergency procedures resolution for adoption by the board.

___   2. **Review Contract.** In particular, review contract for:
   ___ a. Emergency action clause
   ___ b. No-strike clause
   ___ c. Evergreen clause
   ___ d. Sick leave provisions
   ___ e. Health and welfare benefit provisions
   ___ f. Provisions for other leaves of absence

___   3. **Review Board Policies.** Review all existing board policies in light of strike activity.

___   4. **Meet with Legal Counsel.** You should meet with legal counsel prior to commencement of the strike to draft emergency resolutions and to plan a course of legal action to be reviewed by the superintendent and presented to the board for approval.

___   5. **Meet with the Board.** Along with legal counsel, you should meet with the board and inform them as to such issues as the legality of the strike, actions to be taken against striking employees, and the seeking of a restraining order. Authorization should be secured from the governing board instructing legal counsel to take all necessary legal action to prevent or terminate the employee strike.

___   6. **Gather Evidence.**
   ___ a. Provide individual school site administrators with standard report forms on absence from assignment.
   ___ b. Provide each individual school site administrator with report forms that record all incidents listing dates, times, names, etc. Make a file of all activities that are disruptive in nature and that are impediments to the normal functions of the school or that endanger the health and safety of students. [See exhibits 9.25–9.28.]
   ___ c. Make a file of all statements by employee organization leaders mentioning withdrawal of services with times, dates, and witnesses.
   ___ d. Make a file of all statements by the employee organization relating to the number or percentage of employees who threaten to strike with times, dates, and witnesses.
   ___ e. Provide tape recorders and cameras for observers at each school. Photographers, however, must be instructed not to take pictures of peaceful picketing or other peaceful activities as this may constitute an unfair labor practice. Confine photography to incidents of mass picketing, violence, and other unprotected strike activity.
   ___ f. If a temporary restraining order is granted, notify as many of the striking employees as possible, especially the employee organization's leaders that the strike has been enjoined and that they are required to return to work. Make a file of all such employees contacted, setting forth who was contacted, by whom the contact was made, and at what time the contact was made.

___   7. **Service of Process**
   ___ a. Determine the total number of certificated employees in the district.
   ___ b. Determine the total number of certificated employees in the employee organization.

Exhibit 9.24.   Checklist for the Legal Coordinator (*Continued*)

    ___ c. List the names and addresses of all employees, broken down by:
        ___ (1) School
        ___ (2) Classification
        ___ (3) Status
    ___ d. Update list of all union representatives. This list should include addresses, telephone numbers, and pictures, if possible.

___ 8. **Prepare Copies of Applicable State Laws, Penal Code Sections, Local Ordinances, and/or Board Policies.** Examples of laws, etc., which may be duplicated for administrative employees include:
    ___ a. Vehicle code sections on blocking right of ways, free movement of pedestrians and vehicles
    ___ b. Creating a public nuisance
    ___ c. Disturbance at a school site
    ___ d. Willful damage to school property
    ___ e. Unauthorized personnel on campus
    ___ f. Pertinent language of the collective bargaining agreement
    ___ g. Applicable court cases on the legality of strike
    ___ h. Citizen arrests

Consult your legal counsel to determine which of the above might be most useful in your district's situation. You should identify those items that will assist the school principal in maintaining order at the school site, with police help, if necessary.

___ 9. **Develop Procedures for Closing Schools.** Procedures for the closing of schools should be developed and distributed to individual school site administrators prior to the strike. But remember, *only* the superintendent can close a school.

___ 10. **Notify Other Agencies.**
    ___ a. Maintain a list of the officials in the community and county, particularly the chief of police, sheriff's office, city attorney, etc. In the event of a strike, these individuals must be contacted and made aware of the situation, and where appropriate, the district's position.
    ___ b. Prepare to contact the State Employment Development Department (EDD) to prevent payment of benefit claims by strikers.

___ 11. **Review Policies Governing Attendance, Leaves, and Leave Verifications for Bargaining Units Not on Strike.**

___ 12. **Determine If Insurance Benefits Will Be Discontinued during the Strike or If Alternative Arrangements Can Be Made.** Draft form to be executed by striking employees authorizing district to continue insurance benefits at employee's own expense. [See exhibit 9.29.]

___ 13. **Issues to Address Prior to Concluding State of Emergency.** Consider making recommendations to superintendent and board regarding:
    ___ a. Amnesty for strikers
    ___ b. Provisions in settlement prohibiting employee organization's retaliation against or discipline of non-strikers
    ___ c. Disciplinary action against strikers
    ___ d. Withdrawal of unfair practice charges and other legal actions filed by employee organization of district

Exhibit 9.25.   Administrator's Observation Form

Name: _____   Office Phone: _____

Title: _____

Date of occurrence: _____   Time: _____

Location of occurrence: _____

Where were you? _____

What did you personally observe? (List names of the people involved, if available.)

_____

_____

_____

_____

_____

_____

What were you told? (List name of person telling/time told.)

_____

_____

_____

_____

(Use extra pages, if necessary.)

Names of other persons witnessing event.

_____

_____

_____

_____

_____

Exhibit 9.26.   Principal's Draft Declaration

Draft Report of _____

I, _____, declare:

    I am Principal (<u>or Other Title</u>) at _____ School of the Serendipity City Unified School District. The school is located at _____(address)_____.
The school includes grades _____ through _____. Students attending the school are ages _____ through _____.

    This site normally has _____ teachers. Only _____ of those teachers reported for work today. Of those teachers absent, only _____ called in to the school to provide notice of their absence. There were _____ substitute teachers working at the site today. Of approximately _____ enrolled at _____ School, there were approximately _____ students in attendance today at 9:00 a.m. _____ students came to school but went home before 10:00 a.m. By the end of the school day, approximately _____ students remained in attendance. I personally observed the following effect on the <u>(operation of the school / students / parents arriving at the school / persons attempting to make deliveries at the school)</u> caused by the strike today. (Please explain any incidents in the above categories which you have personally observed, or any incidents which have been related to you, including the name of the person relating the incident.)

_____

_____

_____

_____

_____

_____

_____

_____

_____

_____

    I personally observed _____ teachers picketing the school site today. The teachers' names are:

_____

_____

_____

    Teachers did _____ / did not _____ put their cars in the parking lot. Teachers did _____ / did not _____ enter upon school property. (Describe any incident of teachers being on school property or parking cars on school property.)
    I did _____ / did not _____ observe any incidents of violence at the picket line. The incidents of violence were:

_____

_____

_____

This site normally has _____ classified employees. _____ classified employees were absent today. Of those classified employees absent, only _____ called in to notify the school of their absence. _____ classified employees notified the school that they would not report because they refused to cross the teachers' picket line.

Parents (indicate names of parents below) told me today that teachers on the picket line told them:

_____

_____

_____

_____

Students (indicate names of students below) at the school told me that teachers on the picket line had told them:

_____

_____

_____

_____

The strike has had the following effect on our ability to perform the following actions:

_____

_____

_____

Any additional comments:

_____

_____

_____

_____

I have read this draft declaration and would declare under penalty of perjury that a final declaration including these statements is true and correct.

Executed this _____ day of _____, 20_____, at Serendipity, California.

_____

DIRECTIONS: Complete only those portions of the draft of which you have knowledge and which are applicable based upon events occurring at your school. If your knowledge is based upon statements of another person, state the information and the name of the person. Strike out any printed statements of fact that are untrue. Leave blank statements that are inapplicable. Please make additional copies of this blank report to be used in the event the strike lasts more than one day.

Exhibit 9.27.   Parent Report

Report of _____(Parent)_____

I, _____, declare and state:

1. If called as a witness, I could testify from personal knowledge as to the following:

   _____

   _____

2. I reside at: __(address)_____

3. I reside within the boundaries of the Serendipity City Unified School District. My child,
   _____(name)_____, age _____, is currently enrolled at
   _____ School, a school operated by the Serendipity City
   Unified School District.

4. At _____ a.m. / p.m. on _____(date)_____, 20_____, I observed the following events relating to (a) taking my child to school / (b) observing picketers / (c)
   statements made by my child relating to his or her experience at the school:

   _____

   _____

   _____

   _____

   _____

   _____

5. Based upon the following experiences, I believe that the school was _____ safe and
   that my son or daughter should continue attending during the strike—OR—the school
   was _____ unsafe and that my son or daughter should not continue attending.

6. I believe that if teachers at my son or daughter's school remain on strike, his or her education will suffer irreparably because of these circumstances.
   I have read this draft report of _____ typewritten pages and would declare that the
   facts I have stated are true and correct.

Executed this _____ day of _____, 20_____, at Serendipity, California.

                                                _____
                                                                      Signature

Exhibit 9.28. Witness Statement

Your Name: _____   Home Phone: _____

                                         Office Phone: _____

Business Address: _____

Occupation: _____   Employed by: _____

Date of occurrence: _____   Time: _____ a.m. / p.m.

Location: _____

Where were you? _____

Names of other persons observing incident: _____

_____

Explain in detail what you saw and heard (give names of persons involved):

_____

_____

_____

_____

_____

_____

_____

I declare under penalty of perjury that the foregoing is true and correct.

Date: _____   Signature: _____

Exhibit 9.29.   Request for Continuation of Insurance Benefits

I, the undersigned, am currently participating in a collective withholding of my personal services as an employee of the Serendipity City Unified School District.

I hereby authorize the Serendipity City Unified School District to continue my insurance benefits during my participation in such activities.

I understand that I am personally financially obligated for the cost of such benefits during any such absence from my duties.

I specifically authorize the Serendipity City Unified School District to deduct from my present and future salary warrants (if I am reemployed by the District) at the amount necessary to pay the full cost of premiums which accrue(d) during such absence.

NOTE: Failure to execute this authorization will result in lapse of coverage and may result in future loss of coverage entirely.

Name	Social Security No.
Classification	Work Location
Signature	Date

RECEIVED BY:

Signature of Supervisor	Date

10

A Tale of Two Districts: The Birth of a Successful Collaborative Model

In this chapter, I describe the successes and failures of two school districts attempting to establish collaborative labor relations between the teacher unions and the school boards. Their experiences dramatically illustrate the principles laid out and discussed in the previous nine chapters of this book. The events related are, to the best of my knowledge, accurate and true. Only the names have been changed to protect the privacy of the participants.

FARMERSTOWN PUBLIC SCHOOLS

Armed with a brand new Ph.D., and spurred by a compulsion to show the world he knew how schools should be run, William Newman abandoned his comfortable suburban high school principalship in 1977 to become the superintendent of schools in Farmerstown. At the time he had no clue that conditions were nearly ideal in the district for major reform of both labor relations and the instructional programs. Years later he would understand why these two important aspects of school district operations go hand in hand. Along with his success, the superintendent would also taste a generous portion of failure in dealing with a teachers' union not ready for reform.

The Farmerstown Public School District was actually two separate districts with two separate school boards. One was a union high school district encompassing several rural elementary school districts. The other district was the largest of the elementary districts within the high school district's boundaries. The school boards for these two districts did not trust each other entirely; however, they recognized that they could save money by consolidating their district-level operations and hiring one superintendent to run both districts. The result was what Californians call a "common administration." The new superintendent was inexperienced in school district labor relations, but this didn't seem important since collective bargaining was only two years old at the time in California. Dealing with two very different teacher associations and two very different school boards soon made William a veteran.

Labor relations with the teachers in the high school district had been strained. The elementary district teachers' union, on the other hand, seemed less hostile, even though their salaries and benefits were inferior to those of the high school teachers. Newman saw the high school district as his greatest challenge. Looking back, years later, he recognized that the social dynamics at work in this district made it ripe for labor relations reform.

Both of Newman's two school boards wanted significant reform, but most of the demands centered around the high schools. Elementary school board meetings often drifted from elementary school matters to discussions and criticisms of the high school operations and staff. Board members confided to Newman that his extensive, successful experience as a high school principal was one of the reasons he was selected to be the superintendent. They also felt that the aggressive ex-football coach could "handle" the unruly high school union. In retrospect, none of these qualities had anything to do with the success achieved during Newman's tenure as the superintendent of the Farmerstown Public Schools. What mattered was that the two boards earnestly wanted their school district organizations to do well, and they were willing to do whatever necessary to accomplish that goal.

Like many small school districts in the nation, Farmerstown was proud of its schools and their history of service to their children. Teachers and school administrators were among the most respected citizens in the community, although some of this had been tainted by belligerent union pronouncements since the advent of collective bargaining for teachers two years earlier. The Farmerstown High School Teachers' Association (FHSTA) president was by all measures a powerful union leader. He was knowledgeable and experienced with school district negotiations and had a reputation for being tough when necessary. Above all, he was respected as a skilled teacher with high professional standards. The new superintendent quickly recognized that Jake, as the president was known by the faculty, was the authentic leader and true representative of the teachers. Jake, along with two or three of his seasoned union board members, could be counted on to relay accurately the union's position and, more importantly, to speak for the union.

Jake and his board were honestly concerned about the stressful state of relations in the district. Their strike threats were true signs of desperation in this small community. Jake was sorely aware of the "union bad guys" who were being identified by administrators and leaked to the community. In the meantime, the teachers, who had not had a significant raise since collective bargaining was initiated, were beginning to feel beaten down by a community they once believed was supportive. Since negotiations had been deadlocked for more than a year, high school teachers saw themselves losing ground. Once in the top ten among the fifty districts in the county, the absence of a raise had dropped the district to the middle of the pack. At the same time, the members of the fiscally conservative farm community feared that union-controlled teachers would result in increased costs and decreased services. Battle lines were being drawn. Pushing the local teachers' union leaders were strident, antagonistic, and inexperienced NEA Uniserve advisors feeling their oats after the passage of the state's collective bargaining law. Their rhetoric and "training" sessions stirred up some of the Farmerstown High School faculty and moved many of the thoughtful members to action. Fueling this fermentation was a growing distrust of the former superintendent and his administrators. The union found it easy to characterize the administrative staff as being primarily interested in finances and facilities rather than teaching and learning.

At first glance, Newman's task appeared daunting. In fact, it would be nearly impossible if Newman's mission were to restore the system to its former homeostasis. To his credit (or perhaps because of his inexperience), he decided to work hand in hand with the teachers' union leadership to forge a new relationship. He soon began to realize that the most fearsome foes could be allies and that the most desperate circumstances could be fertile seedbeds for authentic reform. Immediately, he learned that the distrust of the old superintendent, which had been widely circulated by union leaders among the staff, made it hard for them to immediately transfer that distrust to the new superintendent without losing their credibility. Newman also found himself free of the inevitable comparisons to a popular, successful superintendent. After all, it's hard to succeed when you follow Johnny Wooden as coach at UCLA. Newman also found out that a powerful and savvy union president is much easier to deal with than one who doesn't know how to play the game—especially if the union leader possesses a combination of savvy and integrity.

In contrast, elementary teachers in the Farmerstown Elementary School District seemed satisfied with their wages and working conditions. The president was a gracious woman serving her last year as president. She was respected as a teacher but not considered a tough union leader. Although their wages were still less than those of the high school faculty, teachers felt happy that they had received a raise while high school district negotiations were deadlocked. Newman's first meeting with the elementary district union president included the members of her board as well as the incoming president. The leaders described their relationship with the district as much less contentious than the high school district's, although they also shared a distrust of the old superintendent. The meeting reinforced Newman's perception that the high school district was where the problems were. He made up his mind at this point to concentrate his labor relations efforts on the high school district. In retrospect this was a mistake. The elementary district leadership failed to keep pace with the high school district and fell prey to the inflammatory anti-administration and anti-board member union rhetoric popular in those early days of collective bargaining.

THE BIRTH OF A COLLABORATIVE LABOR RELATIONS MODEL

Newman set about the initial task of developing a solid professional relationship with Jake, the high school district's union president. His first effort had included both formal and informal meetings—times for Jake and the new superintendent to share perceived problems and ideas. Newman felt that the informal relationship was important since trust had been a major problem with the former superintendent. Cutting down the distance between the two leaders would at least give trust a chance to develop. Jake and his chief negotiator eventually decided to settle the impasse with a compromise on the issues, including salary. The idea was to give the new superintendent a chance to make good on his promise to work with teacher leaders to create a better place for teaching and learning.

At this point it is fair to say that neither Newman nor Jake knew exactly where they were going. They both, however, were convinced that there was a better way to negotiate wages and benefits than the traditional industrial model rapidly being adopted by the teacher unions. At this time in history, both the AFT and the NEA were each trying to prove that they were the "meanest bastards" representing teachers. At the same time, districts were schooling their administrators in traditional labor relations using private-sector union negotiators to conduct the in-services. Teachers were being counseled to get up and walk out of faculty meetings lasting more than the time stipulated in the contract, while some school administrators contemplated requiring teachers to punch a time clock.

Setting up advisory councils, composed of the superintendent with his assistants and the union presidents with their executive boards, seemed to be the first logical step. The first item on the agenda was a study of salaries and benefits.

After pouring over the data derived from the salary schedules of the fifty school districts in the county, the high school council concluded that Farmerstown High School salaries were at about the fiftieth percentile. Further study revealed that the district had formerly been in the top ten among the county school districts (above the eightieth percentile). District leaders claimed that Farmerstown High School District salaries had "traditionally" been in the top 20 percent. Council deliberations eventually revealed the relative position of salaries to be the major interest of the teachers' union and the rank-and-file teachers who had formerly been proud of their status. Losing ground was equivalent to losing force and pride. Newman was intrigued by the fact that the teachers were not interested in some of the more prominent inequities. For example, none were bothered by the prolonged salary schedule, which prevented qualified teachers from earning full salary for fifteen years. Nor were they bothered by comparisons with big-city school districts. Losing ground—or the perception that they were losing ground—made them angry.

True, salary is a bread-and-butter issue, and in private industry unions have traditionally been the force for raising wages. But it became clear to Newman that with teachers, at least these teachers, being treated fairly was more important than the size of their salaries. Their feelings of self-respect and support were all wrapped up in their district's effort to keep teachers paid at a rate commensurate with others in the county. Like most professionals, teachers are more interested in what they do than what they get paid. However, they all want to be treated fairly—and that means they want to be paid at the *going rate*.

Two major challenges emerged from the initial advisory council meetings: first, how to establish the acceptable, traditional rate of compensation, and, second, how to stay there. The first step was easy. The council agreed that fair would mean a return to the traditional top ten position. A discussion of this concept revealed an agreement that as long as the last regularly scheduled step with a master's degree on the salary schedule was one dollar or more above the eleventh place district in the county, the schedule would be fair. Getting there would simply be a matter of scheduling raises to accomplish this benchmark over a number of years.

Thus the foundation was laid for what is now called "interest-based bargaining" of salaries in the Farmerstown High School District. The interest was to maintain teacher salaries among the top ten of the county as measured by an index step on the salary schedule common to all salary schedules in the county.

Newman felt comfortable with this index and this goal since all of the school districts in the county had similar revenue foundations. All were rural, agricultural-based economies. Almost all of the school districts paid similar wages. The difference between salaries in the top 10 percent and the median salary in the county was slightly more than 5 percent. Had there been districts in the county sitting on oil fields or with other large tax bases, the advisory council would have been forced to select an index of "similar districts." However, since the county districts were already similar, and since Farmerstown salaries were traditionally in the top ten of these districts, the decision was easy.

The next problem was how to stay there. Newman and the advisory council recognized this was a far more difficult task. Other districts around the county would raise their salaries from time to time, each making independent decisions. How could Farmerstown High School District stay abreast? Calculating the top 10 percent at the end of the year and giving a raise for the following year doesn't work because the teachers are perennially playing catch-up. They are underpaid each year by an amount roughly equal to the average raise in the county. Calculating the raise and giving the teacher a "catch-up lump sum" at the end of the year plays havoc with budgeting since employee salaries are approximately 85 percent of a district's budget. If all districts would settle their contracts in July and August before school starts in September, there would be no problem. But this was not the real world.

Newman and the advisory council soon came to the conclusion that some method of accurately predicting salary raises in the county was necessary. Accuracy in the prediction was crucial since paying increases not justified by income leads to radical cutbacks in program and eventually bankruptcy. At some time during this debate, Newman and the advisory council adopted the hypothesis that paying "the county average" raise would maintain the high school district's relative salary position among the county's districts. Although they recognized this standard was not precise, it was close enough.

What was emerging from these discussions was a process for achieving a mutually agreed upon bargaining goal—namely, keeping Farmerstown teacher salaries in the top ten districts of the county. A comparison index had been established. The district would pay at least one dollar more than number eleven of the county's fifty districts. Each year the district would pay the teachers a raise equal to the average raise among the other county districts in order to maintain Farmerstown's traditional position continuously over the years.

All that remained now was a method for predicting the average salary raise in the county a year before the data were in. But how? Some districts settle early, some late, some don't settle at all! The $64,000 question was "What sort of data are available that can be used to predict salary increases accurately?"

As a first step, the council collected all the raises from the previous year. As it turned out, this was a difficult task. Some districts were at impasse, others had huge increases that represented a settlement from three years of impasse; others included off-the-schedule bonuses, extra columns, M.A.s added, half-year or partial-year settlements, and multiyear settlements.

The council sorted out all of these issues and came up with actual (or nearly actual) settlements for each district for the year. Large raises for multiple-year settlements were divided out, and off-the-schedule bonuses were ignored. Extra columns added to the salary schedule, masters degree, and partial-year on-schedule settlements were all counted fully. Raises in the districts that had not settled were approximated based on confidential phone conversations with the superintendents (usually very accurate). The raises were added up and divided by fifty (the total number of districts). The result was 4.1 percent. The figure was interesting to council members, but seemingly useless. After all, the year was over. Raises had been given. It was simply interesting history.

William Newman had a different reaction. He had heard that number before: 4.1 percent was the cost of living increase allowed by the state for its district equalization calculation, known in California as the revenue limit calculation. The previous year's cost of living adjustment, or revenue limit COLA, had been 4.1. A coincidence? Newman and the council felt it was worth checking out. A subsequent investigation revealed that the prior year's average raises were very close to the prior year's cost of living adjustment by the state to the district's revenue limit. In the spring of 1978, Newman and the council realized they had discovered something very important. It was the critical information needed annually to predict raises in the surrounding districts and derive a collectively bargained salary increase.

As finishing touches, the council agreed that "What's good for the goose is good for the gander." In other words, if the actual raises turned out to be more than predicted, the district would make up the difference the next year. The council was convinced the difference would be trivial (probably less than two-tenths of a percent). By the same token, if raises were lower than predicted, the teachers would subtract a small fraction from the following year's raise. Probably most important, the council agreed that the actual tentative agreement each year should be between the union president and the superintendent. This feature allows for the unforeseen.

The council recognized that the "formula" was not flawless. It depended upon the integrity of the union president and superintendent. But the members also recognized that now the conditions were different. Both leaders benefit from an accurate prediction—the more precise, the better! If the prediction is too high, the teachers would benefit from an inflated raise; however, when the inflated amount is subtracted from the following year's raise, the rank and file feel disappointed that their leaders did not do as well as surrounding districts. On the other hand, if the estimate is low, the teachers receive slightly less than the going rate, but the district must come up with a higher than average raise the next year, putting financially strapped school boards in a bad light with a spending-conscious public. This forces both the union president and the superintendent to consider all the factors that may in the future impact salaries. Usually, these come in the form of "strings" in the yearly school finance appropriation law, which cause districts to receive a greater or lesser increase than that specified by the COLA.

SELLING THE IDEA TO THE BOARD AND THE TEACHERS

Superintendent Newman now felt the pressure. His board was composed of conservative leaders of a farming community. Each of the members in some way was connected with farming except for the CEO of a local manufacturing firm and the community activist wife of one of the community's doctors. Passing through cost of living adjustments sounded a lot like the big mistake General Motors made several years ago when it agreed to pass on a raise tied to a cost-of-living index. "What about servicing the salary schedule? Don't we automatically give teachers automatic raises for years of service?" board members queried.

The questions about servicing the salary schedule by giving automatic raises for years of service each year along with additional raises for advanced preparation were the most difficult to answer. Teachers moved across the schedule until they reached a maximum salary in about fifteen years. Newman had to convince the board that once teachers reached the top of the schedule they stop advancing. Over the years, retirements will equal new hires, and the average teacher's salary will remain somewhere in the middle of the schedule, resulting in an *actual* cost of servicing the salary schedule—0 percent. Naturally, this is not always true, especially in smaller districts or districts with rapidly declining enrollment. Some years, no one retires. In others, a larger percent begin drawing their pensions. However, Newman reviewed the new hires each year and pointed out that rarely did the district know who comprised the 10 percent before the end of the fiscal year on June 30. Many, if not most, teachers decide to move away, change districts, make a career change, take leave for health reasons, or retire *after* the last day of school. The result, Newman argued, was an average 10 percent retirement and 10 percent new hire each year after adjustment for growth. At the same time, Newman advised the board to resist practices that corrupt this balance of teachers entering and leaving the system, such as golden handshakes. In the long run, these are pure expenses that add to the cost of the average teacher.

One of the board members challenged Newman. "If I understand you right, during the lean years we might have to cut back on supplies or services to students to pay the teachers. Is that correct?" Newman had to admit that lean years might create those choices. In this farm community, however, he used a convincing analogy. "If the price of oranges barely covers the costs of picking and packing, resulting in almost no profit for the year, what will the farmer pay the pickers?" Every trustee in the room agreed that the farmer would pay the pickers the "going rate" whether prices were high or low. In this conservative farming community, the idea of paying teachers the going rate was not challenged.

Jake had an easier time with the high school teachers. His hard-earned credibility paid off, and the teachers trusted their union leadership to make a deal that was fair.

MEANWHILE, BACK IN THE ELEMENTARY DISTRICT. . . .

While the high school board and teachers' union were patting each other on the back and punching the air for what seemed to be labor peace in our time, the teachers in the elementary district were expressing only mild interest in what the high school was doing. The new elementary union president, Daisy Blusher, had taken office, and Newman was busy orienting her to what was happening in the high school district. At about the same time, Daisy was being oriented by NEA's Uniserve and attended a "training" sponsored by the California Teachers' Association (CTA). Wooed by the excitement of the CTA office and the dedication of its professional staff, Daisy began spending more and more time with the union business and causes. Soon it was rumored that she was dating the Uniserve bargaining specialist. Newman's courtship with the elementary district was not blossoming into the romance he had achieved with the high school district. Rather, it was eclipsed by Uniserve's courtship of Daisy Blusher. At first, Daisy and her elementary union board began to develop a traditional salary opener for the upcoming school year. She told Newman that teachers in the elementary school desired to be paid on the same scale as the high school teachers. Newman, sensing this was his chance to begin the earnest dialogue for an interest-based salary agreement, took the opportunity to explain in one sitting all of the insights developed over the previous year with the high school union leadership.

William Newman was a fairly persuasive personality, and because he understood so clearly the rationale for the new process developed with the high school union, he was particularly persuasive and thoroughly sincere in his more than two-hour meeting with President Blusher. After the meeting, he had the warm feeling of accomplishment that only happens after a competent professional skillfully applies his trade. You can imagine his surprise when a visibly agitated Daisy burst unannounced into his office the next afternoon proclaiming with angry righteousness, "I know now what you were doing to me! You were trying to 'co-opt' me." She continued by informing him that collaboration between union leaders and administrators undermines her, her union, and the world's labor movement in general. Salary formulas rob unions of their right to bargain this matter at the table. Setting salary targets, placing a district in the top ten, was also grossly unfair. "It makes us depend on teachers from other districts to bargain for us."

Newman tried to explain that in the public arena, available revenues determine salary increases to a far greater extent than any bargaining team. He began to review the high school advisory council's data.

Daisy interrupted, "Why should we settle for the top ten? Why not first? You always say we are the best teachers around. Why not pay us the best salaries?" Newman stuttered and began to explain some of the political realities of dealing with communities and school boards. He was just beginning to explain how little difference there was between position one and position six when Daisy turned around and stormed out exclaiming, "I've heard enough double talk for one day!"

Newman was crushed. He could see he was in for an uphill battle with one of his two districts.

During the final three years of Newman's tenure, the high school district continued to thrive. Morale grew to a point described by both teachers and classified employees as the highest in their recollection. Curriculum development flourished; test scores soared (from below the twentieth percentile in 1977 to the sixtieth percentile in 1981—just four years later!).

At the same time, the elementary district remained static. Negotiations were settled more or less fairly (as they always are in the long run), but only after much unneeded angst and tension haggling over absurd demands. The elementary school board became impatient with a union that showed little appreciation for its attempt to pay good salaries. Board members began to confide that they felt they were being "strung along" by insincere teacher leaders. Teachers, on the other hand, openly expressed their dismay over what they perceived as the superintendent's favoritism toward the high school teachers. Test scores continued to rise as a result of the sophisticated curriculum development efforts by talented and dedicated curriculum developers but not, however, at the same rate as those of the high school. In fairness, the demographics of the elementary district were not the same as the high school's, and the high school district's curriculum and test scores had more room for improvement. Moreover, some of the high school district's teacher enthusiasm spilled over into the elementary district during cooperative curriculum development activities. However, Newman's failed efforts at establishing collaborative labor relations in the elementary district resulted in a negative impact on the job satisfaction of the faculty. The teachers perceived that they were not being treated with the same high regard as the teachers in the high school district.

LESSONS LEARNED

Newman's initiation into the world of school labor relations gave him a taste of what can go wrong as well as what can go right.

- He learned that "It takes two to tango." Any knowledgeable superintendent can provide leadership, but without the cooperation of a union leadership that is both capable and credible, nothing will happen.
- He also learned that teachers are far less concerned about the amount of money they earn than they are about the commitment of a school board to pay the "going rate." Making the school district employees the board's first financial priority, Newman discovered, may be the most cost-effective action a board can take.
- With the question of salary removed from the table at the high school district, Newman observed less focus on the negotiations process and more concern about the business of teaching and learning.
- Finally, Dr. Newman learned the hard way that reasonable solutions to salary negotiations must be worked out collaboratively with the teacher leadership. This can't be rushed. There simply is no way to install cooperation and trust using brute force. Sometimes, no matter how hard you try, no matter how many things you do right, the dragon still wins.

11

✛

Restoring Public Confidence in the Schools: One District's Experience

In this chapter, I describe how union leaders and district leaders forged a highly sophisticated collaborative labor relations model more than two decades ago that has survived to this day. This long-term organizational stability has contributed significantly to the success the district has achieved over the years. As in the previous chapter, the events related are, to the best of my knowledge, accurate and true. Only the names have been changed to protect the privacy of the participants.

LOS VALECITOS UNIFIED

When Adin Willingham accepted the superintendency of Los Valecitos Unified School District in 1981, he saw an opportunity to accomplish some of the reforms he had envisioned over the years. The district was a newly unified, middle-sized, suburban, K–12 school district. For a number of reasons, it never really got off the ground politically. Nearly every system in the district needed repair. Several months before Dr. Willingham was hired, the district was declared bankrupt by the county business officials. The district's embarrassed school board was forced to petition the state legislature for a bail-out loan. The bankruptcy served to further discredit the embattled superintendent, especially after it was revealed that the fund shortage was a result of the district's mistakes in counting students. At the top of the list of woes that beset the Los Valecitos Unified District was a well-organized and hostile teachers' union that had been almost permanently at impasse with the school board since the district's genesis five years earlier. The constant turmoil led to a predictable community response. A reform board led by three aggressive and well-qualified citizens was elected the year before Willingham's appointment. The old superintendent's contract was not renewed, and Willingham, an experienced superintendent known for his strong background in curriculum and labor relations, was hired.

Immediately prior to the bankruptcy and changeover of superintendents, the teachers' union was preparing for serious job action. Salaries had slipped over the past several years until the district now ranked last among unified districts in the county. Various minor concerted actions had been planned and carried out to demonstrate to the board that the union was unified and ready to act. For example, on one occasion this union called for the "earthquake drill" described earlier. At precisely 10:30 a.m. one morning, all teachers in the district escorted their classes out of the building and onto the lawns to the surprise and consternation of the unwary administrators in the district. At the same time, every school board meeting featured crowds of teachers involved in the pre-planned disruptive activities. Negotiations for the year were stalled and confused by the announcement of insolvency.

In addition to the paralyzing personnel and business problems faced by the district, teaching and learning in the district were also slowing. District-wide test scores had slumped below the fiftieth percentile—a condition considered intolerable by the trio of well-educated professional reform candidates and similarly deplored by the two members of the board minority.

From the outset, Willingham knew he must accomplish three broad goals: first, he must establish a strong, rational organizational structure;

second, he must reestablish fiscal solvency along with safeguards to prevent future budget crises; and, finally, he must develop an approach to union relations that would eliminate the district's tradition of permanent labor unrest. Even though his primary strength and interests were in developing the curriculum and instructional program, the new superintendent recognized that this higher goal would not be achieved until order was firmly established. As he had learned many years before in the classroom, discipline and classroom management are not the most important classroom objectives, but nothing else will happen until these objectives are addressed and order is firmly established.

In keeping with his vision of what needed to be done, Willingham relieved or reassigned several of the top managers of the district who had been involved with the fiscal crisis and the general organizational dysfunction. He replaced them with a talented business manager and operational leaders with demonstrated ability, training, and experience. Managers in every corner of the district were put on notice that strict adherence to fiscal policies and procedures would be an absolute condition for continued employment in the management of the district.

Not unexpectedly, Willingham found a sincere willingness on the part of all remaining members of the management team to play the game the way the superintendent had outlined it. In a short time, the superintendent and his new business manager established a workable fiscal recovery plan with the County Office of Education business officials charged with overseeing the district's bankruptcy. In the district, the dust settled and a temporary atmosphere of normalcy prevailed as relieved staff prepared to begin the new school year. The next task was to forge a relationship with the unions, especially the teachers' union, which would allow the district to progress with its mission of educating the young citizens of Los Valecitos.

"I want to meet with the meanest son-of-a-gun in the union," Willingham told the board president when asked about his approach to the difficult negotiations deadlock. Willingham knew he had some advantages as a newcomer: first, the strike buildup had lost some of its steam with the news of the district's bankruptcy. The old superintendent, who had been the focal point of union strike preparation rhetoric, had been assigned to a classroom and was completely out of the picture. The community was running out of patience with the constant turmoil, and the support from parents for teachers was beginning to wane. Faculty support of the union leadership was also lessening as teachers began questioning the years of conflict with little to show for it. Teacher salaries now were near the bottom of those given in the county.

Willingham was pleasantly surprised to find the top union leaders to be conscientious, thoughtful educators who seemed honestly more interested in the welfare of the district and its employees than their own self-aggrandizement. From the beginning, the president and the chief negotiator were brutally candid with the superintendent. The superintendent, with equal candor, explained his position: "I won't straddle the fence," said Willingham. "I'll work with you to help you accomplish the legitimate needs of your members, but I won't bargain with you. If you want to bargain, you can fight it out with the board's hired gun."

Willingham went on to explain that he really didn't care which direction the district pursued. There were advantages to either. Willingham's experience had shown him that a cooperative labor relations model results in a more satisfied and content staff, but places extreme demands on the superintendent and his staff in working through a multiplicity of personnel matters amounting to year-round negotiations. On the other hand, the traditional industrial-style table negotiations afford more opportunity for the superintendent to work with curriculum development and instructional program improvement, but results in a less professionally satisfying organizational climate. As far as Willingham was concerned, it was a trade-off. His primary goal was to establish order and bring the stalled negotiations to a conclusion.

The union president agreed to call an afterschool meeting of the executive board to discuss with the new superintendent some of his ideas for advancing labor relations in the district. The meeting, held in a high school classroom, was attended by a dozen building reps and members of the executive committee board. Most of them viewed the new superintendent with suspicion. All of them were skeptical that anything important would be said, but they were curious about the person responsible for the large-scale changes in the district's administrative structures. The meeting was marked by only one noteworthy accomplishment: a day-long meeting of the executive board and building reps was scheduled for the purpose of informally discussing the deadlocked contract talks.

The meeting began at the union president's comfortable home early Saturday morning. At the top of the agenda was a 14 percent salary increase demand. The union leaders carefully described their rationale. Their salaries had lagged behind as a result of settlements in previous years. Moreover, they had not settled last year's contract, resulting in an even greater disparity. Even though the district had been declared bankrupt, the union leaders felt they needed at least 14 percent to "make progress."

Taking his cue from this statement, Willingham queried, "Progress toward what?" Responses around the room ranged from "a livable wage" to "a fair salary." Willingham pressed on, "Define a fair salary for me." Frank, the union president, had already had some preliminary discussions with the new superintendent and took a leadership role in the discussion. By noon the group had decided that "fair salary" could reasonably be defined as a salary schedule that ranks number four among the ten unified school districts in the county. Moreover, the group had decided that a long-range plan to achieve that goal over a four-year period of time would also be reasonable. In other words, a plan to gradually raise salaries in relation to other districts in the county could be initiated, resulting in a salary schedule that ranked number four among the unified school districts in the county at the end of the fourth year.

Adin Willingham had become aware through conversations with Farmerstown superintendent William Newman that the state's cost of living adjustment (COLA) to the appropriation to local school districts had a close relationship to salary increases for all school district employees. Furthermore, he was well acquainted with Newman's salary formula worked out in the Farmerstown High School District four years earlier. (See chapter 10 for a description of the Farmerstown formula.) The Farmerstown formula stipulated that the statewide school district revenue COLA would be used each year as the basis for salary increase predictions and calculations. This number would be augmented or diminished based on a calculation of the average raises actually given to the nine other unified school districts in the county. The idea was to establish the average county unified school district raise as the basis for the Los Valecitos Unified School District salary increases each year. To this number would be added a small increment designed to accelerate their salary increases in order to place their salary schedule in the number four position among the county's unified school districts in four years.

The union reps attending the meeting were visibly enthused. "It sounds too good to be true. What's the catch?" asked one skeptic. "Simple," replied Willingham, "abandon positional bargaining."

Abandon positional bargaining? Isn't this what unions had fought for? How could a group of union leaders abandon the concept of "making progress" on the contract? "Making progress" on the contract was a part of union lexicon in 1981 that had been drummed into every unionist's mind. Abandoning the concept would be tantamount to high treason. If positional bargaining were to be abandoned, what would take its place? The afternoon was focused on that question, along with the remaining contract issues of the deadlocked negotiations.

Willingham conceded that positional bargaining gave union members a forum to air changing organizational needs and conditions that affect their lives as employees. He posed a rhetorical question: "If these issues are really important, why should the district wait for the yearly negotiations process to discuss them? In fact, it's common practice to put contract changes on a *three*-year cycle. Doesn't it make more sense to deal with the problems as they arise?" Willingham went on to propose a council composed of his top administrators and the union executive board that would "negotiate" regularly throughout the year—at least once per month. These "negotiation sessions" would address the union concerns as well as management's concerns and "negotiate" solutions. These agreed upon solutions would not become part of the formal contract but would be recorded in formal minutes. When appropriate, they would become formal administrative procedures.

The union leaders remained skeptical. However, most of them admitted that positional bargaining strategies had not made much progress for them over the previous five years. In the final analysis, they were only gambling a year. They could always return to the traditional positional bargaining the following year if things didn't work out. This logic, combined with the favorable four-year plan for salary improvement, tipped the scales, and the teachers agreed. The rest of the day was spent discussing possibilities for prep time for elementary teachers, binding arbitration, and other more ordinary union agenda. The evening was capped off with a dinner at a local restaurant where the newly forged compact was celebrated with several bottles of expensive wine (at the union's expense, of course).

That 1981 meeting marked the beginning of a governance process in the Los Valecitos Unified School District, which more than any single factor led to an explosion of employee productivity. Removing the money from the table convinced the teachers that the board was committed to their welfare and provided a foundation for a very positive organizational climate.

The council established to review employee concerns and devise appropriate solutions proved to be as important as the salary and benefits formula. Union reps from every building became an active part of the governance of the school district. Employee concerns were being addressed not only by school administrators but also by union leadership. The result was a greater attention toward professional tasks serving children and serving the community.

Not surprisingly, the grateful community responded. A foundation was established to raise money solely for the purpose of helping teachers accomplish their dream projects. Praises of the district were heard in service clubs throughout the community and were reflected in cooperation with the various governmental agencies in the area. Within four years, state test scores for the district soared into the eightieth percentile and public confidence in the Los Valecitos Unified School District was restored. Twenty years later, the district is still on a roll.

Today the district has grown to more than twelve thousand students. I had an opportunity last year to interview the former union president and the chief negotiator for Los Valecitos Unified. Both men are still fairly actively involved in union business. I asked them why, after twenty years, the Los Valecitos cooperative labor relations model is still going strong. Many others around the country had collapsed, resulting in strikes and, in many cases, worse relations than before the attempt at collaborative bargaining. The former chief negotiator, Juan, replied,

> I think the board is very, very important in this. The school board doesn't want to take the chance of losing it. They will go beyond what school boards would normally do in order to keep this process working. I think they prefer everything good that comes out of it—you know, the good relations that we have in the community, the fact that there's never any bad press. Teachers are not jumping on the board, and vice versa. And I think they have a big stake in it, too, because we have this history. We have this history where it's worked.

Frank joined the conversation and added, "The only threat to the system now is politics. Politics could harm cooperative labor relations. If somehow it's perceived that we are doing poorly in any particular segment of the community, because of this cooperative model, that could harm it."

I was intrigued. I asked if there were any steps that could be taken to compensate for the political frailties in a community. Frank shrugged, "I don't think so. The longer something lives, the more likely it will continue, because people don't want to interrupt it. But there is no way of legislating good judgment."

I was curious about the role of the state and national unions, the CTA and the NEA. I asked the two veteran leaders how they saw the role of the Uniserve advisor. Could the advisor screw things up? Their replies were unequivocal, "Certainly."

I wondered why they were so sure of the potential negative role that the Uniserve advisors could play. After all, Los Valecitos was successful in its reform effort. Frank explained, "That goes back to the first point I made. You have to have union leaders who are sophisticated enough and self-confident enough to stand by themselves."

Frank went on to explain that when union leaders lack this self-confidence, they must depend on the Uniserve advisors or other state and national union officials, who have their own agenda. He allowed that the union advisors would do their best for the school district unit, but the chances of moving toward collaborative labor relations reform would be nil.

This last comment led me to wonder whether the Los Valecitos union was being advised by the CTA during the period of time they were hammering out the collaborative agreement with superintendent Willingham. Juan clarified this: "Frank and I committed ourselves to this: we decided that we would use them, CTA, when we needed them, but that they would never be able to ever again take control over what we did."

I laughed, "You guys were mavericks back in those days!" Juan agreed and added, "When I was elected as a state representative, I would go to Burlingame [CTA headquarters], and there were people who wouldn't even talk to me. Others would walk up to me and say, 'My God, everybody else is doing your negotiations for you.'"

Twenty years ago, at the onset of the summit meeting between the superintendent and the union leadership at the president's home, incoming superintendent Adin Willingham had taken a hard-line approach with the union by saying, "It's all or nothing. If you want to work cooperatively with me, then I'll work with you. But if you don't, we'll do it the other way." Dr. Willingham reinforced this position in subsequent years at workshops throughout the state. He would propose that the district only had money to offer and the union had only labor. He was fond of saying, "It doesn't make sense to bargain cooperatively on the half the union has to give and positionally on the half the district has to give." I wondered why twenty years ago these militant union leaders were willing to buy that logic. Juan's comment was insightful. He explained, "It was the crisis. I think that you need to offer something better than what they already have. Willingham gave us promise for the future, you know. That's one of the reasons why the formula looked so positive and looked so good to us. But going down a road of 'all or nothing' [in the absence of the crisis], that would have worried me."

I was intrigued. The two union architects of the Los Valecitos collaborative labor relations model were claiming that *without a crisis,* a collaborative model would never have been installed. I wanted to hear more. Juan continued, "It would have worried me because I think you build trust gradually. You don't go into a room and say, 'Hey, you guys, you have to trust me immediately.'"

Frank interrupted, "When you build that kind of trust, you take risks."

Juan nodded in agreement. "I took my name, Frank took his name, and we put them out there for everyone to see. And so when someone criticized Dr. Willingham, Frank and I were the first to stand up and say, 'Wait a minute. We're your leaders. This is what we think Dr. Willingham wants to do, and we're going to support him on it.'"

Both Juan and Frank expressed concern that as time goes on fewer and fewer teachers remember the "bad old days" when morale was low and the union was forced to wage an anti-board and anti-administration PR campaign year after year in order to muster the political pressure necessary to force raises and improve working conditions. "The association membership needs to be constantly reminded of what the alternative is," said Juan. "They have to know what the gains are in cooperative bargaining. And they have to be educated to what it is."

Unquestionably, the concept of cooperative labor relations is a disadvantage to unions in power. After all, one of the reasons for the existence of unions is to "protect" the workers. Unions are strongest when management is threatening. Cooperative labor relations undermine this basic union purpose. Moreover, when salaries are formulized, it is difficult to get most employees concerned about the other trivialities of school district working conditions—especially since the most important working conditions are guaranteed by state law rather than contract.

Willingham left for a larger district after five years. Since then, two new superintendents have presided over the district. Both educators have understood the concept of "paying the going rate," and they have been able to convince their business managers and other money-conscious stakeholders of the advantages in terms of educational productivity of committing to this principle. Frank and Juan have become folk heroes as a result of their vision and strength. They also constitute a major portion of the school district's institutional memory. What happens when these men retire in a few years is anyone's guess. My bet is that new leadership steeped in the traditions of cooperation will take the reins and carry on. In the meantime, Frank and Juan continue to make a major contribution to teaching and learning in the Los Valecitos District.

Appendix A

Sample Strike Manual

The following pages contain the actual text of a strike manual compiled by a California school district faced with the possibility of a teacher walk-out. Materials for the manual were obtained by the district from the Association of California School Administrators (ACSA) *Strike Manual* (1987, 1995) and are provided here with the permission of the association.

EMERGENCY PROCEDURES MANUAL
2001 (REVISED 1/26/01)

TABLE OF CONTENTS

FOREWORD: DISTRICT POSITION AND POLICY

It is the position of the Board of Education that a strike, work slowdown or other type of harassment by any public school teacher is illegal; consequently, the Board of Education has directed that employees who participate in such actions shall be disciplined. The Board of Education also believes that students have a right to a safe, supervised environment and an appropriate educational program on every day of the approved school calendar. Consequently, the Board of Education has established that schools are to be kept open and operating.

The primary responsibility of all District personnel designated as management during any period of unrest is to implement the policy of the District, keep the schools open and operating and to provide the best possible educational environment. Accomplishing this must be the major concern—not responding to the issues of the strike or harassment.

Administrators should not attempt to deal with such issues as the justification of the strike or harassment, the professional attitudes of the involved teachers, whether their demands or grievances are realistic, etc.

These concerns should be divorced from the primary mission, which is to continue to offer a meaningful educational program. To accomplish this during a time of concerted employee activity, emergency operating procedures may have to be put into effect in order to:

1. Ensure the welfare, safety, and education of the pupils;
2. Ensure the rights and safety of all employees;
3. Ensure the protection of public school property; and
4. Provide the necessary staffing and support to fulfill the mission of the Board of Education.

This manual is an outline of the emergency procedures and responsibilities to be effected under strike or harassment conditions and provides for a sequence of authority, communication and responsibility until the disruption ends.

INTRODUCTION

The manner in which a District administrator conducts himself/herself before or during a strike can affect his/her relationships with teachers, students, parents, fellow administrators, and the community for years to come.

During a strike, *the administrator's* problems increase in number and complexity. He/she may be forced to make important decisions instantly. His/her routine and normal school operations will undoubtedly be constantly changing and unpredictable.

The striking teachers also will be under tremendous stress. They will feel righteously justified for their actions, yet tense about the acceptance of their actions by others and about the possible consequences of their actions. This stress will move some to an emotional peak that will produce behavior unlike any normally associated with that person. These behavior changes may prevail for some time. Many will become hostile in defense of their behavior. This hostility could be directed toward the administrator, office personnel, the nonparticipating teachers, noncooperating pupils, emotional parents, and/or anyone else with whom they may come into contact.

The non-striking teachers also will be tense. Some will be critical of their participating peers. They also may become hostile in defense of their own positions on nonparticipation. If the strike lingers, there may develop a resentment or disgust toward the whole situation directed at both the striking teachers and the Administration for being unable to resolve the matter.

Students may be confused by the situation, frustrated because their schedules are disrupted, or active in supporting one side or the other. Those confused may face the divided loyalties represented by respected teachers, administrators, parents, peers, and their own desires. Those frustrated may realize their educational programs are being seriously handicapped by an event over which they have no control and that they may have increasing amounts of work to "catch up." Pupils who become active on one side or the other may become antagonistic toward teachers and other pupils of different convictions and blame the Administration for not settling the problem to their satisfaction.

Parents and the community-at-large also will feel a sense of frustration because they may feel powerless in a situation of direct significance to them. Some will be antagonistic toward the striking teachers for disrupting the education of their children; others will be antagonistic toward the Administration for not avoiding the situation in the first place or resolving it quickly in the second place. Virtually, all will be antagonistic toward "the school" as having failed to maintain "normalcy" in their children's educational programs. In such a complex and tension-laden situation, the school principal is the most important person on the scene.

WHEN THE DISRUPTION IS OVER, PRINCIPALS WILL ONCE AGAIN BE WORKING WITH ALL THESE PERSONS TRYING TO MOLD THEM INTO A SINGLE COMMUNITY WITH A UNITED PURPOSE: THE EDUCATION OF YOUTH.

Suggestions for Administrators

Following are some suggestions based upon behavioral evidence that may contribute toward keeping the school open and operating, toward maintaining a safe and profitable environment for pupils and toward a conciliatory period of reconstruction:

1. Keep "cool" before, during and after the unrest. Function from a rational, mature and unemotional posture, even though others may be irrational and emotional. *If necessary, avoid or delay a response to avoid an impulsive or emotional reaction.* Concede the other party may have a point that deserves consideration and express the need for time to ponder it or to gain information. Those seeking change or to discredit their "opposition" often try to provoke the administrative leadership into overreaction. Such overreaction often is a more valuable aid to their cause than the stated issues; especially when the overreaction is (or appears to be) violation of the existing policies, rules or regulations the administrator is obligated to follow.

2. Deal with specific problems as they arise, and not the issues behind the disruption. The administrator should be willing to discuss them and to state his/her views on the matter openly, honestly and without emotion. He/she must not argue the matter or attempt to have his/her views prevail, but he/she must fulfill his/her responsibilities to pupils, parents and the nonparticipating teachers.

3. Refrain from judging the motives of others. Respect their views and their right to hold such views. A difference of opinion should be no barrier to courtesy, respect and mutual trust.

4. Avoid being defensive, even though it will come naturally while under emotional attack from teachers on both sides, pupils, parents, and citizens. Most may be merely venting their emotions toward the most available symbol or "ear" of the system which either seems opposed to them or ineffective. By "lending an ear," the administrator may be providing a "safety valve" and avoid a larger explosion at another time or place.

5. Do not let your opinion of a disruptive tactic influence your opinion of the participants or nonparticipants as teachers.

6. Rumors and exaggerations will run rampant. Believe nothing until it has been checked with an authoritative source. Remember also, that even the principal is under tension and emotional strain, and that these factors and his/her personal opinions on the issues and tactics of the disruption will influence his/her interpretation of what he/she sees and hears.

7. Select your words and "tone of voice" with care in answering questions or discussing the situation. An emotional listener can grossly distort your meaning. Answers and comments should be brief without embellishments, adjectives, illustrations, or figurative speech. If you *do not know* the answer to a question, admit it.

8. Do nothing to encourage or contribute to alienation between individuals or groups. Do not criticize one individual or group before others. Avoid "taking sides" other than the one to which you are obligated—to keep the schools open and operating. The deliberations to resolve the situation must be accomplished away from the individual school setting by those representing many points of view. If the principal "takes sides" he/she compromises his/her potential effectiveness once the disruption is over and reconciliation efforts begin.

9. Develop a flexible plan with clear delineation of the roles and responsibilities for all concerned. Try to anticipate the various types of incidents which may occur and prepare to meet them. Unused plans are not wasted. Unplanned action frequently may not only be wasteful but counterproductive.

10. Keep channels of communication open. Be available to all. Hold frequent informal meetings to keep all informed and to pass on accurate information of what is going on. Keep the parent leaders and other interested parties informed and solicit their regular input. Student assemblies may be held whenever there is an indication that such action could alleviate pupil unrest, confusion or frustration.
11. Avoid ultimatum-type statements. They can lead to unnecessary confrontations.
12. In group discussions where differences of opinion exist, be sure that all persons and views are heard. Discourage any effort by a minority or majority group to "put down" or dominate others. The administrator during such a meeting should express his/her own position openly, fairly and objectively while demonstrating an understanding and appreciation of the views of others.

ORGANIZATIONAL PATTERN

Principals

The most important District administrator in implementing the policy of keeping the schools open and operating is, undoubtedly, the school principal. The school principal is at all times an agent of the Board of Education. He/she is responsible during a period of unrest, as during any other time, for implementing the Board's policies regardless of his/her own sympathies. This will be very difficult for the principal during any disruptive situation initiated by the teachers. He/she will be called upon to act as the Board's agent and administer these polices impartially with respect to his/her own school and personnel, whether he/she feels the tactic employed is justifiable or abominable.

Superintendent's Emergency Team (E Team)

Although most of the burden of keeping the schools open and operating will fall upon the school principal, the Superintendent's E Team will strive to serve the principal. Among the areas of need with which the Superintendent's E Team can help the principals are personnel, transportation, communications, legal counsel, police assistance, and any other problems, which may result from disruption.

Contact with the Superintendent's E Team is from the principal to the Directors of Elementary and Secondary Education through the emergency telephone number.

In the event of a teacher strike, harassment, or at any other time at the discretion of the Superintendent, the Superintendent's E Team will become active upon notification of its members by the Superintendent or the Assistant Superintendent.

The Superintendent's E Team shall consist of the following District officers:

A. *Superintendent* (Smith)

   Responsible for developing and implementing policies regarding the conduct of affairs related to the situation; for keeping the members of the Board of Education informed; and for counseling with them as the situation develops.

B. *Assistant Superintendent, Personnel Services* (Hall)

   Responsible for assisting the Superintendent as directed; for being available to other members of the E Team; for providing legal assistance; and for communications with representatives of the teachers' union, and the public.

C. *Assistant Superintendent, Business* (O'Hare)

   Responsible for implementing policies in the support services of the District in assisting school principals to keep the schools open and operating; for providing police assistance; for the general conduct of food service, maintenance and operations, transportation of students and employees, business office functions, grounds, mail, telephone service and computer network services.

D. *Assistant Superintendent, Instruction* (Gray)

   Responsible for implementing policies in the elementary and secondary schools as directed by the Superintendent; for meeting the emergency instructional needs of the elementary and secondary schools caused by the situation; for directing the efforts of support personnel in the instructional division; and for the general conduct of affairs in the schools during the period of unrest.

E. *Directors of Elementary and Secondary Education* (Nelson and Grant)

   Responsible for communications with the principals; for processing of complaints from the public about school operations; and for collecting documentation and reporting to the Assistant Superintendent, Personnel Services any employee incidents that should be considered for disciplinary action.

F. *Director of Personnel* (Matting)

   Responsible for providing the certificated and classified personnel necessary to keep the schools open and operating; for employee attendance accounting; and for the general conduct of affairs in the Personnel office.

Throughout the period of unrest, the Superintendent's E Team will meet each day in the Board Room at a time designated by the Superintendent, and will be prepared to meet immediately at any other times upon call by the Superintendent. Daily meetings will be held with principals each day instructional services are withheld.

PRINCIPAL'S RESPONSIBILITY

In cases of emergency, the primary responsibility for the continuation of the instructional program and the safety of the staff and students rests with the principal. The ability to make fast, accurate decisions is essential. The statements below and the actions outlined in the rest of this plan are primarily to support decisions at the local school site.

1. It is the obligation and duty of the school's administrator(s) to keep the school open and operating in order to fulfill their responsibilities.
2. The Principal is responsible for the organization of a dependable strike management team of teachers, instructional assistants, aides, volunteers and classified staff.
3. Administrators will not encourage any staff member to withdraw his/her services.
4. Administrators shall encourage employees and students to stay in school.
5. The principal will recommend altering the schedule or closing the school to the Director of Elementary or Secondary Education only when the health or safety of staff or students is in immediate danger.

EMERGENCY PROCEDURES PRIOR TO AND DURING A STRIKE

It is necessary to be prepared for emergencies at all times to ensure the success of the District policy to keep schools open and operating.

The following conditions have been identified and labeled to assist the management team in their activities:

1. Condition—NORMAL

The District is functioning without the threat of a strike. No action is necessary.

2. Condition—AGITATED

Employee organizations are "beating the drums." Meetings are taking place. Negotiations are stalled. It is apparent that unrest is occurring. Publications are being sent from the organization to employees and the press.

Superintendent will hold management team meetings to review emergency procedures when Condition—AGITATED is determined.

3. Condition—CRITICAL

Strike funds are collected. Demonstrations take place. News media articles mention strike or walkout. Rumors indicate that picket captains have been appointed. Strike signs are painted. Community information attempts are being made by the Teachers' Association.

Each principal should consider Condition—CRITICAL as the signal to prepare to institute emergency procedures. No overt action should be taken other than emergency preparedness procedures. Each principal should do the following:

a. Review the building emergency plan checklist (attached).
b. Put alternate communications systems in a state of readiness.
c. Initiate extra security measures relative to key control, building and grounds.
d. Forward any information regarding possible future actions of employee organizations to the Director of Elementary or Secondary Education.
e. Contact key community people, such as volunteers and school site committee members, PTA, site council, etc. regarding critical condition.

Building staffs are to be informed regarding the critical situation. Standard information will be made available to principals for this purpose from the Superintendent's office.

4. Condition—STRIKE IMMINENT

A strike vote has been taken or the employee organization leadership has been empowered to call a strike. It is almost certain that a strike will occur. Prepare to implement Emergency Procedures as follows:

a. *Identification of Non-Striking Personnel:* On notification of STRIKE IMMINENT condition, the site manager, using a checklist with every site-based person's name on it, should ask each person directly whether or not they will report for work the morning of the first day of the strike. The day before the strike is called, the list must be reaffirmed, as late as possible in the day, but early enough to make contact with every person on the staff. (This should include classified as well as certificated.) From this list, the site manager will be able to identify the number of people he/she will need to keep the site open and operating the following day. Complete "Substitute Teacher Request Form," and return to the Personnel Office before 5:00 p.m. Food service, transportation, and maintenance and operations departments will secure substitutes according to their own procedures.

b. *Plan for Getting Non-Striking Personnel on and off Site:* It may not be possible for an individual to cross a picket line, particularly if there is harassment or verbal abuse aimed at the person crossing. Alternatives to get staff and students on campus are enumerated below.

(1) Consideration should be given to parking cars on the school grounds within fenced areas. If this is not possible, provision needs to be made by the principal to escort substitute personnel from the street, or some other location close to the school, to the school site.

(2) Security guards will be provided by the District to patrol the on campus parking lots at each school during the working hours, approximately 7:30 a.m. to 4:00 p.m. These guards will be authorized to prohibit entry of unauthorized persons into the parking lot during those hours. Any person found to be committing acts of vandalism to personal property would be prosecuted.

(3) As an alternative, if parking seems unsafe at school, advise the substitutes to park in a non-school location. Identify the most appropriate parking site and determine the time which will best meet the needs of your school and advise your substitutes that transportation will be provided from the parking site to your school at that hour. Any substitute who cannot arrive at the designated time will, of course, have to provide his/her own transportation to the school. Designate a member of your staff, either classified or certificated, who will not be involved in the strike to provide the necessary transportation between the parking site and your campus. Mileage will be paid to District personnel providing this service upon submission of the proper monthly allowance form.

(4) Bus transportation may be provided for moving personnel to the sites from a central location. Working with the Transportation Department, principals will need to develop schedules that will get personnel to the schools prior to the time the busses will be needed for the transportation of students.

c. *Additional Personnel:*

(1) Substitutes will be assigned to specific locations in advance of the strike. They will be dispatched *centrally* unless other arrangements are made.

(2) All certificated personnel not regularly assigned to a specific school will be dispatched centrally to be used in the schools as needed.

(3) All available substitute aides and noon-duty supervisors will be on duty. They, too, will be dispatched centrally.

(4) Despite everything that is done, you may be short of substitutes. Some may arrive late.

(5) Volunteer parents, instructional assistants, aides and classified employees may be used to assist a credentialed employee in any duties assigned by the principal.

(6) Principals and teachers are not required to call substitutes, but the principal should ask substitutes if they will return the following day and request additional substitutes as needed on the Substitute Teacher Request Form.

(7) Student teachers should be given the choice to leave or substitute. They should seek guidance from their college supervisors prior to a work stoppage regarding credits, pay, etc.

(8) No person may assume full teaching responsibilities for pay without approval by the Personnel Department. Credentialed parents or credentialed non-District employees who volunteer to teach should be referred to the Personnel Office. Regular or substitute aides may be assigned to work with a group of students under supervision of a teacher or the principal.

(9) Every certificated person on campus, except the principal, may be assigned to teach. The principal needs to be available for duties other than teaching.

(10) Contact parents, college students, or other people as to their willingness to serve as substitutes or aides under strike conditions. Their employment must be processed through the Personnel Office in order for them to be paid. Paid personnel are more desirable than volunteers because (1) they are more likely to come to work every day, (2) any legal problems generating out of accidents are more difficult to deal with if the adult involved is not an agent of the school and (3) coverage for state workers' compensation, etc. is provided.

(11) Parents may be scheduled for as much or as little time as they are willing to accept. If they are working strictly as volunteers, do not put them into positions where their absence would jeopardize the functioning of the school.

(12) Back-up first aid personnel must be identified in order to cover the school in case the school nurse or secretary is out. Non-striking personnel need to be cognizant of the medication needs of students.

d. *Emergency Key Control:* Upon notice of a STRIKE IMMINENT condition pick up all keys. Those people who are non-striking personnel may possibly be insulted by this, but explain carefully the reasons for it and be particularly careful to pick up all master keys. *The principal must maintain complete control of keys and have the only available master key.* Keys for light switches and water faucets are not as vital, but make sure that you have duplicates available for usage. Remember to pick up keys for closets and desks as well as keys for office doors from teachers who use duplicating equipment on weekends. It is recognized that employees may be uncooperative in terms of turning in keys, roll books, etc. These materials are school district property and employees may be required to surrender them. Failure to do so is a basis for disciplinary action. Supervisors must be sure to write and submit to the Personnel Office a report of any refusal to cooperate.

e. *Alternative Plans for Instruction of Pupils:*
   (1) Flexibility in assignment of substitutes must be maintained. Group sizes may vary, depending upon the number of substitutes available. Assignments may be changed during the day as the situation warrants. Have a daily meeting with your staff to make assignments and plan the next day.
   (2) Preprint the school schedule for distribution the morning of the strike. Maintain the library and other activities as much as possible. Cancel all scheduled extracurricular activities. Community use permits should be cancelled if custodial service is not available.
   (3) Provide adequate supervision at recesses to prevent students from making contacts with pickets. Pickets on campus *shall* be asked to stay on sidewalks at entrances to the campus. If they will not, contact the Assistant Superintendent, Business through the emergency number.
   (4) All itinerant teachers will be assigned by their District-level supervisor.
   (5) Keep in mind that classified employees can serve as supervisors. This may include aides, custodians, secretaries, clerks, or cafeteria staff. These staff people should be thoroughly briefed in relation to the job to be performed and what to do in case an emergency situation should arise, such as a fire, injury, power or water shutoff, etc. Also, remember that while it is not legal to place these personnel as "teachers," they may supervise a class that is working on tasks previously assigned by a teacher or administrator.
   (6) Note the number of school-based classified substitutes needed on the Substitute Teacher Request Form.
   (7) The District has made provision for extra high-interest films that can be used with large groups of children. Contact the IMC Coordinator if you need them.

f. *Double Check Substitute Folders:* When the STRIKE IMMINENT condition is called, request and pick up the current lesson plan from each teacher. Non-striking personnel will find these lessons valuable in preparing instructional plans or implementing the teachers' planned instruction. Document and report to the Director of Elementary or Secondary Education any regular teachers who do not provide lesson plans.

g. *Attendance Form Packets:* Forms for recording attendance of students, or any other records needed, must be in packets and given to substitutes on arrival. Accuracy in the use of these forms is imperative. The simplest and most accurate way of recording attendance is to report positive attendance, i.e., those who are there, not those who are absent.

h. *Building Security:* Upon notice of STRIKE IMMINENT condition, personally pick up all attendance records, registers or any other materials that record student attendance and grades to that date. Maintain these records in a place under your control, and do not let unauthorized persons have access to them. At the end of the strike, accurate attendance registers or grade records will be vitally important.

(1) Remove from the school site, preferably to some place in your home, an accurate and up-to-date set of class lists. The list should have the name, address, telephone number, and name of parents of each child. Maintenance of these lists will be important should the District desire to mail reports or communications to parents or need a set of telephone numbers that may be called, as well as being able to reproduce a school class list if other class lists have been destroyed.

(2) Make a copy of all student grade information to date. Keep these copies at home. When the strike condition is over the grades provided by substitute employees may have to be added to the regular teacher information.

i. *Anti-Sabotage Plans:*

(1) Learn the location of and how to operate all water and gas valves and electric power switches in your building. These valves and switches may not be located according to your school's plans. Frequently during construction, locations of valves and switches were changed and no indication was recorded. The Maintenance Department will be available to help you locate each of these switches and to learn its function.

(2) Following a STRIKE IMMINENT condition, place all classroom audio-visual equipment in a locked closet or in a central storage area to prevent theft or damage of lenses, bulbs,

needles, batteries, cords, or related items. All scheduled audio-visual equipment should be collected and secured while not in actual use in a central area. You might want to consider limiting use of this type of equipment. Also, consider maintaining an ample supply of cord replacements.

(3) A sufficient amount of basic supplies for at least three weeks should be maintained in a secured area of the school. While it is true children can bring supplies from home, don't depend upon parents to provide their children with this material. Lock supply room. Dispense only necessary supplies daily.

(4) Remember that you have collected all keys. Besides your master key, which will open all rooms, you will need a set which will open all desks and closets.

(5) Attempts may be made to jam switches or keyways, or to make them inoperable. Unless you are experienced, don't attempt to clean out switches due to the danger involved. Maintenance people will be available for repair. Bulbs may be broken or loosened to make them inoperable. A sufficient number of replacements for at least a three-week period should be maintained.

(6) Depending on the situation, you may want to lock student bathrooms except during certain designated intervals. Emergency maintenance personnel will be available if necessary.

(7) In many schools, a power drop prevents a furnace from operating. Unless you are qualified, it is extremely dangerous to attempt resetting and igniting the furnace. Emergency maintenance personnel will be available, if needed. If time permits prior to an emergency situation, request operating instructions from the Maintenance Department.

(8) Familiarize yourself with the operation of the alarm system so that in the event it is triggered you can shut it off and reset the alarm.

5. Condition—STRIKE

Employees strike, stage a mass walkout or disrupt school procedures. Implement Emergency Procedures. This condition indicates that a strike or work stoppage has begun and all procedures for continuation of the instructional program should be instituted.

Upon notification of the Condition—STRIKE, the principal needs to immediately go through his/her checklist and verify that each activity is completed and ordered into action. The principal's familiarity with his/her local situation and personal judgment are of essence during this phase. The following four conditions should provide some help in determining possible courses of action as they relate to your local decision. Be advised that the criteria outlined in each condition give a general picture. When most or all of the criteria listed become apparent, then it can be assumed that the condition is in operation and this should be reported to the Director of Elementary or Secondary Education.

a. *Normal Instruction Being Maintained:*
   (1) Almost all of staff on campus working full time
   (2) No vandalism or damage to buildings and grounds that would impair normal school
   (3) No pickets or other disturbances at school
   (4) Children arrive in good order at appropriate times
b. *Instruction Being Maintained at Minimal Level:*
   (1) Teacher absence high—substitutes available and in classes to bring complement to 90%
   (2) Legal pickets. No harassment of staff or students
   (3) Vandalism requiring immediate service from maintenance crews
   (4) More than 25% student absenteeism
   (5) Work slowdown by teachers
c. *Marginal Ability to Maintain Instructional Program:* Modification of schedule may be necessary. Call Director of Elementary or Secondary Education for decision.
   (1) Most of staff absent. Substitutes providing marginal coverage, less than 75% of complement
   (2) Pickets unlawfully advocating strike and harassing teachers and students
   (3) Damage to facilities which is dangerous to students and staff
   (4) Students and staff unable to enter building
   (5) Threat of bomb or arson
   (6) Total disruption of instructional program
   (7) Extensive parent concerns for safety of children
d. *Close School:* Contact the Director of Elementary or Secondary Education or the Superintendent's office at the emergency number immediately.
   (1) Danger to staff or students seems imminent
   (2) Aggressive actions or confrontations of a physical nature between staff/strikers/parents
   (3) Arson or any other overt act of a hostile nature

6. Condition—RETRACT TO LESSER CONDITION

Strike, walkout or other disruption has been terminated. Extent or degree of termination will determine what former condition is called. Management team reverts back to identified condition.

The retract signal will be given only by the Superintendent or his/her designee. The retract signal signifies that the strike or action has passed and you may officially retract to the former condition called. This action should be performed in a low-key manner so that school can function at a normal level as soon as possible.

7. Condition—SETTLED

When a final settlement has been reached, several steps undertaken during the strike will need to be continued temporarily.

The Superintendent's E Team will continue to meet at a time designated by the Superintendent on a daily basis until such time as it is no longer deemed necessary by the Superintendent to meet that frequently. The principals shall also meet daily at the Education Center until notified otherwise. Each principal should continue to convene a daily meeting of school site administrative staff until it is determined that such action is no longer necessary.

During the post-strike period, it is important that continuous communication continue so that details which need to be resolved and recorded immediately following a strike or walkout can be handled in a uniform manner throughout the District.

INFORMATION FOR MANAGING STRIKES OR SLOWDOWNS

Attendance

1. Students—The student absence rate will increase. The percentage of absence and number of teachers present may suggest changes in grouping and scheduling. Have a series of alternative plans for this. An attendance report will be required daily. (See Strike Report.)
2. Teachers—Based on experience elsewhere, we may lose up to 90% of the teachers. You will be asked to make a daily estimate of teacher attendance for the following day. (See Substitute Teacher Request Form.) Ask teachers if they plan to work.
3. All Personnel—Attendance of employees will be recorded each day of the strike on forms distributed to each principal. (See Strike Report.)

Discussion

1. Discussion with Teachers—Do not hesitate to discuss with teachers facts relative to the strike. If asked, you may say that:

    a. Schools will remain open.

    b. Teachers who work will be paid; those who don't will lose a day's pay and a pro rata amount of the District contribution to benefits for each day absent without leave.

    c. All normal duties must be performed.

2. Discussion with Students, Parents and Public—Communication with students, parents and public should be handled very carefully. Communications should stick to facts; e.g., "The Association is discussing the possibility of a strike; school will be open; an instructional program will be provided."

Communication

1. The Superintendent's office will make every effort to communicate official messages to public media. Local radio stations, television stations and the press will be asked to cooperate regarding general announcements to parents and by working through the District's spokesperson.

2. A mail distribution service will operate daily during the walkout. If necessary, the daily all-management meeting will be the vehicle for mail service.

3. Use the regular telephone system first. If the regular system is inadequate or nonfunctional, use emergency numbers to be given to you later.

4. In the event of an emergency call your Director or the Superintendent's office at the emergency number first. Do not call police or other emergency services directly unless, in *your best judgment*, failure to do so would jeopardize life or property. A list of such numbers will be supplied by the Superintendent's office.

5. Make arrangements, in advance, to use telephones at the homes of two neighbors near your school in the event your telephones are inoperative. Do not use these numbers unless it involves an extreme emergency and it is the only way of reaching the Superintendent's office.

6. The emergency radio system will be tested and the appropriate uses will be discussed and provided to principals in writing.

7. All official communications from the central office will be sequentially numbered and provided in written form to all administrators.

News Media

1. Be careful of statements to representatives of news media. Stick to the facts. All press people should be directed to the District's

information center, in the Assistant Superintendent, Personnel's office.

2. The principal may allow properly identified media representatives access to the building before and after school, but restrict photographs, quotes or recordings to those working teachers and students who are willing to participate. K–8 students who are to be identified by name must have parent permission before their picture or quotes can be used. 9–12 students should be asked by the media if their name and/or picture can be used. Media representatives must agree to this prior to obtaining permission to enter the building. Call the Assistant Superintendent, Personnel if you have any problems in this regard.

3. If it is necessary to make a statement, the sample listed below should be used as a guide:

    "The_____School is currently open and classes are being held for all grades with the certificated staff which has reported for work and available substitutes and aides. It is our conviction that teachers who desire to teach should be permitted to do so, and students who desire to come to school and learn are also entitled to do so. We will keep the school open as long as it is a safe environment. Parents are encouraged to contact the District's information center for information and may do so by calling _____. The school will be operating on schedule until further notice. Parents are welcome to visit the school at any time and their assistance during this emergency situation will be appreciated."

MAINTAINING THE TEACHING/LEARNING CLIMATE

Organizing for Teaching

1. Provisions should be made to maintain for children the regular school day and instructional activities as near to normal as possible. The supply of substitute teachers may not be plentiful enough to achieve the ultimate emergency service in all buildings. In all cases, however, the activities engaged in should be instructional and purposeful in nature.

2. Students should be made to feel that school is being carried on in the most normal fashion possible. Teachers who are present should help youngsters keep their minds on their school activities; teachers are to be prohibited from discussing the strike with students.

3. Each principal will make plans for his/her own building. There will likely be similar circumstances in several buildings; therefore, these are some general patterns that may be useful:
   a) Staff members, paid aides, parent volunteers, and student assistants may be used to direct students into the building *upon arrival* and to give special directions. Principals should be prepared to document incidents of harassment and obstructiveness.
   b) Take attendance as early as possible (but not later than 45 minutes after the opening of school).
   c) Personnel assigned to a single building may utilized by the school principal at his/her discretion.
   d) Double up classes of the same or sequential grade with one teacher in one room, if large enough. Wherever possible, assign instructional assistant teacher aides and student supervisors to a teacher who has overall supervision of two or three classes.
   e) If a large number of students cannot be accommodated in single classrooms or on a reasonable double basis, schedule them into a large area (multipurpose room, library, cafeteria, etc.) view good, educational films for an appropriate block of time. After that time, schedule the children into smaller groups in classrooms when other large groups are scheduled to view films.
4. Do not deviate from existing practice and policy regarding the supervision of students.
5. If excess staff exist at a building, notify the Personnel Office for reassignment as required. NO NON-STRIKE TEACHERS WILL BE REQUIRED TO GO TO ANOTHER SCHOOL.
6. Minimum days and the elimination of staggered session may be authorized by the Superintendent or his designee only.

Pickets

1. Informational picketing is constitutionally protected as long as it is peaceful and does not disrupt the orderly educational process.
2. Pickets may not demonstrate on school property.
3. Pickets may not enter buildings.
4. Pickets may not block entrance to the school site.
5. Avoid confrontations or arguments with pickets. If there is any interference with students or teachers, call the Assistant Superintendent, Business immediately. Do not call the police unless it is impossible to reach the Assistant Superintendent's office or if violence is imminent. Be sure to document harassment, violence or vandalism.

Teacher Aides and Volunteers

1. Teacher aides and instructional assistants are permitted to provide instructional activities under the *indirect* supervision of a teacher or principal.
2. Volunteers may be particularly useful in performing a variety of activities involving students, but they must be directly supervised by a certificated supervisor if they are providing an instructional activity.

Staff Meetings

Principals should hold a minimum of one staff meeting per day. This meeting should come following the day's instructional period. The following are some suggestions for items appropriate for these meetings. Information of a significant nature relative to school operations or strike actions should be forwarded as soon as possible to the District information center. (See Strike Report and Substitute Teacher Request Form.)

1. The teacher's workday and hours of school for the following day
2. Plans for the following day to include classes in session, directions to students, exact designation of holding areas, etc.
3. Role of parents, if any, in assisting on campus
4. Number of substitute teachers available for assistance on the following day
5. Announcement as to class coverage or the combination of classes
6. Announcements relative to supervision and security measures
7. Announcements regarding attendance and accounting procedures
8. Announcement regarding the availability of counseling and guidance services for students.
9. Operation of the cafeteria, or modification of cafeteria services if necessary
10. Necessary announcements to be made to pupils for the following day, including procedures to enable them to go home if the school is closed. Students also need to be informed of functional items such as the availability of lunches and bus transportation, etc.
11. Thank the substitutes and determine if they will return the next day
12. A status report relative to the situation in other schools
13. Status of negotiations and the District position

Leaves of Absence

In the event of a strike, all employee absences must be substantiated by written proof of the need for the leave. Pay will not be granted for leaves of absence unless the employee worked or was validly excused from work both the workday before the absence and the workday after the absence.

Sick Leave

Employees requesting pay for sick leave must complete a signed affidavit of illness and provide a doctor's certificate of illness. (Affidavit forms will be provided by the Personnel Office.)

Personal Necessity Leave and Personal Welfare Leave

Employees requesting personal necessity or personal welfare leave must receive permission to take the leave from the responsible administrators. In the event of an emergency where advanced notice cannot be obtained, the employee must complete a signed affidavit and present written documentation of the personal necessity. During the period of a strike, personal necessity leave will only be allowed for emergency reasons. (Affidavit forms will be provided by the Personnel Office.)

Other Leaves

Permission to take other leaves must be received in advance of the leave.

Reduction/Withholding of Services/Striking

In the event a person, or persons, not responsible for the administration of your school announces that an adjusted day will be followed rather than the regular full-day schedule, the following procedure shall be strictly adhered to:

1. In the event it becomes evident that teachers are dismissing classes early, the principal and/or assistant principal will attempt to document as many teachers as possible who have dismissed classes. The question to be asked is: "Did you dismiss your class earlier than the prescribed time?"
2. Record the answer and proceed to the next room. Do not ask why the teacher dismissed his class and do not engage in argument or prolonged discussion.
3. After the principal and/or assistant principal have made their assessment to the best of their ability, a progress report is to be made to the Assistant Superintendent, Personnel.

4. The principal will then announce to the entire school:
   "Some teachers are violating school policy by dismissing classes earlier than allowed. You are hereby notified that you should remain in your classroom until _____. The regular schedule for the school is:_____."
5. If teachers persist in dismissing class early, repeat steps one and two, documenting teacher actions and reporting to the Assistant Superintendent, Personnel.

Miscellaneous

1. Administrative staff, clerical staff, paraprofessionals, non-striking teachers and substitutes should arrive at least one hour prior to start of classes. Clerical staff, paraprofessionals and non-striking teachers may be paid for this extra time.
2. Building should be open 30 minutes before classes and if students cannot be accommodated, they should be kept together under supervision.
3. No rooms should be left unlocked without supervision.
4. Be prepared for bomb threats and other unusual activity. The fire department will not schedule unannounced drills.
5. Principals should remain in their buildings all day.
6. Classified personnel are expected, with very few exceptions, to be present.
7. Principals should determine whether their secretaries will report for duty.
8. Central office personnel will be moving from school to school to give assistance. If you need to talk to the Superintendent, contact his office.
9. Principals will be required to assist substitutes in completing appropriate forms making them eligible to be paid. These forms will be completed only on the first day a substitute is employed by the District. Directions and forms will be carried by each substitute.

TYPICAL QUESTIONS AND ANSWERS REGARDING EMERGENCIES

To help anticipate some of the questions you or your staff may have, the following questions and answers are provided. These seem the most typical questions. They by no means represent all possible questions. Further questions should be directed to the Assistant Superintendent, Personnel.

Q. *Under what conditions would schools in the District be closed and who would have the authority to close them?*

A. An imminent safety hazard to students/staff and/or insufficient staff to provide adequate supervision are reasons to consider the closing of a school. The Superintendent or his designee are the only ones with authority to close schools.

Q. *Will classes be combined within any school as necessary at the discretion of the principal, or is authority of central office required?*

A. Principal's discretion.

Q. *Will two or more schools be consolidated into one school plant so as to make maximum utilization of school personnel? If this is a viable alternative would standby pupil transportation be made available be central staff? Also, who will make the decision with regard to the implementation of such a combined schools plan?*

A. Probably not, but Superintendent's discretion.

Q. *What contingency plans have been developed by central Staff in the event that bus drivers, custodians, cafeteria employees, and others decide to honor picket lines or otherwise refuse to carry out their responsibilities?*

A. Emergency crews of non-striking classified personnel will be standing by.

Q. *What will be the District policy with regard to parent organizations, members of the news media or certain elected officials who wish to enter school buildings to inspect "conditions?"*

A. Same as under normal conditions. Permission of the principal is required.

Q. *Will the District seek an injunction against the strike?*

A. Yes, documentation of harassment, student safety, legal violations, vandalism, and violence is essential to support the injunction.

Q. *What will the District's policy be with regard to restraining orders issued by courts? Will it be necessary for the building administrator to establish violation of the restraining order or will the District office perform this function?*

A. The District will take appropriate action on violations of restraining orders as need appears—both principal and District office will establish violation if necessary.

Q. *What will be the District policy with regard to strikers propagandizing students and harassing non-strikers?*

A. District will not tolerate and will seek legal restraint and take disciplinary action if it occurs.

Q. *What will be the District policy with regard to picket line control, particularly as it relates to access to the school plant by pupils and non-striking teachers?*

A. District will not tolerate picket lines out of control or blocking access to the school and will seek legal restraint and/or police assistance if it occurs.

Q. *What is the District policy with regard to actions a principal should take with respect to disruptions, disorders or demonstrations in connection with the strike by pupils, non-striking employees of the District or adults who are not District employees?*

A. Principal should take appropriate action to keep school open and protect safety and welfare of employees and students. The principal should also document all such occurrences. If police assistance is necessary, contact the Assistant Superintendent, Business.

Q. *What will the District policy be with regard to utilization of law enforcement agencies on or in the vicinity of school campuses during a strike? Who is to make the final decision with regard to employment of police?*

A. Police agencies will be used as needed. The principal may call if an immediate hazard is apparent. If a hazard is anticipated, use of police is to be cleared through the emergency number of the Assistant Superintendent, Business. Private security officers may also be employed in the same way.

Q. *What will the District policy be with regard to the utilization of bereavement, illness and/or personal necessity leaves during the period of the strike? Will there be any modification of forms or other procedures for the processing of such leaves during the period of work stoppage itself?*

A. All leave policies will be amended by Board resolution and restricted to essential leaves only, subject to careful verification.

Q. *What will be the policy of the District and the teacher training institutions with regard to student teachers assigned to schools of the District, particularly those student teachers whose master teachers are not present? Specifi-*

cally, will student teachers be directed to cross or not to cross picket lines by the college coordinating their training? Will student teachers be allowed to staff positions where the regular teacher is absent from duty?*

A. Principal's discretion. Student teachers should contact their college supervisor. Questions about eligibility to substitute should be directed to the Personnel Office.

Q. *Will the District hire student teachers to work as aides outside their hours of student teaching?*

A. Yes. Student teachers will be hired as teacher aides under the Education Code provision allowing them to work with children under supervision (but not necessarily under direct supervision).

Q. *Can wives or husbands of non-striking District employees be hired as aides?*

A. Yes, on a "temporary" basis during an emergency through the Personnel Office.

Q. *May principals be authorized to hire aides directly and immediately at site locations?*

A. Yes, but before they can be paid they must be cleared by the Personnel Office.

Q. *What will be the District policy with regard to parent organizations, members of the news media or certain elected officials who provide assistance to employee groups who support a work stoppage?*

A. The District will attempt no direct interference but will continue contacts and attempts to have various groups understand the facts of the situation.

Q. *What are the physical boundaries for "on school grounds" in dealing with pickets?*

A. The public sidewalk and/or fence around the campus borders will be the boundaries for enforcement purposes and pickets will be so informed by site-level administrator; access to the school cannot be blocked legally.

Q. *What will be the District's policy with regard to restraining orders, if any, issued by the courts? That is, what will be necessary to establish violation of a restraining order with regard to an overt act repeated contrary to the first order to desist?*

A. Principals should make a citizen's arrest and pursue all legal means to stop the violation. The District will assist with legal problems resulting from such an emergency.

Q. *What guidelines are to apply relative to the adult/student ratio and possible resulting liability of supervising staff?*

A. The District will try to stay within student groupings that might be considered reasonable. However, we often bring larger groups together for various events, and will do so if necessary during an emergency. All supervising staff are covered by the District's insurance.

Q. *Will the District give extra pay to on-duty teachers for duties within their normal assignment (conference periods, Kindergarten in double session)?*

A. No. All employees will be expected to meet all emergencies without additional compensation. *Prolonged* periods during an emergency that require work hours beyond normal would be considered for additional compensation.

Q. *Can an attorney meet with principals to discuss legal restraints and liability in the event of work stoppage?*

A. Yes, arrangements for such a meeting will be made by the Assistant Superintendent, Personnel.

Q. *Does the Board consider a work stoppage to be an individual breach of contract by those teachers participating?*

A. Yes.

Q. *Will principals be permitted to alter custodians' schedules and to authorize overtime?*

A. Yes, principal discretion.

Q. *Will steps be taken to provide principals with unlisted phone lines before a work stoppage?*

A. Yes. A Communications network plan has been formalized.

Q. *Will the striking employee associations be permitted to use District and site mail services?*

A. In the event of a work stoppage, approval for distribution of employees association communications will be suspended.

POST-STRIKE TRANSITION

The principal has the responsibility for easing the transition from a strike situation to normalcy. Aside from the interpersonal relationships that need attention, there are a number of operational functions that need to be performed.

1. All keys need to be collected from substitutes and from non-striking staff if they have been working in areas other than their own classrooms.
2. All keys should be inventoried.
3. Each staff member or substitute who has worked with students other than his/her own should provide a summary of work covered including any grades earned by students.
4. All grade/roll books should be collected unless a teacher has worked only with his/her regular students. A copy should be made of all grades recorded by substitute teachers. This copy should be kept in a safe place in the event there is a dispute about earned grades.
5. Reports of any personal loss or damage should be submitted.
6. Reports of any physical or mechanical damage to the facility should be submitted.
7. After administrative review, roll/grade books, keys, etc. should be returned to returning teachers.
8. Alternate or revised procedures having to do with day-to-day operations or new contract provisions should be discussed with returning staff.

At the conclusion of a work action, we must attempt to resume the constructive attitudes and establish the program we enjoyed previously. Each principal will face a different situation depending on the experience at that school and the level of activity of those employees. The principal is to avoid harsh statements and do everything possible to restore unity and harmony as quickly as possible. How well the strike is handled may determine the success of the post-strike adjustment.

APPENDIX I: PRINCIPAL'S EMERGENCY PLAN CHECKLISTS

IA: Principal's Emergency Plan Checklist

Condition—NORMAL

____ 1. Be familiar with Emergency Plan

_____ 2. Review employee organization rights and responsibilities documents
_____ 3. Update school emergency procedures
    a. Fire alarms and drills
    b. Utility control
    c. Telephone number update
_____ 4. Develop plan for substitutes to arrive/park
_____ 5. Prepare for civil disturbances
    a. Signal/communication system
    b. Building security
    c. Safety for students and staff
    d. Telephone access
_____ 6. Prepare substitute staff materials
_____ 7. Develop back-up staffing plan
_____ 8. Plan an alternate instructional program
    a. Class organization
    b. Materials
    c. Roll taking
    d. Grade reports
_____ 9. Provide for a building management system
    a. Issuance of keys
    b. Custodial service
    c. Secretarial service
    d. Assistance to substitutes
_____ 10. Prepare a plan to communicate with parents
_____ 11. Identify alternate administrator/manager

Condition—CRITICAL

_____ 1. Double-check all plans
    a. Emergency procedures
    b. Arrival of substitutes
    c. Civil disturbance
    d. Availability of alternate staffing
    e. Alternate instructional program
    f. Building management
    g. Communication with parents
_____ 2. Advise Superintendent/District staff of site developments
_____ 3. Obtain documentation supplies and equipment

Condition—STRIKE IMMINENT

_____ 1. Determine disposition of staff
_____ 2. Undertake support activities for potential non-strikers

____ 3. Implement emergency key control system
____ 4. Obtain roll books, lesson plans, etc.
____ 5. Secure all A-V equipment

Condition—STRIKE

____ 1. Identify non-striking personel
____ 2. Assess staff needs and notify Personnel Office
____ 3. Implement plans for arriving substitutes and students
____ 4. Activate building security and anti-sabotage plan
____ 5. Implement alternate instructional plan
____ 6. Complete Strike Report Form by 10:00 a.m.
____ 7. Undertake contingency plans as needed
  a. Parent communication
  b. Food services
  c. Transportation
  d. Etc.
____ 8. Apprise alternate administrator/manager of status of school each day
____ 9. Turn in Strike Report and Substitute Request Form each day
____ 10. Meet with site staff daily
____ 11. Attend daily principal's briefing at District Office

I-B: Principal's Emergency Plan Checklist Detail

Condition—NORMAL

1. Review, revise and update building emergency plans annually.
2. Familiarize yourself with:
  a. All Board policies and contract provisions relating to employee organization rights and responsibilities. (Employees' duties, leave polices, right to withhold pay, substitute pay, etc.) Have copies of Board policies on hand to share with employees who ask. Any questions on interpretation should be referred to the Assistant Superintendent, Personnel.
  b. The Principal's Emergency Procedure Manual.
  c. All emergency procedures pertaining to the physical operation of your building (your custodian or maintenance supervisor will help with these):
    1) Location of the main gas, water and electrical shut-off valves and switches,
    2) Telephone relay locations,
    3) Security control locations,
    4) Fire alarm locations,

     5) Sheriff or police and fire department emergency phone numbers, and

     6) Develop an alternative parking system for protection of substitutes. Take into consideration the following, wherever possible:

       (a) Secure on-grounds space

       (b) Alternate off-site parking site and transportation to and from

       (c) Supervised movement of traffic in and out

       (d) Arrangement and encouragement of car pools

       (e) Arrangement of reporting and departure time, so as to minimize the number of times personnel will need to cross the picket line (suggest that non-strikers bring a lunch)

3. Be prepared in case of civil disturbance.

    a. Develop an alternative signal system to alert the staff to:

      1) Secure all outside doors,

      2) Stop all outside activities and

      3) Return all children to supervised inside areas.

    b. Consider the possibility of locating classes as close to the office as possible for easy communication.

4. Due to the likelihood of many substitutes from different areas being assigned to your building, develop a plan to allow them to function with as little personal guidance as possible. The plan should include a folder for each substitute containing:

    a. A building map

    b. Time schedules

    c. Fire drill procedure

    d. Class lists

    e. Roll taking and reporting procedures

    f. Cafeteria procedures (if applicable)

    g. Key control directions

    h. Grade recording procedures

    i. Sample daily lesson plans and guides

    j. Bell and alternative signals

5. Develop a plan for utilizing adults for supervision of children:

    a. Aides, instructional assistants

    b. Custodians

    c. Clerical

    d. Parent volunteers

    e. Community volunteers

6. Develop an alternative program for assigning children and for taking roll.

7. Develop a plan to require turn in of:

    a. Keys (especially outside doors and gates)

    b. Roll sheets

    c. Lesson plans, and grades to date
    d. Substitute information folders
8. Develop a plan to keep parents informed about:
    a. Strike proceedings,
    b. Daily changes,
    c. Lunch arrangements,
    d. Getting permission to remove child from school during the day,
    e. School closure procedures,
    f. The need for volunteer help and the areas of need,
    g. Emergency plans, and
    h. Local information services—radio stations, phone recordings, etc.
9. Select another site administrator/manager to serve in your capacity in case of an emergency. In the event of a strike, close contact should be maintained with the administrator/manager.

Condition—CRITICAL

1. Prepare to implement emergency plan.
2. Review building level emergency plan checklist.
3. Put alternate communication system in a state of readiness.
4. Initiate extra security measures.
5. Forward any information regarding possible actions of the employee associations to the Director of Elementary or Secondary Education.

Condition—STRIKE IMMINENT

1. Determine, as nearly as possible, the disposition of the staff (teachers, custodians, secretary, aides, noon-duty supervisors, etc.).
    a. Develop alternative plan to supplement their services; e.g., bring in parents.
    b. Notify Director of Personnel of personnel needs.
2. Because non-striking employees may face external pressures from their peers, the administrator must:
    a. Communicate with the total staff their commitments to the Board's position.
    b. Develop with the staff an alternative educational program for children.
    c. Be prepared to send any questions from the staff, parents or yourself to Director of Elementary or Secondary education for official interpretation. If an immediate answer is required, phone.

Condition—STRIKE

1. Identify non-striking personnel. Determine staff needs; reassign personnel and/or students as required. Notify Director of Personnel of personnel needs by 5:00 p.m. the day before.

2. Institute emergency key control system.
3. Activate plan for receiving and directing students.
4. Activate plan for getting non-striking personnel on and off site, if needed.
5. Activate plan for use of substitutes and instructional support staff.
6. Activate building security and anti-sabotage plan.
7. Take attendance and employee count and phone into Director of Elementary or Secondary Education office by 10:00 a.m. Use Strike Report form as guide.
8. Activate organization plan and procedures.
9. Turn in Principal's Log each evening.
10. Activate parent communication plan.
11. Activate other contingency plans developed as needs become apparent.
12. Call into Director of Elementary or Secondary Education at the emergency number immediately upon your arrival at school each day to assure your presence. In addition, indicate the presence or absence of the day custodian.
13. For future staff morale, the principal should avoid making public pronouncements by referring the press and TV people to the Assistant Superintendent, Personnel. He/she should avoid needless confrontations with school employee pickets. Essentially, they must always gauge their statements and their actions by the firm knowledge that soon the strike will be over and they will have to recreate, from the disruption, a sound teacher/parent/pupil relationship.
14. Keep alternate administrator/manager involved and knowledgeable in case you are unable to be on the job.

APPENDIX II: FORM AND REPORTS
TO BE USED DURING AN EMERGENCY

Strike Report*

School _____ Person Reporting _____ Date _____

GENERAL INSTRUCTIONS FOR SCHOOL SITE ADMINISTRATORS:

A. Time schedule for completion and transmission of reports to Education Center:
   1. Information contained in Part I, A, B, and C must be telephoned in to the Director of Elementary or Secondary Education by 10:00 a.m. each day until otherwise notified.

2. All of the following information must be completed in writing on this form and delivered by school site messenger or runner to School District Strike Headquarters by 2:00 p.m. daily.

PART I. Phone in Parts A, B, and C by 10:00 a.m. to the Elementary or Secondary Director's office.

A. Teachers (Regular Classroom):
No. Present _____ No. Absent _____ No. of Subs. _____
No. Declared Ill ——— No. Absent for Other Reasons _____
No. Absent without Leave _____

B. Students:
No. Present _____ No. Absent _____

C. Pickets Present (after school has begun):
Yes _____ No _____ Approx. No. _____
List the names of any pickets that you recognize on a separate piece of paper and attach.

D. Please list below the unusual things that are happening in your school that are disruptive in nature and that are impediments to the normal functioning of your school.

*Please make report in duplicate and keep one copy for your files.

STRIKE REPORT

PART II. Complete the following information.

A. Operating as usual: No. Present _____ No. Absent _____
B. Secretaries: No. Present _____ No. Absent _____
C. Aides: No. Present _____ No. Absent _____
D. Custodians: No. Present _____ No. Absent _____
E. Administrators: No. Present _____ No. Absent _____
F. Cafeteria: No. Present _____ No. Absent _____
G. Harassments: Yes _____ No _____

(Explain under Part J who was involved: Students, parents, teachers, citizens, etc.)

H. Busing: No Problems _____ Problems _____
Describe: _____
_____
_____
_____

I. What are your needs?
1. _____
2. _____
3. _____
4. _____

J. Explanation of Problems:

_____

_____

_____

Substitute Teacher Request Form
(To be completed daily and delivered to the Personnel Office)

_____

School   Telephone Number

_____

Date   Contact Person at Site

Designate the number of substitute teachers at specific grade levels or in specific subject areas that you will need *tomorrow*. Keep all the substitutes that worked at your school today unless other arrangements are made with the Personnel Office. Specify the desired number of substitutes as well as the minimum number with which you could function. At the bottom of the sheet, please note the number of paid instructional aides at your school. Overestimate the "desired" number, but accurately specify the minimum which would allow you to remain open.

Grade/Subject	Desired No.	Minimum No.	New	Continuing
_____	_____	_____	___	_____
_____	_____	_____	___	_____
_____	_____	_____	___	_____
_____	_____	_____	___	_____
_____	_____	_____	___	_____

Designate, by name, and the reason for release of any substitute teacher assigned to your school who has been released for the succeeding day:

_____

_____

_____

Number of paid instructional aides on your campus: _____

NOTE: Be sure your site contact person receives a completed copy of this form daily and is knowledgeable to answer questions which may come from the Personnel Office.

APPENDIX III: MISCELLANEOUS INFORMATION TO ASSIST PRINCIPALS IN PREPARING FOR EMERGENCIES

Typical Duties for Personnel Assigned to Schools during an Emergency

Teacher aides, instructional assistants, and volunteer laypersons are permitted to engage in instructional activities under appropriate supervision of a teacher or principal.

Teacher aides may be particularly useful in performing these functions during a strike in addition to supervising instructional activities prepared by a teacher or administrator:

1. Direct students into the building when they arrive and give them special directions where to report.
2. Assist in taking student attendance when they are in a central meeting area or during the first period after deployments.
3. Supervise groups of students who are doing noninstructional activities before and after school
4. Escort children to and from the bus loading area and help supervise bus loading.
5. Assist in keeping halls clear.
6. Help supervise bicycle racks and parking lots; keep areas clear of students.
7. Assist in answering the phone and refer calls to proper person.
8. Take children home when they become ill, if parents cannot come to school.
9. Help supervise in cafeterias, on playgrounds and in large group instruction.
10. Assist in media centers and libraries in checking out materials and in delivering materials to classrooms.
11. Operate audio-visual equipment.
12. Operate duplicator and do typing for staff.
13. Assist in distributing mail and in storing incoming supplies.
14. Help collect and count cafeteria money.

Utilization of Auxiliary Staff during Work Stoppage

Most schools have certificated staff assigned who are not carrying a full classroom load of students. In case of an emergency, these people may be utilized to protect the safety and welfare of students. *Care must be taken that the members of the staff funded by categorical federal or state funds continue with the function for which they are funded.* Although they may supervise additional students on a temporary basis, they must continue to provide service to the children for whom special funds are being received.

The following are some suggestions regarding how special teachers might be utilized in an emergency:

1. Resource Specialists, ISGI teachers, and ROP teachers should have their regular students, but may be assigned additional students on an emergency basis.
2. District reading teachers may be assigned full time to classrooms without restrictions.
3. Special day class teachers should be assigned the students they usually work with and integrate additional children into their classrooms on an emergency basis.
4. Aides—SIP, special education and other paid aides may have their time extended and can be assigned to work with groups of children under the supervision of a credentialed teacher.
5. Nurses—The school to which the nurse reports on the first day of the work stoppage will retain that nurse until no longer needed. The Personnel Office will otherwise reassign the nurse as necessary. The nurse will return to the assigned school after leaving for any emergency health service in other schools.
6. Psychologists, Speech Therapists and Music Teachers utilize as described for nurses. Personnel Office will reassign these people if they are not needed in the schools to which they report on the first day of work stoppage.

Other certificated persons, not responsible for classroom groups of students, may be assigned at the discretion of the principal.

Assignment of Building Responsibilities

Perhaps the heart of the administrative emergency plan is the establishment of specific responsibilities for each member of the staff during the strike. It is paramount that all non-striking members and volunteers know clearly who is responsible for the execution of certain specific and necessary responsibilities and functions. Such an assignment sheet should be in effect on the first and any subsequent days of the emergency.

A typical responsibility list may include:

1. Substitutes—All substitutes to report to administrator's office for specific assignment.

2. Daily and Special Bulletins—Administrator to prepare daily bulletin notices for faculty and students, giving daily information on status of school operation. Daily bulletin notices must remind teachers to sign in on the special sign-in sheet provided, call their attention to the Faculty Handbook requirements and make special announcements as necessary.

3. Bell Schedule—Administrator to determine whether special bell schedule for the day is needed, and plan accordingly. Administrator's office will authorize all bell signals. No bells are to be rung without specific authorization.

4. Class Coverage—All class coverage will be assigned through the administrator's office.

5. Communications—Administrator's office to maintain runner system for rapid communication between major student holding areas as needed. Reliable pupils may be used as runners for this purpose.

6. Check of Personnel—Every work station is to be checked and a head count made of all personnel. Personal contact with all personnel is to be made daily.

7. Supervision—Administrator to provide security and supervision for campus area.

8. Police Liaison—Administrator to authorize and coordinate all liaison with the police.

9. Restroom Security—Administrator responsible to ensure restroom facilities remain operable.

10. Holding Area—Overflow from classes without teacher or aide will be directed first to the auditorium/multiuse room. Administrator to supervise initially and determine subsequent action to be taken.

11. Picketing—Administrator to assign supervising staff to cover the front of the school to supervise pupils coming and going and to observe picketing and record significant events.

12. Locks—Administrator to prepare contingency plan to ensure access to all school facilities during the strike.

13. Buses and Transportation—Administrator to contact the Transportation Office and arrange for early or late pickup of students as appropriate. Ensure that students have an opportunity to make proper arrangements for transportation if necessary.

14. Parking Lot—Administrator to ensure that proper security is maintained on faculty parking lot, including locking of gates, and to observe and record significant events.

15. School Secretary Responsibilities
    a. Parent Inquiry—Set up phone service desk with an adult to receive incoming calls and transmit necessary information.

b. Teacher Calls—Keep special log of incoming calls from teachers indicating absence and reason therefore.

c. Sign-in Sheet—Prepare special sign-in sheet for strike date and every day thereafter that the strike may continue. Teachers coming to work should sign in on this sheet only. Transfer information to attendance reports and attach special sign-in sheets.

d. Payroll Information—Prepare faculty bulletin notices regarding payroll, necessity for signing in, absentee calls, etc., reminding the faculty of proper procedures in all these areas.

e. Daily Log—Keep daily log of significant events in the main office, such as bomb threats, false alarms, etc.

f. Substitute—Packets should be made up that contain:
   1. A building map
   2. Time schedules based on the emergency plan
   3. Fire drill procedures
   4. Class lists
   5. Roll taking and reporting procedures
   6. Cafeteria procedures (if applicable)
   7. Key control directions
   8. Sample daily lesson plans and guides
   9. Grade reporting procedures
   10. Bell and alternative signals

Appendix B

Emergency
Procedures Resolution

WHEREAS, the Board of Education finds that a substantial number of employees are engaged in, or are about to engage in a strike, work slow-down, sick-out, work stoppage, or other withdrawal of services which would interfere with, impede or have the effect of interfering with or impeding the normal operation of the school district which would result in great and irreparable damage to the schools and the pupils of the school district:

NOW, THEREFORE BE IT RESOLVED that the Board of Education hereby determines that a legitimate emergency exists as defined by (Article _____ of the current collective bargaining agreement), as well as California law, Board of Education Policy and Administrative Rules and Regulations;

BE IT FURTHER RESOLVED that all unauthorized absences shall result in the deduction of salary and paid benefits for each day of absence as specified in the Education Code;

BE IT FURTHER RESOLVED that the superintendent or his/her designee(s) is authorized to employ substitute certificated and classified employees at a daily rate (not to exceed the pro rata daily rate of the top step of the appropriate salary schedule for that classification);

BE IT FURTHER RESOLVED that the Superintendent or his/her designee(s) is directed that all student grades given during the emergency will stand as recorded and will not be made up or modified at the end of the emergency;

BE IT FURTHER RESOLVED that the Superintendent or his/her designee(s) shall undertake appropriate action to implement this resolution, including, but not limited to, action necessary to ensure and protect the physical and educational well-being of all students and the safety and property of the school district, including its agents, employees, representatives, and all persons acting for or on behalf of the school district. Any such action shall prevail to the extent it amends, modifies, or rescinds provisions of (the current collective bargaining agreement as permitted by Article _____ of said agreement), Board of Education Policy and Administrative Rules and Regulations;

BE IT FURTHER RESOLVED that the Superintendent or his/her designated representative shall be the sole district employee authorized to close any of the district's educational facilities. Such facilities shall be closed when, in the opinion of the Superintendent or his/her designated representative, the physical welfare of the students or staff on that school site is in jeopardy because of the inadequate staffing or disruptive activities which take place on or within the vicinity of the site;

BE IT FURTHER RESOLVED that the superintendent or his/her designated representative may authorize any appropriate legal action or defense in regard to matters relating to the emergency;

BE IT FURTHER RESOLVED that the law firm of _____ is authorized to represent the district in legal matters relating to actions arising out of this emergency;

BE IT FURTHER RESOLVED that this resolution is an emergency measure within the mandate and jurisdiction of the Board of Education and is necessary for the immediate welfare of the schools and pupils thereof. Therefore, this resolution shall become effective immediately upon its adoption and shall remain in effect until repealed by formal Board action.

ADOPTED this _____ day of _____, 20___, by the following vote:

AYES: _____

NOES: _____

ABSENT: _____

ABSTAINING: _____

Appendix C

Delegation of Authority to Superintendent

WHEREAS, the Education Code permits the Governing Board to delegate to an officer or employee of the District any of the Governing Board's powers and duties; and

WHEREAS, the Governing Board is desirous of delegating to the District Superintendent or designee certain powers and duties;

NOW, THEREFORE BE IT RESOLVED that the Governing Board of the Serendipity School District delegates the following powers and duties upon the District Superintendent:

1. To give the required public notice of all meetings, actions, activities, or conduct of the Governing Board or District in the manner provided by statute.
2. To enter into any lease, permit, or agreement for the use by District of buildings or other facilities if the use is to be granted to the District without charge.
3. To solicit and receive bids for the sale or lease of any surplus real property of the District. The Governing Board retains the power to accept bids.
4. To contract on behalf of the District provided that no contract made pursuant to this delegation shall be valid or constitute an enforceable obligation against the District unless and until the same shall have been approved or ratified by the Governing Board.
5. To purchase supplies, materials, apparatus, equipment, and services involving the expenditure of funds less than the amount specified in the Public Contracts Code. All transactions entered into by

the Superintendent shall be reviewed by the Governing Board every 60 days.

6. To employ substitute employees at a daily rate not to exceed 10 percent over the pro rata daily rate of the top step of the salary schedule for that classification.

7. In the event of an emergency, the Superintendent is directed:

   a. To require that all student grades given during the emergency will stand as recorded and will not be made up or modified at the end of the emergency.

   b. To deduct salary and paid benefits as specified in the Education Code for each day of unauthorized absence during the emergency.

   c. To undertake appropriate action to implement this resolution, including but not limited to action necessary to ensure and protect the physical and educational well-being of all students and the safety and property of the District, including its agents, employees, representatives, and all persons acting for or on the behalf of the District.

   d. To authorize closure of any of the District's educational facilities.

8. To allow, compromise, or settle a claim against the District, its officers and employees upon the recommendation of and on the terms proposed by the District's insurance advisor. Any allowance, compromise, or settlement authorized by the Superintendent shall not exceed $10,000.

9. To enter into agreements admitting to the schools or classes maintained in the District any pupil who lives in another school district.

10. To issue and file written notices of unprofessional conduct or incompetency involving any certificated employee of this District, pursuant to the provisions of the Education Code.

11. To seek legal counsel to represent the District legal matters, action, or defense in regard to matters relating to the emergency.

12. To accept the resignation of any employee. The resignation shall become effective and binding at the time of acceptance, although the employee may remain in paid service until the agreed upon last day of service.

BE IT FURTHER RESOLVED, that the delegations of the powers and duties set forth above shall not modify or reduce any powers and duties delegated to the Superintendent by prior action of the Governing Board.

PASSED AND ADOPTED by the Board of Trustees of the Serendipity School District of _____ County, State of _____, this _____ day of _____, 20___, by the following vote:

AYES: _____

NOES: _____

ABSENT: _____

ABSTAINING: _____

Appendix D

Emergency Regulations of the Serendipity School District

WHEREAS, it is the responsibility of the Board of Trustees of the Serendipity School District to provide for the operation of the schools of the District for the purpose of education of the pupils thereof; and

WHEREAS, any strike, walkout, slowdown, or other type of work stoppage by the employees of the District could materially disrupt the operation of the schools of the District; and

WHEREAS, any strike, walkout, slowdown, or other type of work stoppage by the employees of the District is unlawful; and

WHEREAS, the Board intends to keep the schools of this District open and operating;

NOW, THEREFORE, IT IS RESOLVED by this Board, if an emergency exists with respect to the operation of the schools of the District because of the above-cited reasons, that the following EMERGENCY REGULATIONS shall be in effect:

1. INTERESTS OF PUPILS, EMPLOYEES, COMMUNITY, AND PROPERTY. In the event of an employee strike, walkout, or other work stoppage, the District intent shall be to keep the schools open and operating. To accomplish this, emergency operating procedures will be put into effect in order to:
   a. *Ensure the welfare and safety of the pupils;*
   b. *Ensure the rights and safety of all employees;*
   c. *Ensure the protection of public school property; and*
   d. *Provide the necessary staffing to fulfill the intent of the Board of Trustees.*

2. ORDER OF AUTHORITY. This regulation is an outline of emergency procedures and responsibilities to be put into effect by the superintendent or his designee when he determines that such conditions exist and provides for a sequence of authority, communication, and responsibility until the Board of Trustees determines the disruption is ended.
3. LEAVE OF ABSENCE.
    a. *Personal necessity leave or personal leave.* Personal necessity or personal leaves are authorized for district employees only when the same is taken due to:
        (1) Death or serious illness of a member of such employee's immediate family; or
        (2) Accident involving such employee's person or property or the person or property of a member of such employee's immediate family.

        District employees who take personal necessity or emergency leaves for one of the above reasons may be required to file with the Board satisfactory evidence of entitlement to such leave.
    b. *Sick Leave.*
        (1) In order to be granted sick leave for any absence claimed to be due to illness or injury (other than pursuant to an industrial accident or illness leave), a district employee must file with the Personnel Office of the District a statement signed by his or her physician or medical advisor.
        (2) In the event there is a suspected concerted withdrawal of services by employees, it shall be district regulation to require a physician's certification from any employee who is absent on the date of said suspected withdrawal of the services and who files a claim for sick leave benefits for the absence.
        (3) Said certificate must be filed immediately upon return to work. In the event a district employee fails or refuses to furnish said certificate, said absence shall be treated as and be deemed to be unauthorized absence without pay.
        (4) Except as otherwise provided herein, all of the leave policies and regulations of the district shall remain in full force and effect.
    c. *Vacations and professional leave.* All vacations and professional leaves are suspended during the period of the emergency except by special authorization of the superintendent or his designee.
4. ABSENCE WITHOUT LEAVE: WALKOUT, SLOWDOWN, WORK STOPPAGE
    a. *Unauthorized absence.* This is defined as nonperformance of those duties and responsibilities assigned by the district and its repre-

sentatives including all duties and responsibilities as defined by the Education Code, rules and regulations of the State Board of Education, and policies and regulations of the Board of Trustees of the Serendipity School District. Such unauthorized absence may include but is not limited to collective refusals to provide service, unauthorized use of leave benefits, and nonattendance at required meetings.

b. *Disciplinary report.* The superintendent, or such person or persons as he may designate, shall prepare for submission to this Board a disciplinary report setting forth the name and relevant information concerning each employee who is believed to have been:

(1) Absent without authorization on any workday or part thereof;

(2) Engaged in a walkout, slowdown, work stoppage, or other strike-related activity;

(3) Engaged in acts of vandalism directed against real or personal property of the school district or the personal property of others located on school property;

(4) Suggested, encouraged, intimidated, coerced, or by any other means attempted to initiate or aid in a boycott of school by pupils of the district;

(5) Suggested, encouraged, intimidated, or coerced, or by any other means attempted to persuade one or more pupils of the district not to attend school; or

(6) Acted or failed to act in a manner which the superintendent believes warrants disciplinary action by the Board. Procedures with respect to said disciplinary report shall be as follows:

(a) Notice shall first be given to the employee pursuant to the Education code, and he or she shall be given an opportunity to review the disciplinary report and comment thereon.

(b) In the event such employee desires to enter and have attached to the disciplinary report his or her own comments, such employee shall do so within two (2) working days of receipt of notice, or he or she shall be deemed to have waived such a right.

(c) Said disciplinary report shall be submitted to the Board, together with any written comments filed by the employee, for consideration and determination on whether or not the board will commence disciplinary action, including but not limited to immediate suspension and adoption of a resolution of intention to dismiss the employee.

c. *Compensation.* No compensation shall be paid to or on behalf of any district employee unless the Superintendent or the Assistant Superintendent of Personnel, whose duty is to draw the warrants, is satisfied that the employee has faithfully performed all of his or her prescribed duties. The term "compensation," as used herein, shall include but shall not be limited to employer contribution, if any, toward the cost of any health, welfare, or group benefits of the employee.

5. DELEGATION OF AUTHORITY TO SUPERINTENDENT

a. *Authority to contract.*

(1) Substitute employees. The superintendent or his designee is hereby authorized to employ additional substitutes as needed. Substitutes may be paid whatever rate he deems necessary to assure availability of substitutes.

(2) Legal services. In the event of emergencies, the superintendent or his designee is authorized to take all legal steps necessary to obtain the requisite legal services and to cause to be instituted or defended in the name of the District any litigation arising out of or related to any slowdown, walkout, strike, etc., of employees of the District.

(3) Consultant services. The superintendent or his designee is hereby authorized to contract, pursuant to Government Code, for such consultant services as are necessary in order to obtain professional advice for himself and his staff on strike or strike-related matters.

b. *Assignment of District employees.* The superintendent or his designee is hereby authorized to reassign any and all employees as needed in order to keep the school open and operating.

c. *Organization of personnel and resource.* The superintendent or his designee is authorized to organize the District's personnel and its material resources in any manner necessary in order to keep the schools open and operating.

d. *District property.* The superintendent or his designee is authorized to secure necessary legal assistance from county counsel or retained counsel to require that any district property held by District employees be immediately delivered to him or his designated representatives. As used herein, "district property" includes but is not limited to keys, audio-visual equipment, instructional materials, grade books, attendance records, posting charts, and pupil scholastic data.

e. *Emergency communications systems.* The superintendent or his designee is authorized to establish emergency communications systems.

f. *Transportation.* The superintendent or his designee is authorized to enter into contract with public or private agencies for pupil transportation services and may assign District buses to the contracted agency until the resolution of the emergency.

6. OFFICIAL BOARD SPOKESMAN. At the time the superintendent declares an emergency, the superintendent or his designated representative becomes the official spokesman of the Board.

7. CLOSING A SCHOOL. Only the superintendent and/or the strike coordinator has the authority to close a school. If the principal concludes at any time that the school should be closed, this should be reported to the superintendent's office. The report of the situation and recommendation will be studied by the superintendent for a final decision. If the superintendent should order a school closed, the principal will:

a. Notify the staff that closure is occurring.

b. Inform the students at each grade level of any change in dismissal times. If closure is at the end of a regular day, the student should be notified not to come to school until official announcement is made by the district.

c. Take those steps necessary to ensure the safety of students, student records, staff, and the property of the District.

d. Direct staff not participating in the disruption to continue to report, as directed, to be available for other services.

e. Inform the superintendent if he is unable to report for duty.

8. PUPIL REASSIGNMENT. In the event that an emergency is declared, the superintendent or his designee is authorized to provide for attendance of any district pupil at a school other than the school to which the pupil is normally assigned. Such attendance shall be for the period of time until the Board of Trustees determines the emergency is ended.

9. PUBLICATION AND POSTING. In the event that an emergency is so declared, a copy of these emergency regulations shall be published in a newspaper serving the district. Copies of these emergency regulations shall be posted in such places as to make them accessible to all employees.

10. NOTICE TO PARENTS AND EMPLOYEES. When the superintendent or the strike coordinator declares that an emergency exists, the community, parents, and employees shall be notified that these emergency regulations are operative by the most efficient and expeditious means available.

11. EFFECTIVE DATES. These emergency regulations shall become operative immediately upon declaration of an emergency by the superintendent or the strike coordinator and shall remain in effect until the Board of Trustees determines the emergency is ended.

IN WITNESS WHEREOF, we members of the Board of Trustees of the Serendipity School District of _____ County, State of _____, have hereunto set our hand this _____ day of _____, 20____.

Bibliography

American Association of School Administrators. (1975). Work stoppage strategies. Arlington, VA: The Association.

Bacharach, S. B. (1990). Education reform: Making sense of it all. Boston: Allyn and Bacon.

Bacharach, S., Bamberger, P., & Conley, S. (1990). Professionals and workplace control. *Industrial and Labor Relations Review*, 43: 570.

Bovard, J. (1999). Teachers unions: Are the schools run for them? http://www.self-gov.org/freeman/bova.html.

Bowers, B. C. (1991). Teacher involvement in curriculum development. *Research Roundup*, 1:3. Alexandria, VA: National Association of Elementary School Principals.

Boyton, B., & Lloyd, J. (May 1985). Why the largest teachers union puts its staff first and education second. *The Washington Monthly*, 17:4, 24.

Brimlow, P., & Spencer, L. (1993). The national extortion association. *Forbes*, 151(12), 72–84.

Chalker, D. M. (1990, November). School improvement can't be negotiated. Paper presented at the annual meeting of the Southern Regional Council on Educational Administration, Atlanta, GA.

Deming, W. E. (1986). Out of the crisis. Cambridge: MIT Center for Advanced Engineering Study.

Denholm, D. Y. (1999). The impact of unionism on the quality of education. http://www.psrf.org/doc/art2.html.

Eberts, R., and Stone, J. (1984). Unions and public schools. Massachusetts: Lexington Books. Educational Research Service.

Fisher, R., & Ury, W. (1981). Getting to yes. Boston: Houghton Mifflin.

Harju, B. (1996, Jan. 17). Let them buy Cadillacs. SDTA Teacher Advocate. San Diego, CA.

Harju, B. (1996, Feb. 21). Together we did it! SDTA Teacher Advocate. San Diego, CA.

Jones, S. L. (1996, Jan. 26). Settle now: Teachers' strike would hurt kids and teachers. *San Diego Union-Tribune.*

Jones, S. L. (1996, Jan. 27). Schools' strikes plan initiated. *San Diego Union-Tribune.*

Jones, S. L. (1996, Jan. 29). Teachers' frustration boils into a crisis: Their influence has ebbed with centralizing of power. *San Diego Union-Tribune.*

Jones, S. L. (1996, Feb. 9). We're glad it's over: Teachers expected to ratify pact today. *San Diego Union-Tribune.*

Kerchner, C., Koppich, J., & Weeres, J. (1997). United mind workers. San Francisco: Jossey-Bass.

Koppich, J. E. (1993, April). How professional unionism challenges public bureaucracy. Paper presented at the American Education Research Association annual meeting, Atlanta, GA.

Lieberman, M. (1997). The teacher unions. New York: The Free Press.

Loveless, Tom (Ed.). (2000). Conflicting missions?: Teacher unions & educational reform. Washington, D.C.: Brookings Institution Press.

Maitland, C., & Kerchner, C. (1986, April). The tone of labor relations in schools: Correlates of teacher reception. Paper presented at the American Education Research Association annual meeting, San Francisco.

McDonnell, L., & Pascal, A. (1988). Teacher unions & educational reform. Santa Monica, CA: Rand Corporation.

Murphy, Joe, & Hallinger, P. (1990). Characteristics of instructionally effective school districts. *Outcomes,* 8(4), 26–33.

National Education Association. (1998). Estimated average salary of teachers in public elementary and secondary schools: 1959–60 to 1997–98. Digest of Education Statistics, http://nces.ed.gov/pubs2000.digest99/d99t078.html.

Shreeve, William, et al. (1990). Reflections of a strike as seen through the eyes of superintendents. U.S. Department of Education research report, ERIC ED 319 104, EA 021 734.

Streshly, William, & DeMitchell, Todd. (1994). Teacher unions & TQE: Building quality labor relations. Thousand Oaks, CA: Corwin.

About the Author

William A. Streshly is a professor of educational leadership at San Diego State University. Prior to coming to the university, Professor Streshly spent thirty years in public school administration, including five years as principal of large suburban high schools and fourteen years as superintendent of school districts varying in size from 2,500 to 25,000 students. His profound understanding of the social and political tensions shaping our modern-day public school systems stems from his years of work leading successful school reform initiatives, as well as his current research projects at the university.

During his forty-year career, he has "walked-his-talk" as a school district leader. He is known among his peers both for his masterful management of teacher strikes and his ingenious work establishing collaborative school district labor relations. The model he founded twenty years ago in the San Marcos Schools in Southern California has endured through the years and stands as an exemplar among California school districts. The rare combination of distinguished service as a practitioner and important research as a professor of educational administration has resulted in a deep insight into the barriers faced by school reformers.

Professor Streshly is a frequent contributor to the professional literature. He has published articles on character education, staff development, curriculum management, competency testing, school finance, and school labor relations. He is also coauthor of three other practical books for school leaders, including the currently popular *Top Ten Myths in Education.* He has served as speaker and/or consultant for numerous state and national conferences, school districts, and professional organizations, in addition to fulfilling scores of speaking engagements for community service clubs, Chambers of Commerce, alumni clubs, and political groups. He has been active in the leadership of numerous community/civic organizations and has served as an educational advisor to county, state, and federal officials.

Professor Streshly also serves the educational community as a Lead Curriculum Auditor for the International Curriculum Management Audit Center, an affiliate of the Phi Delta Kappa educational fraternity. In recent years, he has audited the instructional management operations of more than twenty-five school districts in fifteen states.